"Those of us who were on the bus in the sixties and took that magical and dangerous trip came out of that experience with a code that would guide us for the rest of our lives. The lesson was to live your life as if there was something bigger than your own mortality at stake. That art, for example, gifted by the muse, is bigger than the artists who create it. I am forever grateful to John Densmore, not only for enduring the crucible described in this book, but for never wavering from the code that some of us still hold so dear. Because the music that The Doors created is so important to so many people, its worth is much greater than the sum of its parts; and certainly greater than their commercial success. Because John Densmore believes this, we are all in his debt. Not only for renewing our belief in the transcendent magic of The Doors, but for staying true to the best ideals of our generation." —Jim Ladd, DJ and author

THE doors

UNHINGED

JIM MORRISON'S LEGACY GOES ON TRIAL

BY JOHN DENSMORE

AKASHIC BOOKS

BROOKLYN, NEW YORK

Published by Akashic Books
©2023 John Densmore. All rights reserved.

Paperback ISBN: 978-1-63614-157-2
Hardcover ISBN: 978-1-63614-155-8
Library of Congress Control Number: 2023933929
First Akashic Books printing

Cover design by Shepard Fairey
Front cover photo by Joel Brodsky
Back cover photo by Fredric Goodich, ASC
Back flap photo by Jeff Katz Photography

Akashic Books
Instagram, Twitter, Facebook: AkashicBooks
info@akashicbooks.com
www.akashicbooks.com
www.johndensmore.com

To Danny Sugerman,
Who used to drive me crazy,
But at his final crossing,
Checked out like a
Bodhisattva

Table of Contents

We feared that the music which had given us sustenance
was in danger of spiritual starvation.
We feared it losing its sense of purpose,
we feared it falling into fattened hands,
we feared it floundering in a mire of spectacle,
finance, and vapid technical complexity.

—Patti Smith, *Just Kids*

Preface

Money is not evil. It's a potent energy that can be used to feed negative or positive impulses. Ever since rock and roll was born, a tradition has been building on the idea that our music means something more than money, and if it's compromised, its power could be lessened. That's the underlying thread of this book.

Even though turning down the big bucks makes me weak in the knees, I've remained consistent with my stance about music and money. I was offered a good deal for this book by a major publisher; I took it, but it didn't work out for me. "Give us some gossip about Jim," they kept saying.

"I've already written about Jim in my memoir, *Riders on the Storm: My Life with Jim Morrison and The Doors*," I said. "It was released in 1991 and it was a *New York Times* best seller. You should pick it up."

"There's gotta be more stories about him," they persisted. They wanted to destroy my baby by chopping off a couple of arms, but I wouldn't allow it.

"Look," I told them, "I'm sorry I didn't shoot heroin like Keith Richards or have seven wives like Greg Allman, but this book is the antithesis of sex, drugs, and rock and roll. That could be your marketing campaign."

They weren't buying it, so I returned the advance, took the manuscript back, and self-published it. When it was initially released in 2013, I was a little ahead of the curve, but it seems that the time for this book is right now. As of 2019, the following artists have sold their songs or recording rights for BIG bucks: Bruce Springsteen, Paul Simon, the Beach Boys, Neil Young, Tina Turner, Ray Charles, Stevie Nicks, Whitney Houston, David Crosby, Dolly Parton, David Bowie, John Legend, James Brown, ZZ Top, Taylor Swift, Shakira, Mick Fleetwood, Lindsay Buckingham, Mötley Crüe, Neil Diamond, Bad Company, and America. Some of them have sold parts of their catalog and a few have disallowed certain songs from being exploited to sell products. Even our great poet-prince Bob Dylan has succumbed to the temptation. I think his reasons are different, though. Money is an addiction, but for Dylan it's not about the dough. He just hates being put on a pedestal, so he deliberately does things to throw us all a curveball.

In the book, I write about how Bruce Springsteen is one of the few left standing, but now, I can't help but wonder what his hero, Pete Seeger, would think about "The Boss" selling his songs for $500+ million. Maybe he will give a bunch of his dough to charity. I know, it's nobody's business what someone does with his or her $$. It's a free country. But those songs were soundtracks for people's lives, and it would be weird for them to hear, "Born to Run . . . to WalMart." It's disturbing, but artists strive so hard to catch the brass ring that when they get there, it can be blinding. That could be one reason for the dark glasses: you don't want the fans looking into the windows of your soul and seeing nothing!

I would only sell The Doors's catalog if we could abide

by Jim Morrison's wishes to not allow any of the songs to be used in commercials. Ever. *In perpetuity*. That's safer than hanging on to it until I'm not here anymore. My kids know my wishes, but several generations down the road, they might not, so I can lock it in right now, *in perpetuity*. Those two words. That means no one would ever be allowed to use the music in an ad. Then I could put the obscene amounts of front money toward green energy, social justice, and the environment. Money is like fertilizer: When hoarded, it stinks. When spread around, things grow.

In the history of rock, whenever it started to lose its integrity, renewal was always in the wings. Each new creative wave that came along challenged the previous modus operandi. Elvis shocked Eisenhower's generation with sexuality. The hippies were too grubby for the early sixties crowd. The punks were too angry for the "flower power" folks. Reggae and rap are strong offshoots of this energy, yet all these musical movements had the same message:

Vitality. Don't compromise the life force.

Yes, to be human is to be humiliated, but in the face of that, spirit transcends the physical. In recent years, the Rock & Roll Hall of Fame has openly sought to represent a big-tent definition of rock and roll (as opposed to its more guitar-oriented offspring, rock). At N.W.A's induction Ice Cube said, "Rock and roll is not an instrument, rock and roll is not even a style of music. Rock and roll is a spirit."

When my generation got too intoxicated with self-importance, the punks came along and yelled at us. It was a wake-up call. Patti Smith was fed by The Doors artistically, but when complacency became the main course for hippies, she wrote, "We feared that the music which had given us sustenance was in danger of spiritual starvation."

Most of the groups in the sixties wanted to say something about the human condition. Of course, we wanted to make money, but that wasn't the primary impulse. The country was polarized by the Vietnam War—not unlike today, where we are polarized by the red states and the blue states. Back then, the war was so disturbing that politics seeped into all genres of art, whether it was music, films, or books. The negativity of people dying in a war coalesced into a positive energy in art. There have been a lot of people dying in the past few years due to COVID, so hopefully as we come out of it, there will be a lot of positive impulses that we learned from the lockdown. At this very moment, Russian president Putin is learning that the world won't tolerate dictators anymore.

As I write about my struggle to keep doing what I think is right, I know the blowback will be fierce because I'm practically the last man standing. Artists not only sell their catalogs for the money, they also worry as they get older how the songs will be managed after they're gone. Yeah, it's lonely . . . do I hear violins behind this rap? "It's lonely having deep pockets, John"? Actually, in a way it is. Jay-Z nails the feeling with a rap he graciously let me reprint here:

> *What do I think of success?*
> *It sucks, too much stress . . .*
> *I used to give a shit, now I don't give a shit more*
> *Truth be told I had more fun when I was piss-poor . . .*
> *All this stress, all I got is this big house*
> *Couple of cars, I don't bring half of them shits out . . .*
> *How many times can I go to Mr. Chow's, Tao's, Nobu? . . .*
> *I got watches I ain't seen in months*
> *Apartment at the Trump I only slept in once . . .*

I think we need to let the flame burn through hypocrisy as we keep seeking the truth, but you can read the following pages and come to your own conclusions. I do think there are thousands of fans out there who are disappointed in their musical heroes, and would be eager to read about another way to do this. Since this book was originally published, we have lost Ray Manzarek. I will forever miss this remarkable, gifted musician. Now, there are only two "Doors" left out of four, and at this juncture it seems assured that the music we made will outlive all of us, something we are all very proud of. I believe that part of this longevity is due to our being very careful with the fruits of our labors—which is what I have always tried to do.

John Densmore
July 2023

Introduction

"**F**uck you!" Jim Morrison yelled.

His outburst shocked the rest of us. It was 1968, we were on a break from rehearsing, and Jim had never raised his voice at us like that before.

"Fuck you guys!" he repeated. "I thought it was supposed to be all for one and one for all. I thought we were supposed to be brothers!"

"Jim, we *are*, man!" Ray responded meekly. "Nothing has changed."

"Everything has fucking changed, Ray!" Jim said. "Everything!"

"Why?" Ray asked. "I don't understand. Just because we signed a contract to get a load of money for a fucking song in a Buick commercial . . . why has everything changed?"

Jim spoke from a deeply wounded place, pulling a knife out that he felt *we* had stabbed into the band's unspoken mission statement:

A band of musicians (warriors) who used musical notes instead of arrows, and always aimed for the listener's heart.

In Ray's autobiography, he described this next comment as Jim stabbing The Doors in our collective heart:

"Because I can't *trust* you anymore," Jim snapped. "It's fucking industry! It's corporate! It's the devil, you asshole. We always agreed that our music would never be used in commercials. You guys just made a pact with the devil."

Robby got defensive: "The hell we did."

"Oh yes you did, Robby. He shows you what you want and then he puts a little twist in it. Makes you say yes to him when you know you shouldn't . . ." Jim was pacing. "But you go along with it because the deal's just too good. It tastes too good." He stopped and stared at our keyboard player. "It's too much *money*, isn't it, Ray?"

Ray's fur arched up along his back. "Fuck you, Jim."

"I know you, Ray," Jim said. "You're only in it for the money."

Ray retaliated: "I just wanna make music. And if we can make some money at it . . . that's cool with me."

Ray was trying to smooth things over, but his feeble attempt at "fathering" was failing. In his book, he described Jim during this period as "over the top, gone," while he described himself as "trying to maintain the dream" ($?), hoping Jim would snap out of this phase he was in. Hoping that it *was* a phase. A momentary aberration. Hoping that Jim would come to his senses and we could resume our grail quest together (for more $?). The four of us. The Doors.

"Lots of money," Jim mumbled loud enough so we all could hear.

"What'd you say?" Ray responded.

"You heard me."

Robby tried breaking the tension: "Well, it's too late."

"Oh yeah? We'll see about that." Jim upped the ante: "I'm

gonna smash a fucking Buick to dust onstage. It's gonna be part of my new act. 'Smash a Buick to Smithereens.' We'll see how they like that. And then I'm gonna get Abe [our attorney] to sue their asses. For big fucking bucks, Ray. For a lot more than their shitty little contract. Then let's see if they still want to use a Doors song to sell a sports car."

Jim grabbed the phone on the spot and called our lawyers. "Threaten them with a lawsuit!" he bellowed into the receiver. "Tell them I'm gonna smash a Buick with a sledgehammer onstage! Tell them anything! But *stop* the fucking contract!"

This prompted a series of short legal agreements in response to the contract we had approved for "Light My Fire" to be used in a commercial . . . without Jim's consent. We got out of that contract, but it turned out that Jim's angry words to Ray—*You're only in it for the money*—were harbingers of things to come, things that thirty years later would cause The Doors to unhinge.

Jim's trust for us had eroded, although we continued to make great music. Then he left for Paris, where he died. Today, no longer are we "one for all," no longer brothers. Instead, here we are, about to go to court, fighting tooth and nail over the integrity of our name and our music. This time, Jim may not be here to rage against the pursuit of money at the expense of artistic integrity, but his spirit is here, urging me on to "smash that Buick." Well, this time it's Cadillac offering us the big bucks, and a tour without me or Jim that Ray and Robby want to call The Doors of the 21st Century. The Doors, my ass.

Yes, without the spirit of Jim Morrison (the hinges), The Doors don't open. And what was that spirit? In my opinion, it was a spirit infused with creativity, a spirit incompatible with compromise—a pure strand of new ideas, unpolluted by circumstance. It's hard to live in this world with that kind of integrity.

A few years before Jim's death, when he commented on the passing of Jimi Hendrix and Janis Joplin, I think he was commenting on himself as well, although maybe he wasn't conscious of it. My intuition tells me that toward the end of his life Jim had entered a state of ennui, a world-weariness manifested in a deep sadness and lack of energy, and thus his comments about Hendrix and Joplin were also comments about himself. In reflecting on Janis and Jimi, he jokingly said, "You're drinkin' with number three!"

That was *Jimbo* talking—Jim's tortured alter ego who had become an alcoholic. The younger Jim, vibrant as any twenty-year-old could be, had been determined to say something with his words and determined not to let the message become diluted. So determined that when we, his self-proclaimed brothers, in the vehicle for his words (The Doors), suggested compromising a song that Robby had mostly written by selling it to advertise a product ("Come on, Buick, Light My Fire"), Jim went ballistic. When that happened, the pure trust among us, the shepherds of The Doors catalog, was never to be the same.

Later, when huge success had befallen us four lads from Venice, California, there was no time for the original gestation period of a song. Our fans were demanding the newborn "Light My Fire," along with the rest of the songs on our first LP, every night. Gone was the time for the womb-like incubation in the garage that we liked giving to each song. That was when Jim suggested moving to an island and starting all over. He alluded to that idea in our song "Strange Days," saying that our old way of making music was being destroyed and we should find a new town. He was trying to get back, to renew that elusive quality that was with us in the rock and roll garage many years before.

I always knew that the lyrics to "Hello, I Love You" were great, all the way back in the garage when we first started. Incidentally, this song was not about Ray's girlfriend, as he falsely reported in his memoir. The very provocative line about Jim seeing an extremely attractive Black woman on the boardwalk killed me:

Sidewalk crouches at her feet,
Like a dog that begs for something sweet
Do you hope to make her see, you fool?
Do you hope to pluck this dusky jewel?
("Hello, I Love You")

The lyrics were powerful from the start, but the truth is that we'd been struggling with the musical arrangement for years when our producer, Paul Rothchild, finally said, "Damn it, we need a hit, and this one could fit the bill. Let's write the music in the studio."

Paul was correct that we should make an attempt, even though it would have been cheaper to do it in rehearsal, but that intimate, personal time together to incubate a song had been long gone, ever since the huge success of "Light My Fire." Fans demanded to hear the hits, and the organic method of adding a leaf here and a leaf there to the nest of a new song was now in overdrive. Our group started to feel like a runaway train, with Jim as the locomotive in the front, Ray shoveling coal into the engine, Robby on the fence in the middle, and I was the caboose (drummers are in the back), trying to avoid an accident by putting the brakes on.

When Jim sang us "Crystal Ship" back in the garage, that song formed immediately as we figured out the chords and rhythm in a few hours. But "Hello, I Love You," even with its tantalizing words, simply wouldn't go to bed.

She's walking down the street
Blind to every eye she meets
Do you think you'll be the guy
To make the queen of the angels sigh?

Robby and Rothchild overdubbed so many distorted guitars, it sounded like a snake with a buzzer for a rattle. But as the snake wound its way to #1, I was amazed that we pulled it off. It was too poppy a sound for my taste, but as usual, I couldn't get enough of Jim's fabulous lyrics!

A true artist Jim was . . . but by the time he made his way to Paris, he was also a man with a disease. A disease so strong that his pals (Ray, Robby, and me) couldn't hang with him anymore like in the old days. We really didn't want to go to that island with him . . . There was trouble in paradise. There were rummies. Plus, we were a little intoxicated ourselves . . . with fame.

Suckcess (as Bob Dylan spells it) has a dark side. We were seduced by the limelight and Jim was addicted to the juice. God knows how many folks try everything possible to keep it together. But no one—myself included—seems to escape the dark underpinnings of the human condition . . . intoxication, greed, grabs for power. As Jim's pals, we wanted more success . . . and Jim wanted less, but more of the drink, since the sticky web of liquor had already been woven tightly around him.

But none of this, NONE OF THIS, can ever take away

from the magnificence of the muse that visited us four guys in a garage in Venice, infused by Jim's voracious spirit, which, when denied, he substituted with the spirit in the bottle. So this story is a tragedy.

When I look back, I wonder, how does such a magical union go sour? Why do good people get divorced? These questions can't be fully answered, but I'm going to do my best by telling the story from my viewpoint . . . from the drum stool. Maybe it's the alignment of the stars . . . maybe it's just fate.

> *We asked for signs*
> *The signs were sent:*
> *The birth betrayed*
> *The marriage spent*
> *Yeah the widowhood*
> *Of every government . . .*
> *Ring the bells that still can ring*
> *Forget your perfect offering*
> *There is a crack, a crack in everything*
> *That's how the light gets in.*
> —Leonard Cohen

PART ONE

THE SETUP

Chapter 1

THE GOOD OLD DAYS

July 6, 2004

It's early morning and I just parked in the courthouse lot, where I paid the usual seventeen-dollar parking fee. This charge benignly drops to a mere six dollars after eleven a.m., but who goes to court after eleven? It's not like I can't afford the tariff. I can. But what about the unfortunate folks who dominate this building in the mornings, with their woes of immigration, traffic tickets, and petty crimes? *Let's rip off the poor one more time*, must be the motto here.

As I approach the heavy front doors to the ominous Los Angeles courthouse, I'm keenly aware that this is quite a different venue than I'm used to playing. Compared to the smoky clubs where I spent my lonely youth, this is pretty antiseptic. As a kid, I was hoping that a girl might notice me behind my gleaming set of drums, but now I don't have my musical security blanket. It's just me entering this courthouse, armed with my determination to make right what I believe is a wrong.

I stop for a moment when I pass through the recently

installed metal detectors at the entrance to the courthouse. I get frisked by security as I gaze down the long marble hall-way with the bright neon lighting, winding its way to my new prison cell—I'm referring to courtroom Division #36. I expect I'll be here every day for a few weeks. (Not for the entire summer, as it actually will turn out.) I am plagued by thoughts about how my "integrity" led me to this dire hall of justice. Will I actually wind up with any justice? What am I trying to prove here? Am I committing sabotage against my old bandmates? These thoughts won't stop, like maybe I should be less possessive about our brand name. I don't own it. We all do. We're all in this together. Is it unfair for one person to try to stop it? Am I the spoiler?

The truth is that a precious pact inked long ago by our front man, Jim, states quite clearly that if things ever get weird, one of us can and should do something. Well, it got weird and I'm doing something. But now that I've blown the whistle, I'm in the weirdest place I've ever been. Inside the courtroom, people talk real quiet, calling each other "sir" and "Your Honor," while they simultaneously and deliberately stab anyone standing in the way of their agenda . . . in the neck, back, sides, front, toes . . . anywhere. They're dressed in their Sunday best Armani suits, but they act like they're in a brothel instead of church. What the hell am I doing here?

I had no idea that when Jim suggested a four-way split on everything that it was a historic moment not to be dupli-cated by any other band for a very long time. His suggestion was not only magnanimous, but the solidarity turned out to be ironclad. Nothing would crack this fortress. I rest in the knowledge that I haven't sabotaged Jim.

In fact, reflecting back all those years to Jim's violent re-action to the Buick incident, when Ray, Robby, and I nearly sold "Light My Fire" to Buick for a TV commercial, I feel shame. The "greed gene" was flowing through my veins back then when Jim's outrageous burst of passion against our selling a song to an ad agency became etched on my brain, never to be forgotten. For thirty years we were a band of musicians with one of the most unique four-way agreements ever—nothing could be contracted unless we each gave it the okay. And now we are enemy combatants on the fourth floor of the courthouse in downtown Los Angeles.

In a book by James Hillman (Pulitzer Prize nominee, Jungian psychologist, and best-selling author), *The Soul's Code*, he states that individuals hold the potential for their unique possibilities inside themselves already, much as an acorn holds the pattern for an oak tree. I think Jim and legendary Crazy Horse (Native American war leader of the Oglala Lakota) had similar callings—that invisible mystery at the center of every life that speaks to the fundamental question, *What is it in my heart that I must do?* With all the slings and arrows of outrageous fortune that these two endured, they lived out their defining images that were in them from the beginning.

I hate all the Morrison fake-death rumors, but there is a reason that, like Crazy Horse, the whereabouts of Jim's remains still evoke mystery. I'm quite sure that the Père Lachaise Cemetery in Paris is his "happy hunting ground," due to mistaking THE GREAT SPIRIT for the spirit in the bottle, but Jim's spirit is still so strong, the fans want him alive.

As John Neihardt (*Black Elk Speaks*) says in *A Cycle of the West*, the parents of Crazy Horse rode into the Black Hills of South Dakota carrying their son's body behind them. His mother wept for the innocent times "before the great dream" took her son's life. No one really knows where they stopped as the final resting place for their offspring, but to the Lakota, the entire area is sacred.

I, too, look back to the sweet, innocent period when we were a garage band, before our "great dream" took us off to the global stage. But there is very little sacred about this courtroom, which is filled with people whispering secrets to each other. I'm used to loud, inebriated fans yelling out requests for their favorite song. How did it come to this? While I wait to enter the courtroom, I travel back in time to the beginning . . .

It was 1965. Ray Manzarek and Jim Morrison had met and become fast friends while attending film school at UCLA in beautiful Westwood Village in Los Angeles. At that time, people were becoming interested in Eastern philosophy and so my good friend Robby Krieger and I decided to attend a seminar on Transcendental Meditation (TM), which Ray, whom I hadn't yet met, also attended. I was obsessed with music, taking piano lessons at eight years old, playing drums in the high school marching band, the dance band, and the orchestra. I went to Tijuana and got a fake ID so I could play in bars . . . a budding professional. At the TM meeting, Ray introduced himself and suggested I come to his parents' house in Manhattan Beach to jam. I was down, happy to follow any lead to further the high I got from playing music. The praise that came from fellow musicians was like a dermatologist's salve on my acne.

The gathering at Ray's garage had both a negative and a positive cast. On the downside was the low level of musicianship of Ray's two brothers . . . but the guy lurking in the corner of the garage fascinated me. His name was Jim Morrison, he looked like a modern version of a Greek sculpture, and he moved like one too. In other words, he didn't move at all. I stopped staring at him when Manzarek started a nice groove on keyboards, a blues by Muddy Waters, and I joined in. It must have been true that the guy in the corner had never sung before, just like Ray said, because it was a good half hour before he walked up to the mic. At the time, I didn't think this guy had the confidence to be the next Mick Jagger, but I just couldn't stop looking at him . . . and I wasn't into guys!

Thankfully, after a couple more rehearsals, the two Manzarek brothers quit, convinced that this band wasn't going anywhere with a lead singer who was obviously so uncomfortable performing. I was worried about Jim's stage presence, just like they were, but his lyrics were extremely interesting to me—and they were percussive! I immediately heard drumbeats to his words:

You know the day destroys the night
Night divides the day
Tried to run, tried to hide
Break on through to the other side . . .

It was very risky betting on a singer who had never been in a band, couldn't play an instrument, and was extremely shy. Something was magical about him, though . . . I just couldn't put my finger on it.

The void created by our lack of a guitar player provided me an opportunity to invite Robby Krieger to audition for the group. Up to this point he'd primarily been a flamenco guitar player, but he was starting to get into playing electric as well. Ray was gregarious and knowledgeable about jazz, which was my passion, but he wasn't too passionate about my bringing

Robby Krieger in for a rehearsal. His reluctance came from the fact that Robby's persona was not that of the typical macho rock lead guitarist—strutting the stage, milking the notes, grabbing the audience. Robby had a much more internal style and Ray was concerned that two introverts (Jim and Robby) would not make a rock band. But I pressed for Robby because of his talent. In the end, I was able to convince Ray that what Robby lacked in persona, he made up for in originality. Robby's musical contribution to this band was immense, and once he had joined us, The Doors was complete.

As we continued to meet and rehearse, a fascinating thing happened. One day, in a show of extraordinary selflessness, Jim suggested that all the songs be credited as being written by all of us, even though he, himself, the primary lyricist, was entitled to half of the writing royalties. As a result, no song in our playlist is written solely by Jim Morrison. No song is written solely by John Densmore. And no song is written solely by Robby Krieger or Ray Manzarek. Jim's desire to split the pot four equal ways had never been done by a band in the history of popular music, from Glenn Miller to the Beatles and beyond.

Then Jim took it a step further. During a break in a rehearsal, he sat up on the edge of the couch and declared, "We should all have veto power." That is, if any one of us didn't like something that was proposed, each man had the right to veto it. That's the way Jim thought we could achieve harmony, and we all loved the idea, which worked flawlessly—until this current court battle some thirty years later.

In 1967, during the Summer of Love, Elektra Records released our first album and "Light My Fire" went straight to the top of the charts . . . and stayed there . . . and stayed there . . . for an unheard-of twenty-six weeks. We started touring and recorded a second album, and toured some more, and recorded some more. This was our life over the next several years . . . an incredibly creative period that was a lot of fun, especially because we were all kindred spirits. But then Jim started to go down.

Besides his encroaching alcoholism, there was another divisive element in the air: Vietnam. The folk prophet Bob Dylan whistled into my ears, giving me the courage to get out of the draft, which was blowing in the wind harder every day:

> Temptation's page flies out the door
> You follow, find yourself at war
> Watch waterfalls of pity roar
> You feel to moan but unlike before
> You discover that you'd be just one more
> Person crying.

A napalm storm would reach such a gale force that college kids, married men, and parents with children were forced into a "conflict" we knew was a "terrible wrong," way before Secretary of Defense McNamara would write that phrase in a war memoir. His book exposed the underpinnings of why I narrowly escaped going down with sixty thousand of my classmates and ghetto brothers, not to mention a million and a half Vietnamese. It was a book written in blood, not ink.

Power-hungry men didn't understand that the Dylan lyric, *The warriors whose strength is* not *to fight*, was heralding the beginning of a movement: peace. Jim further defined the underpinnings of the time:

> There's blood in the streets, it's up to my ankles
> Blood in the streets, it's up to my knee

Blood in the streets, the town of Chicago
Blood on the rise, it's following me.

The dread was with us 24/7 and we were desperate every day due to the immoral nature of the enterprise and the growing awareness of the American public. The country was divided "for" and "against," and we were against this war in a big way. At the same time, the seeds of the civil rights movement, the peace movement, and the women's movement were all being planted in the sixties. The Doors were steeped in that kind of stuff, hoping we could sort of level the playing field for everyone else out there. It may have been a pipe dream, but without a dream, one has no sense of direction. We also hoped to make a lot of dough, though we wanted to do it with a sense of social consciousness.

By the time we had reached "arena" status, which is usually reserved for sports and not music, we had acquired a couple of managers, Sal Bonafede and Asher Dann. They were obviously not kindred spirits, however, when they pulled Jim aside one day and said, "Hey, *you're* the money. Let's get rid of these other guys."

They didn't know Jim. At our very next rehearsal, Jim told us, "These guys want me to dump you guys . . . Let's dump *them.*" Which we did.

The businessmen drink my blood
Like the kids in art school said they would
And I guess I'll just begin again . . .
—Arcade Fire

And then a final note of group unity manifested when we were about to go onstage and a DJ introduced us to an audience somewhere as "Jim Morrison and The Doors." Our lead singer dragged the DJ back onstage by the ear, refusing to play until he reintroduced us as just "The Doors."

Those were the good old days. Now, the remaining Doors are ready to tear asunder everything we stood for in the beginning. We used to be a collective body intent on making art, not a bunch of individuals mainly out for ourselves or for the money. Perhaps if Jim hadn't made such a point of us being a "band of brothers," we wouldn't be here in this historic courthouse at all. But he did, and it resonates with me still.

Chapter 2

LITIGATION BLUES

I peer through the tiny peephole in the gleaming mahogany courtroom door of #36. I can see a couple of clerks bustling around and a stenographer sitting in front of the bench—the podium where the judge sits. When I step inside, it seems like things get very quiet. On the right side of the aisle I notice a few friends and family, and on the left . . . nobody. Rumor had it that Ray and Robby would be no-shows, and they are—since they're touring and raking in the bucks as fast and furiously as possible until this trial is over, for fear they will no longer be allowed to use the stolen name: "The Doors."

Once Jim was gone, I think to myself, I suppose we should have known better than to keep on going. But we just couldn't give up the musical synchronicity that the three of us had built over the last several years. Ray was right when he called us a diamond that, without all four points, would not shine as bright. But for the first few years after Jim died, we thought we could continue. We auditioned several singers, yet we swiftly came to the conclusion that no one could fill Jim's skintight leather pants, so Ray and Robby took over the vocal duties with lots of effort and little chops. Then, after two albums, we threw in the towel, walking away from guaranteed advances of $750,000 (in 1971—that would be several million dollars today) because the soul of our band was gone. Without our focal (and vocal) point, we were lost.

Ray embarked on some solo projects, and I joined Robby's band (RKO) for two tours of Europe, where he played half the set of his original fusion jazz, and I joined him for several Doors songs. We made sure the advertising for the tours was very specific about credits:

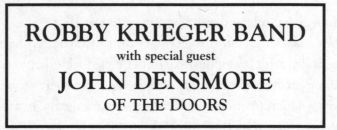

ROBBY KRIEGER BAND
with special guest
JOHN DENSMORE
OF THE DOORS

Of The Doors indicated that we were founding members of the original band—a term that I have never had a problem with. To me, this was a legitimate way to identify ourselves, since we weren't claiming to be the original band. We were founding members of The Doors, whose careers continued to thrive, even though our singer "broke on through to the other side." In fact, we released a greatest hits album that was so successful, *Rolling Stone* put a photo of Jim on the cover saying: "HE'S HOT, HE'S SEXY, AND HE'S DEAD."

I was shocked by the continued interest in The Doors's music, as director Francis Ford Coppola put our song "The End" at the beginning of his surrealist Vietnam epic movie, *Apocalypse Now*. It was an extremely powerful combination of visuals and music, and *Rolling Stone* writer Anthony De-Curtis said, "It is to this day one of the classic uses of music in a movie." So The Doors brand was doing fine, even though Jim was six feet under.

Then we got our own movie, thanks to award-winning director Oliver Stone. Ray had been taking lunches all over Hollywood, trying to drum up interest in a Doors film and proposing to the various studios that, since he'd attended UCLA film school, he should direct it. Robby and I were not surprised that the studios weren't biting. Who wanted to entrust millions of budget dollars into the hands of someone with a student résumé? You can bet we were relieved when Oliver Stone came on board, because his latest film, *Salvador*, had just been released and had impressed us all.

In a last-ditch effort to get his way, Ray criticized Stone's screenplay, which emphasized Jim's demons. He kept trying to hammer home his vision of a movie about the "Golden Doors," which overlooked all of Jim's shenanigans. It was no surprise, then, that Ray's attitude eventually made him less than welcome on Oliver Stone's set. All the while, we were getting offers to lend our music for the soundtrack to sell all kinds of stuff: cars, cigars, cigarettes, computers, a gas company, and tires. Even though we were on high alert about licensing our songs for commercials and endorsements after the Buick episode, the offers kept coming and we were manipulated, begged, extorted, and bribed to make a pact with the devil. And over the years, I have been the stubborn idealist resisting the external pressure of the corporations and the internal pressure of the other Doors to cave in to commercial interests.

I did this with relative ease until August 18, 2000, when Apple called. Without contacting us, they'd had the audacity to spend their own money to cut our song "When the Music's Over" into an ad for their new cube computer, which, incidentally, ended up dying a slow death, one of Apple's rare duds. They wanted our permission to air the commercial the following weekend and offered us a million and a half dollars! A MILLION AND A HALF DOLLARS!

Why not? I thought at first. *Apple is a pretty hip company. We use computers.* Damn it! Why did Jim have to have such integrity? We didn't need the money, I was pretty clear that we shouldn't do it, but the pressure immediately came down.

"Commercials will give us more exposure," Ray argued.

"So you're not for it because of the money?" I asked.

"No," he said.

Then why was Ray's first question always, "How much?" when we got one of these offers that he was almost always in favor of accepting?

I'm pulled from my reverie as twelve people enter from the right side of the courtroom through a door marked *Jury*. The trial becomes real as they file into the room and take their seats, looking like a global village: a couple of white people, several elderly Black women, two attractive young Latina women, and two middle-aged Latino men. A jury of my peers? Hopefully. If they could hear my jazz group Tribaljazz, they might be on my side since my band is as diverse as this group of jurors appears.

I take my seat with my crew. It feels good to have my wife Leslie here, as well as many friends, including Sam Joseph, a fellow writer and longtime friend. It doesn't feel good that there is no padding on the seats, as if I'm back in Catholic church sitting on those hard pews. At least there aren't any Bibles, although I'm going to be singing the hymn "Litigation Blues" over and over for quite a while.

I guess it was just a matter of time until push came to shove—when we got THE offer that would be just too good to refuse, and the gloves would come off once and for all. On

October 23, 2000, an offer came into The Doors's office that would make anyone's knees weak: Cadillac wanted to co-op rock and roll for their new line of cars. New, indeed! I don't think so. They were the same old giant SUV gas-guzzling battleships, old-world Frank Sinatra cars, and a few "sports" Caddies that looked just like the old ones. Apparently, they were trying to attract the youth market and get "hip," leaving behind the "senior citizen cruising Palm Springs" retirees. And they wanted to pay us a ton of money to use one of our songs. Remaining true to my original stance, I vetoed it.

But as the offer doubled and tripled due to my veto (when we didn't bite, what started as six million went to eight and finally topped off at fifteen), I started to feel like my life was in danger. It was a paranoid thought, but after being barraged for weeks by my own lawyers (they were supposed to be working for *all* of us), I was exhausted. I could hardly believe I was paying these attorneys one fourth of several hundred bucks an hour for this kind of abuse, as they spent a great deal of effort hassling me to give in so they could fashion the biggest commercial deal ever put together. They could *smell* history in the making, but their world (that of numbers) was not mine.

Over and over, I tried to explain to these businesspeople about maintaining integrity with Jim's lyrics. My pleas fell on deaf ears, and day after day the lawyers called, emailed, and instant-messaged me. We were looking at fifteen million dollars and even *I* had to admit that the numbers were astounding. But each of us already had nice homes and a couple of groovy cars. I looked at Robby and said, "Okay . . . what do you want to buy? What do you need that you haven't got?"

He had no answer as he straightened out his spine a little. Robby looked like he might cave in, but Ray simply could not believe we were thinking about passing on such big money.

He called endless meetings with our lawyers, which I refused to attend since I knew I was being targeted to be worn down until I relented. But Ray prodded the lawyers to continue calling me. In fact, I wrote a piece on this subject for the *Nation*, a periodical dedicated to politics and culture.

My editor at the *Nation*, Tom Hayden, who served in the California State Assembly and the State Senate, warned me that turning down that kind of money would make some people very angry. He knew firsthand about being the brunt of people's anger since he was *still* being attacked, along with his then wife, actor/activist Jane Fonda, for their anti–Vietnam War stance. I'd already gotten a few negative letters in response to my article, calling me a "wealthy, guilt-ridden rock dinosaur completely out of touch with everyone except rich socialists."

Here is an excerpt from my article:

> *I am reminded of the sound of greed, trying to talk me into not vetoing a Doors song for a cigarette ad in Japan.*
>
> *"It's the only way to get a hit over there, John. They love commercials. It's the new thing!"*
>
> *"What about encouraging kids to smoke, Ray?"*
>
> *"You always have to be PC, don't you, John?"*
>
> *I stuck to my guns and vetoed the offer; thinking about the karma if we did it.*

Around this time, I wrote an autobiography, *Riders on the Storm*, in which I took Ray to task, saying that his crusade to "raise The Doors's consciousness" was a little self-serving. Not only was my book a best seller, Oliver Stone actually waxed poetic on the back about what a visionary I was, but it seemed that jealousy reared its ugly head in Ray's stomach, which he blamed on me. I spoke to Ray's wife Dorothy when he was in the hospital and she reassured me that he was doing better and getting out of the woods, after six hours of exploratory surgery. I wished him well, but obviously, emotionally he still saw me through a group of trees ... probably giant redwoods. A few years later, Ray rewrote The Doors's history with an autobiography of his own, criticizing me for making poor choices in my personal life and calling me "the dumb drummer."

Book critic Teresa Gubbins of the Dallas Morning News made me feel better when she reviewed Ray's book:

> Mr. Manzarek still feels a compulsion to throw another log on The Doors's pyre with his pompous account. His recollections favor his own contributions and downplay guitarist Robby Krieger . . . Drummer John Densmore, whose bummer disposition repeatedly brings down Mr. Manzarek's high, gets kicked again and again. Jim didn't like him either, you see. It leaves you questioning the very thing Mr. Manzarek goes to such great lengths to establish: just how much of a hand he really had in the greatness that was The Doors.

Well, he is a great keyboard player ... but I couldn't have worded that any better myself.

And now here I sit, waiting for the judge to enter the courtroom. I really hoped it wouldn't come to this when I was deposed for this trial on April 23, 2004. When the Cadillac offer finally died, I thought we were through the worst of it. We weren't. The final straw came when Ray and Robby decided to take their act on the road—only it wasn't going to be *their* act. It was going to be The Doors of the 21st Century. No Jim Morrison. No John Densmore. So it wasn't The Doors at all. If anything, it was The Doors Unhinged.

Chapter 3

BEGINNING OF THE END

As I wait for the mystery man, the judge, to enter the courtroom with my fate in his hands, I reflect on how much I've already learned about the court system. First of all, it moves VERY slowly. In my naïveté, I thought you just sued someone and then you showed up in court, the lawyers pled their cases, and the jury reached a verdict. I had no idea about the pretrial world of settlement conferences, ridiculous numbers of depositions, and all the rest of it. Clearly, the word "naïve" is an understatement when I think about all I've been through to get to this point—after I made my unlikely decision to go for it.

It unfolded like this:

The California poppies were blanketing the hillsides in 2002, heralding the spring equinox, when our manager, Danny Sugerman, called to say that Harley-Davidson motorcycles was hosting a gala hundredth-anniversary celebration. They wanted Ray, Robby, and me to perform for really big bucks and I was interested for two reasons: First, I like making money as much as the next guy, so my greed gene would get a good fix. Second, I hoped that Manzarek's pleading for more $ via selling our songs for advertisements would subside.

Dream on, John. Can you believe that during this period in our band's life, Ray was trying to make the case that he was broke?

"But I've been married three times," I challenged him, "paid alimony and child support, and I'm doing fine financially. And *you're* broke?"

Knowing I'd busted him, he said with a squirm, "Well, I'm not broke . . . I just need a few more million."

It turned out that I didn't do the motorcycle gig, not because I didn't want to—I *did* want to—but because I feared for my health. I'd suffered for years with tinnitus, a brutal disease that gives the perception of a constant ringing in the ears, a hellish state for anyone, especially a musician. It was much better these days, but I feared that doing a gig right then might impede my healing process. I passed on the gala and Stewart Copeland, a wonderful drummer formerly with the Police, filled in for me. Little did I know that this gig, which should have been so straightforward, would lead to a major rift between my bandmates and me. It seemed that amid positive reviews for the Harley-Davidson celebration, Ray blurted out during an interview with *Billboard* magazine that "Stewart and Ian Astbury [formerly of the Cult] are playing with us from here on out."

Gosh. It sounded like I had just been fired—in public. A phone call would have been nice. But instead of raging against the tide, I called Robby and said, "Okay, if you guys are going to tour, go ahead. But you have to change the name of the group. Without Jim, it's not 'The Doors.' Call it 'The New Doors' if you want. Whatever. Just make it clear that this band is different from our original band."

Robby agreed, and they booked a number of gigs in Los Angeles, Las Vegas, and Toronto. But a few weeks later, a friend called. "John," he said, "I was just driving through Sin City and I saw a giant billboard promoting an upcoming concert by THE DOORS."

I called Robby immediately, plenty pissed off. "What's the story?" I said. "I thought we had an agreement you'd use a different name. Get it right!"

I also contacted their new manager, Tom Vitorino, who had the gall to berate me by saying, "What do you care about the name, anyway? It's just a logo. Why be so possessive?"

I thought that was abrasive treatment from someone like Tom, who had recently been promoted from The Doors's roadie to manager of the new group, where he could make some real dough for the first time. I tried to ignore his comments . . . until the ads for the upcoming tour started appearing in the newspapers. They had changed their name to "The Doors of the 21st Century," but our original logo was huge, and the new name, "of the 21st Century" (what a mouthful) was one third the size of the old trademark. If that wasn't bad enough, they had superimposed the lettering on top of an outtake of our second album cover, our only cover that did not have a shot of us four band members. This outtake photo got them off the hook for plagiarism, but it looked EXACTLY like our second album cover. To top off the rip-off, a line from Jim's poetry was included: THE CEREMONY IS ABOUT TO BEGIN, followed by the word AGAIN.

It was further implied that the original group was back when they placed ads on the Universal Amphitheatre website, using a famous photo of Jim holding a sparkler. As if he were rising from the dead to perform in the upcoming gigs. To imply that this new band was the real thing to young fans who weren't old enough to have experienced the first round was totally manipulative. The following review in *Variety*, written by Steven Mirkin, reflected the travesty:

> ## DOORS REUNION ABSOLUTELY DEADLY
> *The show was less a concert than dinner-theater rock, an exercise in empty nostalgia without the original cast. When looking for a new name, perhaps Manzarek and Krieger should have opted for "Dormant."*

I had to do something, but begging Robby to correct the misconception came to no avail. He just kept telling me he wanted to perform for large crowds like in the old days, and they booked more and more gigs. Each time I complained, the ads got altered slightly, but the effect was inconsequential and friends began calling me to excitedly say that they were getting tickets to see me play. The legacy we'd built as a group with integrity was being eroded into one of those worn-out sixties groups with two members left, playing for the money. I was deeply troubled when I got hundreds of letters from fans saying they couldn't wait to hear me play again. For example:

May 12, 2003

Dear John,

I know you are extremely busy, but I wanted to thank you for all the years of excellent entertainment. I am a huge fan, always remark how great you are whenever we listen to our classic Doors albums. We are so psyched that The Doors are touring and can't wait to see you at PNC Arts Center this summer!!!!!

Is there any way to obtain an autograph?

Thanks a million and take care,
Jessica

July 23, 2003

Dear Mr. Densmore,
I am a poet/singer who was deeply affected by The
Doors's music as I was growing up. I live in Virginia and
plan to catch you guys in Virginia Beach in August. Have
a great tour.

Sincerely,
Norm

Could anyone doubt that these people were victims of
false advertising? I was devastated, especially when Jim Keltner, arguably the most famous recording session drummer in
pop music history, called me to say he'd stayed up late to see
The "so-called" Doors on Jay Leno, and was appalled at the
misrepresentation. Leno had actually announced, "One of
the greatest rock and roll bands ever has reunited after thirty
years."

Natalie Nichols of the *Los Angeles Times* wrote about
their live show:

Manzarek insisted throughout Friday's show that The
Doors . . . are a new thing. Okay, so what's this new
thing got? A logo that looks a lot like the old Doors logo,
a two-hour set of nothing but old Doors tunes, and the
promise of a new album later this year. Genuine sparks
were minimal, furthering the sense that the whole affair
was a sad replay of something that was once great.

Since my pleas with Robby to modify the name had produced no results, I had nothing left to do but launch my own major offensive—a lawsuit—the hardest thing I would ever do. I would never have believed, when we were back in Ray Manzarek's parents' garage, that eventually I'd be ragging on my fellow musicians, the ones with whom I had created something much, much more than the sum of its parts. These guys were my musical brothers, and it felt like I was turning on my family. I took myself to task, wondering if maintaining my integrity was worth losing millions of dollars in attorneys' fees, which *would* happen if the judge or jury didn't get my point of view. Not to mention losing a fourth of EIGHTEEN MILLION dollars in commercials I'd passed on. Why was I being such a hard-ass?

I couldn't get Jim's spirit out of my mind. That's why.

I called up The Doors's former attorney, Abe Somer, of Mitchell, Silberberg & Knupp, and we met at his office to review some old contracts. Russ Frackman, one of the senior barristers at the firm, told me I definitely had a case. But this firm could not represent me due to the conflict of having represented the entire band in the past. Instead, he recommended a small firm in my hometown of Santa Monica, where I was immediately seduced by the warm personality of attorney Jerry Mandel. As he and I walked from his office on Wilshire Boulevard to a local lunch spot (he wore a Hawaiian shirt, jeans, and he was about my age), I liked him right away. But I was kind of stunned when he looked at me with a smile and said, "We're gonna be friends for life, John."

And you're gonna have your hand in my pocket for life? I thought.

We were from the same era, we had a lot of similar life experiences, but how could I ever have a lawyer for a friend?

I was about to find out. The game was on as Jerry and I initiated a lawsuit to prevent Ray and Robby from using The Doors's name. I put out a press release that read, in part:

> *Los Angeles, Feb. 4, 2003*
> *In a move to protect the legacy of one of rock's greatest musical groups, attorneys representing John Densmore, cofounder and drummer of The Doors, have filed a legal action in Los Angeles County Superior Court today charging breach of contract, trademark infringement, and unfair competition against Ray Manzarek and Robby Krieger, the two other remaining members of The Doors . . .*
>
> *"It's misleading to the fans," stated Densmore. "I'm forced to speak out now and to take action in order to protect the integrity of the great work all four of us created together. My partners are free to play under any other name and any other logo, as the members of many bands from the same era are doing. I am seeking only to end the confusion caused by the deceptive ad campaign they are using on this tour, in order to preserve the legacy of The Doors, and to set the record straight."*

This initial move brought me fairly positive worldwide press and it felt like I was doing the right thing, though my elation was short-lived. A few weeks later, Ray and Robby responded by launching a countersuit of their own against me—for FORTY MILLION DOLLARS.

That's right. Forty million dollars. I called my old pal and said, "Robby, let me get this straight . . . I sued you guys about the name, not the money, and your response is to sue me back for more money than all of us have made collectively in our entire lives?"

"Oh, that's just what lawyers do," was his reply. I hung up quickly, feeling a sting from one of my best friends. Maybe it's naïve of me, or kind of like wearing blinders, to think that everybody who grew up in the sixties was altruistic. That decade really only had a couple of years, from '65 to '67, when that kind of thinking flourished.

We were street scientists, exploring the use of psychedelics, which were legal at the time. By '68, cocaine and the Vietnam War had blown our "doors of perception" off their hinges, but as the dharma bum, Pulitzer Prize–winning poet Gary Snyder, said that maybe the seeds of the sixties (civil rights, peace movement, feminism) wouldn't all sprout for fifty or a hundred years . . . but they had been planted!

Are they growing in your garden, Ray? Robby? Of course we wanted to make money, and fame was an exciting concept, but I think our lead singer was saddened by the pursuit of all that overshadowing the fruit of new, challenging art . . . and ideas. I wanted to remind Robby in particular that we must not forget that we were blessed much more than most. We were part of a great band that was important to and touched millions of people. We made large sums of money that provided ourselves and our families with wonderful and secure lives, allowing me to be generous with others, to donate to charities and the arts, and to help friends. So what is this madness about suing me for forty million dollars?

My new attorney, Jerry, tried to reassure me that they were just trying to scare me (it worked), and that I wasn't really exposed (meaning vulnerable to being wiped out financially), but the feeling that my family was being terrorized wouldn't go away. Reiterating my lawyer's assurances didn't quell my fear for my loved ones who depended on me. Neither did the character assassinations against me in the coun-

tersuit, language that was meant to provide some basis for
Ray and Robby's accusations:

> The legendary performing group The Doors is currently
> being held hostage by the arbitrary, capricious, and bad-
> faith actions of its drummer, Cross-Defendant John
> Densmore. While the other two surviving members of
> the band, Cross-Complainants Raymond Manzarek
> and Robby Krieger, are seeking to revitalize the band's
> legacy and to perform the band's classic songs before a
> new generation of fans, Densmore has engaged in a de-
> structive course of conduct in which he casts his vote on
> issues of band governance in an arbitrary, capricious, and
> sometimes malicious manner rather than voting in good
> faith and in the best interests of the band and its legacy.
> The various damaging effects of Densmore's actions have
> caused Manzarek and Krieger to suffer substantial dam-
> ages which total at least forty million dollars.

I was learning how highly complicated the legal system
can be. Before a trial date, they have these little get-togethers
they call "settlement conferences" where they try to work out
compromise agreements between the warring parties in an
effort to avoid the time and cost of a formal trial.

And so it was onward and downward as I headed through
the bowels of the Century City Towers parking garage to
show up at the law offices of Lavely & Singer for the first
"settlement conference." These famously expensive attorneys whom Ray and Robby had hired had defended such luminaries as Britney Spears and Arnold Schwarzenegger.

Now I was about to enter their lair as I paid my thirty dollars (!) to the parking attendant and headed for the elevator,

walking into a wind vortex as I stepped inside. I pressed the button for the twenty-fifth floor, hoping that one of our famous California earthquakes wasn't about to hit. Not only do these high-rise buildings change wind patterns, they are actually built to *sway* a little bit in case the earth decides to do some mountain-making. Maybe it was vertigo, but I felt the structure moving a little just before I exited on the twenty-fifth floor.

There, I met up with my self-declared "country" lawyer from Santa Monica where we would face the other side for the first time. Even though this settlement conference would end up as an exercise in futility, as with all the rest, there was one positive note. Like a home run hit to left field, the fact that I had started this mess left me with a gift that I never, ever would have expected—meeting Jim's father, "the Admiral."

Chapter 4

THE ADMIRAL

Still waiting for the judge, I know I'm doing the right thing, but my alter ego is feeling remorse. At times, I have doubts about alienating possibly two of the most important people in my life so far. But Ray and Robby didn't exactly call me up and say, *Hey, John, we want to go out on the road and use The Doors's name. Can we make some kind of arrangement?*

They just did it.

"All rise," the bailiff announces. We stand while everyone's attention shifts to see Judge Gregory Alarcon striding into the courtroom. He has a few wisps of dark hair drooping over the top of his ears, sort of like an early, early Beatles mop top. Maybe he's one of us and will side with us! US? It's no longer *us*, John. It's you and them. So what if this judge is asleep at the wheel? You can have good intentions but the "system" can wear anyone down. When I think about it, that's the golden rule of too many lawyers these days: *Forget the truth! Who gives a damn about the truth? Just hit your opponent with a never-ending barrage of paper and con-*

tradicting accusations, and maybe you can confuse the hell out of everybody—including the judge.

Alarcon takes his seat, so do the rest of us, and I have a good look around the courtroom. This is the day I dreaded, the beginning of the trial, and here we are. Well, not all of us. One of us is gone forever, the other two Doors are off relentlessly playing gigs until they are made to cease and desist (or not), and I sit here in the courtroom, waiting for opening statements in a case against my former brothers. I'm here with my attorney, Jerry Mandel. Several of Ray and Robby's attorneys, whom I met during the settlement conferences and the deposition, are at the opposite table, and some of my personal support team are flanking me.

The Morrison family, involved by their own choice in these proceedings, is not in the courtroom on this first day of the trial. I didn't expect them to be. When I passed through the daunting metal detectors at the entrance to the courthouse earlier this morning, I speculated about whether or not Jim's eighty-year-old parents had the *cojones*, let alone the stamina, to make it through all of this. After all, they live on Coronado Island in San Diego County, a long journey to Los Angeles to face such an upsetting ordeal. The irony is that the current beefed-up security at the entrance to this courthouse is not a result of 9/11, which occurred only a couple of years prior. Rather, they cracked down following a somewhat recent divorce proceeding during which a doctor shot his wife on the second floor of this very building.

To be perfectly honest, I was amazed that Jim's estate, consisting of the Admiral, Mrs. Morrison, and Penny Courson (Jim's mother-in-law), actually jumped on board with their own lawsuit to join forces with me. I had worked hard at trying to rally the estate to unite with me in the suit by sending them copies of Ray's and Robby's manipulative ads and interviews. A couple of silent months had passed and I thought they had no interest—then their attorneys finally called and said that the estate agreed to unite with me. For the first time since I decided to take legal action against my former bandmates, I felt gratified and hopeful.

In fact, when I knew for sure that the Morrisons and I had actually teamed up, the mere thought of standing beside Jim's parents at a press conference seemed so powerful, I fantasized about Ray and Robby ceremoniously giving up and handing our name, The Doors, back to the Admiral and Mrs. Morrison. I could imagine the very people whom Jim had declared "dead" (in his first press bio) staring down Jim's old partners and asking them what the hell they were doing with their son's legacy. Of course, it was only a fantasy, but you have to remember that before I'd met Jim's parents at the first of two court settlement conferences a few months prior, they had been phantom people toward whom Jim had directed some pretty powerful and disturbing lyrics.

It was in our song "The End":

The killer awoke before dawn
He put his boots on
He took a face from the ancient gallery
And he walked on down the hall
He went into the room where his sister lived, and then he
Paid a visit to his brother, and then he
He walked on down the hall, and
And he came to a door
And he looked inside
"Father?"
"Yes, son?"

"*I want to kill you*"
"*Mother? I want to . . .*"
WAAAAAA . . .

Now, it turned out that Jim's family were flesh-and-blood real people, and meeting them at the first settlement conference felt like dreamtime.

Jim was *walking down the hallway.*

He went into a room where his sister lived . . .

There was Anne Morrison, Jim's real-life sibling, the one who accepted her brother's trophy at the Rock & Roll Hall of Fame induction. She looked like a pretty, middle-aged former Southern California surfer, clutching her husband's arm in the hallway.

And then he paid a visit to his brother . . .

There was Jim's brother, Andy Morrison, a friendly, nearly bald man who flew in from Hawaii, where he lived, expressly for the settlement conference. Soft, short, white tufts of hair on the sides of his ears made a sharp contrast to the last and only time I'd met him, in front of our studio where we recorded "L.A. Woman" so many years ago. Back then, his thick hair flowed all the way down his back. I suppose I looked different to him as well, with *my* bald spot gaining ground every day.

And he walked on down the hall. Yeah!

And he came to a door and he looked inside. Father . . .

Mother . . .

There they all were. Admiral Steve Morrison was wearing a nice-looking gray suit, his straight-backed posture suggesting his lifelong military career. His wife, Clara Morrison, sporting silver earrings to match her tied-up silver Victorian locks, had a twinkle in her eye. But could this sweet lady in the wheelchair really be the same woman who stomped into our gig thirty-five years ago at a DC arena and interrupted a discussion between our manager and the lighting director, demanding to know what was wrong with her son's lighting crew? Aging has a way of tenderizing even the toughest among us.

And then there was Jim's mother-in-law, Pearl "Penny" Courson. After her daughter Pamela died, Penny had teamed up with the Morrisons, agreeing to share equally in The Doors interests that she owned. Penny and I had recently reconnected since we were on the same side of the fence of this "travesty," as the *New York Times* repeatedly called it when they were giving the new band very bad reviews. I'd been enjoying Penny's sharp wit on the phone during the last few months. "As soon as 'Lawrence of Poland' opens his mouth," she said to me, "we'll win this case," referring to Ray's self-aggrandizement.

I was well aware of who Ray was, but still, I was stunned that Professor Manzarek didn't even blink when he first saw the representatives of Jim's estate. Instead, he dropped into his sugar-sweet charm mode that I knew all too well, shaking everyone's hand as if nothing controversial was going on.

When I met the Admiral, on the other hand, I saw immediately that although he was a military man, he was not packing a rod for vengeance (like that divorced doctor, for instance, a couple of floors below). The Admiral's target was simply the two Doors who were trying to sell out his deceased son's legacy, and were now shaking hands congenially, trying to appease the famously private progenitors. I'd thought (mistakenly) that once Ray was pushing seventy, he would back away from his famous declaration, "The Doors's music is the appropriate vision for the second half of the twentieth century. I won't stop until everyone knows who Jim Morrison is. I might have to do a lot of talking, maybe the rest of my life."

As Ray continued to press for usage of the original name, adding the odd singer to his latest band (anyone in leather pants would do), and was looking to sell our music to the highest bidder, he seemed to have forgotten who Jim really was and what he stood for. But Admiral Steve Morrison hadn't forgotten. After all, he had risen to the level of rear admiral through sheer hard work, only to hit the wall when he should have been promoted to "full" admiral—partially because of his son's aberrant behavior.

It seems that a promotion from rear to full admiral occurs by political appointment only. Rumor has it that Rear Admiral Morrison applied for the promotion several times but was continually shot down by the antics of his antiestablishment son. Each time he scaled to the top through hard work and dedication, Jimbo thwarted his goal with controversial news-making behavior, such as penning the clearly antiwar song "Unknown Soldier," being detained for drunk and disorderly behavior on a flight to Phoenix, and last, and perhaps worst, being arrested for alleged indecent exposure in Miami.

The above minor lapse in decorum (which didn't really happen but might as well have, considering the repercussions) managed to generate a large "Rally for Decency" in 1969, held at the Orange Bowl and attended by thirty thousand people. Such luminaries as Miami "Rat Packer" Jackie Gleason and homophobe Anita Bryant ranted about the decay of American ideals. The grand finale was the reading of a letter from that champion of morality: Tricky Dick Nixon. I was struck at the impact that Jimbo's behavior was having on the culture, but he *did* have an FBI file as thick as the Pentagon Papers. In retrospect, I'm proud that The Doors were on Nixon's hit list. We were tagged not because of any overt political activity; it was just that our songs and personae represented rebellious youth, not unlike the censorship of artists that still goes on today in dictatorial countries.

In any event, the Admiral, who was so proud of his time in the service, offered to retire rather than allow his son's public arrests to generate criticism toward the navy. When they refused to accept his resignation, the Admiral and his beloved navy came to a compromise and he retired to the rear. They offered him the title "Commander in Chief, Marianas," a post that the Admiral relished, as he was able to help thousands of refugees. And now there he stood opposite me, extending his hand as a comrade-in-arms.

"Although these are difficult and awkward circumstances," he said warmly, "it is a pleasure to meet you, John."

I almost wanted to salute. Symbolically, I was the prodigal son, finally returning to complete the circle. So much had happened between the actual father and son, going back to Jim's statement in 1966, in The Doors's first biography, that his parents were dead. And now, despite their subsequent lack of contact and the negative things Jim had said about them, here they were, standing with me, trying to defend the integrity of the "word man's" words, while protecting the purity of the magic created among us four band members. I'd lost my own dad to cancer; he had been a typical fifties male, hiding behind the newspaper most of the time, rarely connecting. Now, I was forming an alliance with a member of the World War II generation, to uphold a mutual vision.

It felt like a healing salve and I took the huge leap of forgiveness (in the sixties, we were dedicated to *hating* anyone over thirty), realizing that if Admiral Steve hadn't been the archetypal military man for Jim to rail against, he would never have blossomed into full-blown James Dean rebellion. I know it's a lofty example, but if Judas wasn't fully himself, Jesus might not have become the Christ. Not that you want these obstacles along your path, but in retrospect, one can see the bigger plan and hopefully get some closure. The Doors's family circle was intact, except two members were on the outside . . . because they had put themselves there.

At the end of the first settlement conference, there were no agreements and Judge Alarcon pressed for another settlement conference, trying very hard to bring together these two divergent groups of people. I learned later that having two settlement conferences was rare, but the good judge was a Doors fan and hoped he could help us come to terms. In the end, unfortunately, the gap only got wider. Our attorneys called Ray and Robby's barrister, Jay Lavely, several times between conferences, but he never returned a call—until Mark Hurwitz, Penny Courson's lawyer, had a wild idea. We offered to *walk*, to drop the entire lawsuit with no money claims other than attorneys' fees—if they would cease using The Doors's name by December 31, 2003. They countered again with the same old proposal of keeping the name "The Doors of the 21st Century" until 2008. In other words, they wouldn't budge.

Penny Courson said later that it had been a very emotional day, with the reunion of these two families that had each lost a child to the abuses of the sixties. The depth of the tragedy is reflected in the fact that Jim and his parents never connected when he was alive. But later, a kind of healing between the families had begun, which only escalated our upset at what Ray and Robby were doing. And it was far from over. Since the settlement conferences had been unproductive, it was onward to the many depositions, the next phase of legal-istic protocol before the trial, information-gathering sessions held in law offices. This was where the principals in a case get to be interrogated by opposing counsel—sort of like a dress rehearsal for the trauma to come.

Chapter 5

THE DRESS REHEARSAL

My deposition started with the formalities, such as listing the names of everyone present: Ray and Robby's rep, John Lavely; my attorney, Jerry Mandel; and the estates' attorney, Jeff Forer. We sat in a large fluorescent-lit conference room at the offices of Lavely & Singer where the atmosphere was stiflingly formal as they laid out the requisite admonishments—that I was under oath and facing the penalty of perjury. I listened, trying to figure out if I was a good guy or a bad guy. I believed I was doing the right thing, even though our hard-core Doors fans were probably incensed at me for initiating this train wreck. Well, that was how I felt when Yoko Ono supposedly broke up the Beatles so many years prior, but my circumstances are much more complicated.

First and foremost, John Lennon was still alive when Yoko entered the scene, and Jim is gone. If they ever found a way to resurrect him, I'd be back in a New York minute. Secondly, I now understand that it was *time* for the Beatles to break up. Nothing lasts forever. In fact, there was latent tension between Paul and George in their *Let It Be* documentary and Yoko was supposedly a powerful catalyst for the inevitable end of the group and the jump-start for John's incredible solo career.

I took a deep breath in the windowless conference room and prepared for the onslaught as I was asked about my cell phone bills and other annoying and prying financial questions. I felt like they were snooping through my dresser drawers, inspecting my underwear, until Mr. Lavely asked me, "Do you know who was talking to Jim Morrison about this dispute, namely the issue of the use of 'Light My Fire' in the Buick Opel commercial?"

Here we were, at the crux of the matter that had occurred so many years ago, when we all got the message loud and clear that Jim was irate that we had even *considered* selling out. I said that it had been Penny Courson's daughter Pam who had witnessed Jim on the phone with Ray, giving him grief about the Buick commercial.

"And what did Penny Courson tell you about that?" Lavely asked me.

"She said Pam noticed that Jim was visibly shaken," I answered, "and a little teary, and he quickly got off the phone. Pam said, 'What's wrong?' And Jim said something like, 'They sold us down the river.' I'm paraphrasing."

"Is that your best recollection of that conversation?" Mr. Lavely asked.

"Yes, it is," I said.

"Did you express objection or disapproval of the hiring of Ian Astbury as singer in connection with any Harley-Davidson concert?" he said.

Now wait a minute here. What about the conversation we were just having about Buick? I was quickly learning that when a lawyer doesn't like an answer, he or she just ignores it and moves on. I moved on too. I had no other choice. "I had a continuing dialogue with Robby about having trouble with one guy doing Jim's part," I said. "I told him if he wanted to go on tour, why not take several singers? Then it would be a tribute, not someone trying to *be* Jim Morrison."

I explained that I had thought Ian was fine for one show. What I didn't say was I had hoped that the money they got for the Harley-Davidson show would calm Ray down and hopefully get him off the "selling out for commercials" track.

"So that whatever was Ray Manzarek's share of $150,000," continued Mr. Lavely, "it would make up for the fifteen-million-dollar Cadillac deal. Is that your theory?"

"No," I said. This man was clearly trying to make me look like an idiot and I didn't appreciate it. "I don't approve of one guy trying to fill Jim's shoes," I explained. "The VH1 show we did was a tribute, and therefore avoided the trap of imitation." I went on to explain that, over the years, we had been approached by numerous people and businesses to buy our music for advertisements. When Jim had angrily and tearfully rejected the Buick commercial, I felt he had set a precedent, and even though he was no longer here, I wanted to honor it.

"And do you recall any conversation about a specific advertisement you talked to Robby about in that conversation about the modifier?" asked Lavely. He was shifting subjects faster than the speed of light.

"Yeah," I said, "I recall saying, 'You're using the logo. You can't do that.'"

"Where did you observe that?" he asked. "Was that a particular ad that you were commenting on?"

"In various newspapers," I said.

"What did Robby say?"

"He admitted it was manipulative," I answered.

"I'm going to move to strike that comment as nonrespon-sive," said Lavely to the stenographer.

What? Did the definition of "responsive" change when I wasn't looking? I had just responded honestly to his question and he was calling it nonresponsive. Is that because I didn't give him the answer he wanted? "That's what he said," I told Lavely.

"He said, 'I admit it's manipulative'?" Lavely asked me again.

"Yeah," I said.

"Why did you post this article or allow the link to the *Nation* article to be put on the official Doors website?" he asked. Another subject change.

"Well," I said, "it's actually on *my* page of the website, not on the front, and then they have to link to another site if they're interested in the subject matter."

This segment of the article is what he was referring to:

Robby stepped up to the plate again the other day, and I was very pleased that he's been a longtime friend. I was trying to get through to our ivory tinkler, with the rap that playing Robin Hood is fun, but the "bottom line" is that our songs have a higher purpose, like keeping the integrity of their original meaning for our fans. "Many kids have said to me that 'Light My Fire,' for example, was playing when they first made love, or were fighting in 'Nam, or got high—pivotal moments in their lives."

Robby jumped in. "If we're only one of two or three groups who don't do commercials, that will help the value of our songs in the long run. The publishing will suffer a little, but we should be proud of our stance." Then he hit a home run: "When I heard from one fan that our songs

saved him from committing suicide, I realized, that's it—
we can't sell off these songs."

So, in the spirit of the Bob Dylan line, "Money doesn't
talk, it swears," we have been manipulated, begged, extorted, and bribed to make a pact with the devil. While
I was writing this article, Toyota Holland went over the
line and did it for us. They took the opening melodic lines
of "Light My Fire" to sell their cars. We've called up attorneys in the Netherlands to chase them down, but in
the meantime, folks in Amsterdam think we sold out. Jim
loved Amsterdam.

The purpose of the article was to recount my dissatisfac-
tion with the corporate takeover of music in general, and my
battles with Ray and Robby to protect the legacy of our music
from overcommercialization. I apparently hit a nerve because
the BBC World News called me for an interview. Addition-
ally, the London *Guardian* and *Rolling Stone* magazine, which
had previously rejected the piece, syndicated it and it was
emailed all over Europe.

Mr. Lavely clearly had an agenda about my article as he
asked me, "Why did you create that link? Did you consider
the fact that you were discussing private business decisions
of the partnership among partners when you agreed to have
that linked?"

My team all objected at once, saying that the question
was argumentative. I would have objected too, but I objected
to *everything* that was taking place, so where would I begin?
I faced Mr. Lavely again as he asked me if what I considered
"lies about me" that Ray had written in his book were the
reason I had posted my *Nation* article.

"No," I answered. "I posted it because it's something I'm

concerned about, and if anyone else wanted to read about what I thought, they could."

"Did you feel you were being critical of one of your band-mates, namely Ray Manzarek, in that article that you linked onto this website?" Lavely wanted to know.

"I hoped that he could see the light about Jim's original message in vetoing the Buick commercial," I said.

"Did you think you were being critical of Mr. Manzarek when you referred to him as 'the hand of greed' and other characterizations like that?"

Now I was getting pissed off. "I did *not* refer to Ray Man-zarek as 'the hand of greed,'" I said. "I referred to *myself* as 'the hand of greed' because my hand was shaking when I wrote my 10 percent tithing checks to charity." He should have read my article more thoroughly if he intended to trap me with it.

"Whatever your understanding, it's about being critical," Lavely said. "Did you think you were being critical of Mr. Manzarek in this piece?"

"I was hoping that I could point out to him that not ev-eryone has a price," I answered quite honestly. "And that our songs are priceless."

"Is that the message you wanted to convey in this piece?" he said.

"Uh-huh. Yes."

"And that Mr. Manzarek had a price and you didn't?"

"Well," I said, "that the stuff we created a long time ago in his parents' garage turned out to be invaluable, and should be carefully nurtured."

"Do you recall making statements a number of places in your book [*Riders on the Storm*] that you hated performing and you were happy and thankful when the group decided to no longer tour after a year and a half of your trying to convince Ray and Robby to stop touring?"

Damn! This guy must have had a really bad undiagnosed case of attention deficit disorder. He couldn't stick with one subject for more than a few seconds. But I was rescued by my attorney, who objected to the question as argumentative and totally out of context.

I answered anyway: "To say I hated playing—this band was fantastic. What I hated was Jim's alcoholism, which deteriorated the quality."

Jerry brought my part of the deposition to an end in the next moment. I was relieved; I'd had enough. But I knew that this was only shades of things to come. The courtroom would be even more intimidating. I took some deep breaths and wondered how Ray would get through a similar going-over by my rep. Would he like it any better than I did?

And that day came.

"Mr. Manzarek," Jerry Mandel said, "as you sit here today, do you understand that you and Robby Krieger have sued John Densmore personally and that you are seeking to recover from him forty million dollars in damages, at least?"

"Yes," said Ray.

"Do you know if he even has forty million dollars?" Jerry asked.

"I wouldn't be surprised," said Ray smugly.

I couldn't believe he was saying that. He knew I didn't have that kind of money. Jerry made it very clear when he asked, "Have you earned forty million dollars from The Doors from the inception until today?"

"No," Ray said.

"Mr. Densmore has the same [financial] interest in The Doors as you. Is that right?"

"Yes."

Jerry went on, "Would you describe for me, please, the components of the forty million dollars that you seek to recover from Mr. Densmore? By that I'm not asking for your factual basis for the various allegations. I'm just trying to understand how the forty million dollars is arrived at . . . Was there, you know, a car that he destroyed that was ten thousand, or this was a million or something else that was ten million?"

"I have no comment," said Ray.

"You can't identify any specific acts?"

"Just Cadillac," said Ray. "Not taking the Cadillac commercial, for one."

"Any others?" asked Jerry.

"Leave it at that," said Ray, sounding plenty annoyed. "Let's see. The Apple television commercial and—I can't recall. Various other things, but I can't be specific at this particular time."

Ray must have forgotten that Robby, with whom he had joined in this lawsuit, had not okayed those two deals either. And when Jerry tried to remind Ray that he himself had vetoed many of the commercial offers, he had to agree that he had turned down Texas Gas.

"That was not what we wanted to use Doors songs for," Ray admitted. "If you want to use Doors songs, use them for something meaningful, something exciting, something artistic, a good product."

This brought to mind another excerpt from my *Nation* article:

It's not a given that one should do commercials for the products one uses. The Brits might bust me here, having heard "Riders on the Storm" during the seventies (in Britain only) pushing tires for their roadsters, but our singer's ghost brought me to my senses and I gave my portion to charity. I still don't think the Polish member of our band has learned the lesson of the (Buick) Opel, but I am now adamant that three commercials and we're out of our singer's respect. "Jim's dead!" our piano player responds to this line of thought. That is precisely why we should resist, in my opinion.

I was alluding to the one commercial we okayed after Jim died. It was a Pirelli tire ad that was aired in England only. Yes, I okayed it and so did the other two, but as soon as I got the dough, I realized what I had done and I gave my part away.

"So Pirelli tires were meaningful?" Jerry asked Ray.

"Good rain tires keep the family alive," Ray maintained.

"Good Texas gas burns in ovens," said Jerry, as Lavely strongly objected that Mr. Mandel was being overbroad, vague, and ambiguous.

"It's rather a silly question," said Ray. "First of all, the idea of Texas Gas and 'Light My Fire' is not where 'Light My Fire' should go. Aesthetically, it's not the right use of 'Light My Fire.'"

So why was he so ready to sell "Light My Fire" to Buick so many years prior? Is he suggesting that "Come on, Buick, Light My Fire" was appropriate for possibly the most important song of the entire sixties?

Jerry pressed on: "Were you ever presented with a commercial opportunity for 'Light My Fire' that you thought aesthetically was appropriate?"

"I can't recall at this time," said Ray, as if Buick had never happened.

"How about for a cigarette company?" asked Jerry.

"Not to my knowledge," said Ray.

"How about for a cigar company?"

"Not to my knowledge."

I think they call this perjury, since Ray had desperately wanted to sell our music for that cigarette commercial in Japan many years ago.

Then Jerry hit him with a hard one: "Isn't it true that you vetoed, literally said 'I veto' . . . accepting an offer from the Muriel Cigar Company for 'Light My Fire'?"

"I can't recall that at all," said Ray, his selective memory taking center stage. We already had deposition testimony from our former accountant, Bob Greene, who had clearly stated that Ray had deemed Muriel Cigars an inappropriate use of the music. In other words, Ray himself had vetoed the use of the song along with Robby and me. The testimony read:

Mr. Forer (the Jim Morrison estate's lawyer): Mr. Greene, what was discussed about Muriel Cigars and the use of the song "Light My Fire" in the commercials?

Mr. Greene: The band, and in particular Ray, said no, it's not appropriate. And my notes say that Ray vetoed the use of the song.

Mr. Forer: So Ray vetoed the use of the song?

Mr. Greene: That's what my notes said.

Mr. Forer: Do you recall if the other three members were for it?

Mr. Greene: I don't recall. I would doubt it.

Mr. Forer: Once Ray vetoed it, it was over?

Mr. Greene: Correct.

But try as he might (or might not), Ray just couldn't remember the offer from Muriel.

When Jerry was through grilling Ray, Robby gave his deposition as well, but for the sake of the reader, I'm leaving it out since he had nothing to say that was particularly monumental or surprising. So let me sum all of this up in a few quick sentences:

Ray and Robby were suing me for more money than our group had collectively ever made. They were also suing me for vetoing commercials that Robby had vetoed and in some cases so had Ray. But they were suing me anyway.

And now, here I am, on July 5, 2004, at Division #36 in the Los Angeles County Courthouse, flanked by my attorneys, as the memories fade and the curtain rises . . .

This is the end.

PART TWO

TRIAL AND TRIBULATION

Chapter 6

ONE FOR ALL

It's July 6, 2004. As I listen to my attorney's opening statement that marks the beginning of this long-awaited trial, I wonder how I found this noble David who I assigned to take out Goliath—the Hollywood law firm being retained by Ray and Robby. The eclectic jury is in place, the courtroom has been silenced, and I'm ready for the journey to justice. Or at least to what I hope will be justice.

"Ladies and gentlemen," Jerry addresses the jury, "we're going to go over forty years of history to resolve these issues. I'm prepared to start telling you about those forty years. So let's talk about it.

"In 1965, Ray Manzarek and Jim Morrison met each other at film school at UCLA. Shortly after they graduated, they met John Densmore and then they met his very good friend Robby Krieger. You'll hear all the details later. Suffice it to say, they all fell in love with each other. They all wanted to be in a band. They were kids in the sixties. Who didn't want to be in a band?"

I relax into my attorney's hypnotic storytelling style as he continues, "Morrison had never been in a band. He couldn't play an instrument. But he was a poet. He could write poetry and he could write his lyrics. And everybody else could write and arrange the music. They weren't kids. They were young adults. They weren't stupid, either. They all went to college. For example, Mr. Manzarek has a degree in economics and a master's degree in fine arts from UCLA.

"Right from the start, they made a very significant and unique agreement. In order to create harmony in the group, Jim decided they were all going to be equal."

No one knows better than I that this was an unheard-of agreement among a highly successful band of four, in which every decision would be made by consensus. Not only did we each own a quarter of the publishing, we also had equal veto power. It was one for all and all for one. I know it sounds like we're talking about the Three Musketeers, but that was also The Doors. We were all equal and there was to be no back-stabbing in this organization. I'm proud of that agreement and my attempt to continue to uphold it, as I place my attention back on what Jerry is saying:

"But today, the defendants in this case want to say, *There is no veto power*. Today the defendants contend that decisions are made and should be made by 'majority rules.' Why? Because the money has gotten bigger. Is the money more important than the principle?"

I have goose bumps, forgetting about the results for a moment and focusing on this journey. I am standing up for what I believe, the only thing that makes me feel at peace in this situation. Only a few months prior, in March 2003, when George W. Bush ordered a preemptive strike on Iraq, I found an opportunity to stand up for what I believed. It was on the eve of the invasion, when the strikingly poised and beautiful

British actress Julie Christie and I were involved in a theatrical performance of the Greek play *Lysistrata*.

"Good for our paths to have crossed on this issue," she said with deep sadness in her voice. "When you live as long as us, you get to see many wars."

The play was about how the Grecian women, led by Lysistrata, got fed up with the men fighting all the time and said they were going to withhold sex if the guys wouldn't stop their war games. Still pertinent today, it seems that artists see the future before other people do. When President Bush declared war on Iraq, granted, we may not have been politicians with inside info from the Pentagon, but our information came from the street, with no agendas attached. There were millions of us across the globe protesting the act of aggression that would result in terrible suffering and innumerable deaths. How perfect, then, at this particular time, to be performing one of the few surviving plays written by Aristophanes in 411 BC, a somewhat humorous tale of a woman's extraordinary mission to end the Peloponnesian War.

It reminded me of the posters from the Vietnam era depicting US generals with missiles coming out of their crotches. And then, in 2003, we were facing yet another travesty of war, and I stood beside the women once again. And what a stellar group of women it was: Julie Christie, Alfre Woodard, Christine Lahti, Mary McDonnell. I didn't feel castrated by the women or the play. I felt like a warrior who had rechanneled his energy into being "a warrior for peace." In fact, I've always been inclined this way. I suppose I'm basically the same person I was forty-five years ago, and yet . . . I'm not. Hopefully, I've evolved a little. It makes me think of the question the members of The Doors were all asked in various interviews over the years: "If you had it to do over again, would you do it differently?"

I remember Jim's answer to that one: "If I had to do it all over again, I think I would have gone more for the quiet and undemonstrative little artist plodding away in his own garden trip." I remember Ray being embarrassed by Jim's answer, wanting him to say that our career was so great, he'd do it all over again, just the same, if he had the chance.

If I could do this over again, the trial, I mean, would I travel down the same path? Yes and no. Yes, for the way I want to stand up for Jim. No, for the strain I'm putting on my family and friends and my health. I'm not sick, but the sickness inside this never-ending cloud of misery might just eat its way right through me. I still think that if one of Jim's masterpieces were downgraded to sell crap, I would get sick. So I suppose I might have done things differently, because hopefully you learn from your experience. But then, if I'd done things differently, I wouldn't be who I am, and the bottom line is . . . I like myself.

I have no idea what will happen in the end here, but I feel proud to be on what I consider the right side of the situation. And I'm even more impressed with Jerry than I ever expected to be, relieved that he is making the point that neither Ray nor Robby tried to sue Jim when he vetoed the Buick deal so many years prior. They followed his lead at the time and allowed the deal to be canceled. They hadn't made any noise or threatened to sue . . . until now, after he was gone.

"What is interesting," Jerry tells the court, "is that you're going to hear from each one of the band members about what they think 'governance' was. You'll hear from John Densmore and he'll tell you that anybody has a veto. Nothing has changed. You'll hear from the estates. They'll say they always understood that in the thirty years or so since they've been involved. You're going to hear from Robby Krieger, who is going to say, 'Yeah, that is how we operated.' And you're going to hear from Ray Manzarek. You'll see his words and you'll hear his words. And he probably has the simplest description of all—something he said less than three years ago before the Cadillac offer. He said, 'The Doors all had veto power. If one guy didn't want to do something, it wasn't done. That's the way it's always worked with The Doors. It was a four-way split of all the money, totally democratic with veto power.'

"Ladies and gentlemen, you're going to see it. You'll hear him say it. And it accurately sets forth the rule of governance of this band and this business called The Doors. The reason for all this 'how we do business' hyperbole is that John's old bandmates are trying for a 'coup' to get the governance changed to 'majority rules,' so they can do all the commercials they want. So you're going to see a fascinating document as we expect Stewart Copeland to come and testify."

When Copeland, the drummer for the Police, with Sting as their lead singer, was tapped by Robby and Ray to join their new touring group, he wrote a memo to Ray, Robby, Ian Astbury, and Tom Vitorino, the new manager of this band. The memo read:

> We have to talk about a few things. We can't really call ourselves The Doors, can we? Isn't everybody really going to get mad about this? Don't we have to pay them if we do something like that? And what about governance? How are we going to govern ourselves? Is it going to be unanimous like the old Doors? But if we don't call ourselves The Doors, maybe we won't get to play the really big arenas and drive around in the chauffeur-driven limousines.

Jerry explained that even though my old bandmates denied ever seeing this memo, Stewart Copeland himself would be walking into this courtroom and testifying under oath that he had written and sent it. He had also talked to people about it, including Ray and Robby.

After all is said and done, it seems like Ray and Robby really want The Doors experience, exactly as it happened in the past. They seem to want to repeat it over and over, including the large crowds, the money, the fame, and the notoriety. That would be fine with me if Jim were still around. But he isn't. Don't get me wrong; I like being admired, but being admired for something new seems more fulfilling than being admired for something I did years ago.

"They knew what they were doing," Jerry assures the jury. "And by January of 2003, the booking agents were selling this other band as The Doors across the country at $150,000 to $175,000 a night." Here he quoted a ridiculous statement from the defendants' lawyers: "They said they were doing this 'to put food on the tables of their families so they could eat.'"

As if things had gotten so bad, Ray's and Robby's families would starve unless they exploited the name of our group. That was so far from the truth, I considered it laughable. What happened to the times when we agreed that it was our mutual responsibility to use our notoriety not just to make money, but also for causes we believed in? Weren't we committed to doing what it took to promote peace and raise awareness?

I turn my attention back to Jerry as he says, "Then, John sees an ad in the *Los Angeles Times* on January 19 announcing that The Doors are going to perform at the Universal Amphitheatre."

I remember this well; as I mentioned, people called to tell me they were excited for the opportunity to watch me perform. But it had nothing to do with me. Suddenly, the name "The Doors" was meant to be Ray Manzarek, Robby Krieger, Stewart Copeland, and Ian Astbury. That wasn't The Doors the last time I checked. Jerry goes on to tell the jury that I got angry at the misuse of the name and called up Robby.

"What are you doing?" I asked Robby. "You promised me that it would be 'The (Something) Doors.' And that you wouldn't use our logo. But you're using the original name and you're using our logo. What's up with that?"

Jerry goes on, "Things don't get much better after that. They go back and forth. There's some yelling and screaming. John wants to try to work it out. It doesn't work. We now know that in Texas they're changing the advertising materials. Supervised by Dave Kirby, we now know that they have one ad mat for everywhere but California that uses the original logo and the name The Doors. There's a plan to try to make sure that John doesn't see that they're using the logo and the name in his backyard. Now, let me summarize by telling you what we want and what we don't want in this lawsuit."

I hope everyone is listening really well as Jerry makes it crystal clear: "We don't want to stop Ray and Robby from performing The Doors's music. They have the right to do that. We don't care if it's 'Ray Manzarek and Robby Krieger of The Doors.' We don't care if it's 'Ray Manzarek, Robby Krieger, founders of The Doors.' What we want is for them to stop identifying themselves as 'The Doors' or 'The Doors of the 21st Century,' because you'll hear experts who say, 'You know, Doors of the 21st Century.' Nobody will say, 'Of the 21st Century.' They'll say 'The Doors.' And you'll see evidence where people do exactly that."

Jerry explains that the name and legacy of The Doors has been harmed. He also states that we aren't asking for financial compensation for the harm that has already been done. "This is not about money," he says, informing the jury that I simply want the other partners to stop asserting authority where they have none, and to stop taking the asset of the partnership for themselves.

"It's wrong," Jerry tells everyone. "It's a misappropriation. Identity theft. And what I am saying is not speculation. I wouldn't stand here and tell you something that we can't show you.

"Thank you very much. Thank you for your patience."

Jerry takes his seat. It's a nice beginning by my counsel. But I know that opposing counsel, William Briggs from Lavely & Singer, who is about to give his opening statement, will be challenging my ability to stay positive and centered.

Chapter 7

IT'S NOT ABOUT THE MUSIC

After a lunch break, the trial continues as Mr. Briggs takes the floor. I find myself wondering why my karma is such that, while I am represented by a white "country" lawyer who wears Hawaiian shirts (not in court, thank God), I am being opposed by a handsome, very tall Black man. Lost in thought, I quickly get jarred into the present by the sound of my own drumming. What the hell? Yes, it seems that while Mr. Briggs stands up to button his double-breasted Armani suit jacket, the intro to "Light My Fire," which begins with my opening snare drum crack, blasts into the courtroom, resonating through the chamber. After the initial impact is made, William Briggs's assistant turns the sound down so the attorney can be heard.

"Good afternoon, ladies and gentlemen of the jury," says Mr. Briggs. "This case is about that music—music that was created by my clients, Ray Manzarek, Robby Krieger, and by John Densmore and Jim Morrison."

My outrage intensifies as I remember that the judge admonished us not to exhibit any emotional response to any statements made by attorneys or witnesses. That was easy for him to say. I somehow manage to stifle my reaction to the beginning of Briggs's opening statement, but the judge must be able to see the smoke coming out of my ears. I fear that if my rage is that obvious, he will ask me to excuse myself from the courtroom. I control myself, but I didn't drum my heart out on this song for it to be thrown back in my face as a soundtrack for some hard-ass lawyer to criticize me with. What makes it even worse is that "Light My Fire" has always been my favorite song to play live. It elicited abandoned joy from our audiences and I loved drumming away to a sea of bobbing heads. *And now there's this,* I think to myself, as I feel the burrito I had for lunch rising like yeast in my stomach.

"My clients," says Briggs, "want to continue to play this music. They want to play this music that was created more than thirty years ago. Great rock music for a new generation of fans. And they want to play this music as The Doors of the 21st Century because we are, after all, in the twenty-first century. And they want to reach new generations of fans so that everyone can enjoy the music that they created.

"Now, Mr. Mandel comes into this courtroom and he tells you, 'We're not here to stop the music.' Let's not be mistaken, ladies and gentlemen, that is precisely why we're here. Mr. Densmore wants to attempt to stop my clients, Ray and Robby, from playing this music. From playing this music not only for the new fans, but for old fans as well."

It's impossible to explain how this sounds to me, as if I believe that anyone can stop anyone else from playing anybody's songs live. There is no law against that and I don't want there to be. I want to yell out loud, *This case is not about music, it's about money! It's about first-class tickets, big concert halls, and shiny black stretch limos!* I hold my tongue, and it's back to Mr. Briggs.

"At the end of the day, ladies and gentlemen, you're going to be asked whether or not my clients, Ray and Robby, can continue to play this music."

This attorney knows full well that you can't stop people from playing whatever they want to play live. There are zillions of tribute bands playing Doors music all the time. Granted, we can prevent people from *recording* our songs without permission, but they can play the music live until the cows come home and I couldn't care less. All I'm doing here is trying to stop the false usage of the name, as I am forced to sit on my hands and listen to William Briggs slanting the truth and stuffing words and my own music into my mouth. I had no idea he would play this dirty, using sound bites, taking things out of context. And for his next act, he is about to share his personally distorted take on our history:

"A month or two after Ray met Jim, my client, Ray, is in a meditation class and he approaches John. John is there to get to higher consciousness without the help of the usual toke."

Is he calling me a drug addict for attending a meditation class that Ray also attended? It appears that he is. He continues to quote Ray as saying, "John, I understand you're a drummer. I have my two brothers playing guitar but it's just not working out."

Briggs explains that I introduced Ray to Robby, the first true thing he's said, but he misquotes me as saying that I grew up with Robby. I didn't. In his version of my life with The Doors, that was all it took and then we were four buddies hanging out in a garage in the summer of '65, and we were jamming. A year later, we signed on to a record company.

"Mr. Densmore is going to get up on the stand," says

Briggs, "and he'll try to tell you that all the partners signed an agreement for veto power in which all decisions had to be unanimous. But ladies and gentlemen, that is not what the evidence shows. In this case, amazingly, Mr. Densmore wrote a national best seller."

I cringe. What is so amazing about my writing a best seller? I guess it wreaked havoc with something Ray said in *his* book, that I was just the stupid kid brother, the dumb drummer. And dumb drummers do not write best sellers. But I did. And still, I had trouble with the idea of calling myself a writer. I knew I was a musician, since I'd been doing it for fifty years. But after my memoir, I wrote a three-hundred-page novel which to this day needs work. Years later, after writing articles and essays in several national and international publications, I wrote a short piece for the *Nation* magazine. I knew I had found my "voice" in the autobiography, and there it was again as I wrote the article for the *Nation*. And it never left me.

And I have to say that, like music, technique is not everything. You have to have enough technique to be able to say what you need to say, but "soul" comes from the other world. It's a gift (call it "the muse") that can't be bought. Well . . . you could try to make a pact with the devil, but you must pay, as Tom Waits portrayed in Terry Gilliam's *Imaginarium of Doctor Parnassus*. It's best to hone your craft as much as you can, and then you'll be ready for "the visitor." Or "the guest," as the poet Rūmī might say.

This line of thought, by the way, is not particular to the arts. It applies to anything, even to making love. What gives the moment "soul" is losing yourself in the experience and not thinking about technique.

Mr. Briggs continues, "His best seller was called *Riders*

on the Storm. And before the book was published, Mr. Densmore said he had all the galley pages checked. He said he sent them to Ray and Robby and other people because he wanted everyone to understand that he was putting out an accurate depiction of what happened. He said he didn't want any mistakes or errors in his book."

In the next sentence, Briggs quotes a section from my book about a conversation in a garage in Venice where we agreed to split all the money equally among the four of us. But since I didn't speak about the four-way veto power in that particular paragraph, Briggs is trying to convince the jury that it never took place. He's really on a roll, trying to make Jim look bad . . . because Jim's estate is also on my side. And now I have to sit here in silence as William Briggs distorts the infamous Miami incident that occurred on March 1, 1969.

"Mr. Morrison arrives late to the Miami concert," says Briggs, "and he's drunk again. He gets up onstage and there are varying accounts and reports about this. But you'll hear the evidence during the course of this trial. Supposedly, he either takes down his pants or opens his pants. And onstage he either pretends or he does play with himself onstage. And he does something else. He pretends to orally copulate Robby Krieger."

Briggs is accusing Jim falsely—guilty until proven innocent. I'm upset that Ray and Robby are not present to listen to this tripe fostered by their representative. We were there and we all know the truth about these allegations, that Jim never broke the law, but there's just too much money to be made on the road for the other two to show up and stand up for Jim. In fact, when all is said and done and verdicts are reached, the codefendants in this trial will have missed all but a few isolated days of this entire three-month trial.

The reality about the infamous Miami incident, which we all three know for certain, is that Jim frequently got down on his knees in front of Robby to get a closer look at his magical "flamenco fingers" flying across his guitar. That is what he was doing that night, but Mr. Briggs speaks as if he was there and saw something that never happened.

So much for getting the facts in order.

In November 2010, by the way, the outgoing governor of Florida, Charlie Crist, got Jim's penis back in the news. The story was covered by the NBC *Nightly News*, CNN, the Associated Press, and the BBC, who all aired stories on the pardoning of Jim Morrison's penis. Hope they feel like they can get back to the important news now. But whatever the news agencies said, whether they called it a crime or a publicity stunt, none of us saw the "golden shaft" revealed.

What actually happened was that the courts got it backward by acquitting Jim of lewd behavior and public drunkenness and finding him guilty of exposing himself. Jim actually did the opposite, but it was a sign of things to come. Before he died of consumption in a bathtub in Paris, the writing was on the wall at Dinner Key Auditorium in Miami. It took a whole lotta beer to give Jim the courage to inject our concert with a major dose of Julian Beck and Judith Malina's "Living Theatre." He'd seen their work in Los Angeles a few nights before, and he felt compelled to emulate the company and rant about politics in the middle of our gig. Unfortunately, his timing was off.

At the time, you see, the entire country was polarized into "for" or "against" the Vietnam War. The national tension was seething as each camp tried to sideswipe the other. "Let's get those grubby rock musicians" was the mantra that was chanted louder and louder during the week after we played Miami. So, although there were hundreds of photos of the concert and plenty of police at the event, no evidence backed up the charges and no arrests were made until a week later. When the momentum swelled to engorgement, the release came at the Orange Bowl, where thirty thousand people expressed their dismay at our country losing its "decency." Meanwhile, behind closed doors, President Nixon was busy laying the groundwork for his future illegal activities. So the court made its decision and the appeal was pending when Jim "broke on through." Governor Crist, who was actually a moderate Republican, felt compassion for the deceased and pushed through a pardon of Jim's penis. But doesn't a pardon imply that the penis was exposed? "Expunged from the record" would have been more appropriate. Maybe someone needs to pardon the pardon.

Clearly, Briggs couldn't care less about the truth as he drones on, "Ladies and gentlemen, this is in the Bible zone. This is in Florida. You don't do something like that in Florida."

Something like *what*? Jim didn't do anything, and it turns my stomach to hear the same lawyerly rant that I heard directed at Robby on the witness stand at Jim's Miami trial many years ago. Robby denied the accusation then, but if he were here now, would he stand by the same testimony?

"So what happens?" Briggs says. "The Floridian police put out an arrest warrant for Mr. Morrison. Once word spreads, concert promoter after concert promoter begins to cancel The Doors concerts. And as you're going to hear and see, because it's in Mr. Densmore's book, he was happy. He was glad, He was happy the music had stopped. He was glad that they stopped touring. So this played right into his hand to stop the music."

My attorney has tried to prepare me for the other side's

misinterpretations and accusations, but I'm still bowled over. The music could never stop; no one ever wanted it to stop. But we were losing control over a man who was increasingly bent on self-destruction. I was worried about Jim as a friend who was drinking too much and it took me a year to convince Ray that we needed to stop performing because Jim was destroying himself.

It was ten months after my initial appeal to Ray and Robby, after an embarrassing concert in New Orleans, right in the middle of a set, when Jim suddenly stopped singing, took a seat on the front of the drum riser, his head in his hands, and wouldn't get up. I stood up from my drum stool, walked around, and sat down beside him. The alcohol on his breath nearly knocked me over as I said into his ear, "Jim, is there anything you want to play next?"

While thousands of people waited, Jim got up and blabbered some gibberish into the microphone. Obviously, the concert was over and Ray and Robby got it. They agreed that we needed to stop—not the music, but the touring. Finally, everyone recognized the elephant in the room . . . and the mounds of elephant shit disguised as our meal ticket. I recall this vividly as Briggs goes on to what he depicts as my "malicious veto of the Cadillac commercial."

"Not only did Mr. Densmore say no to the Cadillac offer," says Briggs, "he decides, 'I'm going to write an article in a national publication called the *Nation*.' And in this article, Mr. Densmore attempts to explain why he doesn't want any of the commercials or the songs used in commercials. He says the whole world is hopefully headed toward democracy. He tells us that Vackva Hobble [sic], when he took over as president of Czechoslovakia after the fall of communism, said, 'We're not going to rush into this too quickly because I don't know if there's much difference between the KGB and the IBM.'

"This is Mr. Densmore's thinking, ladies and gentlemen. This is his philosophy. These are the reasons why he didn't want the music used in commercials—because he equates, as the evidence will show, our system of government with greed."

For starters, I would like to correct Mr. Briggs, who has grossly mispronounced the name Vaclav Havel. It is obvious that Briggs does not understand that Havel, in jail because of his political views and his work as an outspoken playwright, credits his sanity to listening underground to American rock and roll. In fact, communism fell in Czechoslovakia without bloodshed and the era was labeled the "Velvet Revolution," named after the Velvet Underground. Lou Reed, the group's lead singer, told me that when Havel became president of his country, he offered to sit for an interview with the singer. The president wanted to thank him for the music that provided him solace in his darkest prison hours.

It isn't often that a rock and roller is allowed, let alone asked, to "interrogate" the president of a country. And here is Mr. Briggs, trying desperately to paint me (and President Havel) as sympathetic to communism, when my music, rock and roll, has been the best "propaganda" ever to convince the populace of dictatorships to join the "free" world. And now the jury will have false information about what happened and how to pronounce the man's name.

But I am even further stunned by Briggs's labeling me as being un-American. If my distaste for getting the maximum profit at the expense of anything and everything is un-American, Briggs is using Joe McCarthy tactics as he takes Havel's words out of context. The Czech president was actually making a joke about corporate greed. And Briggs's pathetic tactic reminds me of when Joe McCarthy stated that journalist Edward R. Murrow was cited in the foreword of a book by a socialist. He had conveniently left out the fact that the book clearly asserted the fact that Murrow was *not* a communist.

Briggs was tagging me as a liberal whose actions were the result of my anti-capitalist philosophy. It felt like he was a member of the LA gangs who steal around at night spray-painting their monikers all over town like male dogs marking their territory. In my opinion, we haven't fully recovered from the "red-baiting" of the fifties by people who operate out of fear as they tag others as "different, commie, pinko," and a host of other damning names. "If you're not with our tribe, you're different" . . . which leads to George Bush's declaration, "Either you are with us or you are with the terrorists."

Never in my wildest dreams did I think that kind of logic would come out of our keyboard player's mouth, let alone the mouth of his representative. And yet, Mr. Briggs continues: "Ladies and gentlemen, I'm going to tell you—the evidence is going to show—that this is probably the very first case where someone has hired a lawyer to come into court, not to protect their rights but to say, 'No, I've made enough money and I don't want you to make any more either.' Because that's what Mr. Densmore is doing here.

"Now, Mr. Densmore claims that he's here to protect the legacy. He claims that he doesn't want them to use the logo. Mr. Densmore claims that this is a matter of principle. Ladies and gentlemen, I've got to tell you, I'm at a quandary. You're going to have to help me figure out why it is that John Densmore and the estates, who are along for the ride here, want to come into this courtroom and ask you to stop my two clients, the two original members of The Doors, from performing, when they have never taken any action against any of these other groups [tribute bands].

"Most of you have seen my clients here. They're no spring chickens. They're elder. One of them is in his sixties. But they get out there and they work, and they perform, and it's hard work. You may think getting up onstage for maybe a ninety-minute set is easy, but there's a lot that goes into it. And Mr. Manzarek will explain that."

Briggs is suggesting that I am *forcing* Ray out on the road, to work his elderly ass off to put food on the table, or, as Ray himself has stated, because he needed a few more million. But does he really need forty million of *my* money?

"At the end of the case," Briggs says as he finishes his opening statement of untruths, "I'm going to ask all of you to award my clients a substantial sum of money. Thank you, ladies and gentlemen."

The judge declares a recess and we all rise. I leave the courtroom wishing Briggs had actually told the jury the ridiculous amount of money they are suing me for. I understand why he didn't shout it out loud . . . because it is too shocking. He just didn't have the nerve. Talk about greed.

Chapter 8

A SOCIAL PHILOSOPHY

I'm standing in the hallway, trying to get my bearings after hearing so many lies and misrepresentations, when I get a surprise hug from Jerry Mandel. I guess he can tell how shaky I am after hearing the other side's opening statements and he senses I need some grounding. We both know I'm up next. I'm going to be first to take the stand because Jerry wants me to set the stage. "You'll do fine," he assures me. "Just be yourself."

That is exactly what I intend to do when I step up to the witness stand. I raise my hand and swear to tell the whole truth, so help me God. A dank sweat ring is starting to show through the armpits of my monkey suit. At least I refused to wear a tie!

"Mr. Densmore," says Jerry once I'm seated, "are you nervous?"

"Yes," I answer. The witness stand is an extremely intimidating place to be. I have this jack-in-the-box kind of feeling, sequestered on a stool, trapped in a small, four-by-four space, being poked at while everyone watches. I'm on edge, knowing that if my responses don't please the questioners, or aren't what they hoped, they'll walk around and poke me in the back, figuratively of course, until they feel they've extracted from me exactly what they want. I've never been in this position before and Jerry seems to read my mind as he asks, "Have you ever done anything like this before?"

"Well," I answer, "I've been in front of a lot of people before, you know, like at the Hollywood Bowl. But this is different." I go on to explain, "I didn't think I'd ever be suing my musical brothers and it's hard. But circumstances kept mounting and I had to do it."

As Jerry encourages me to talk about my activities and vocations other than being a musician, I discuss my philanthropy. "I give back a lot. Around 1980, when I read that John Lennon gave 10 percent of his money to charity, I decided to do the same thing. Since the other Doors and I have done so well, I upped my tithe to 20 percent, and I spend a lot of time making sure it goes to the right places and gets used properly."

Maybe I'm stuck in the sixties in some ways, but not because I want to go out and play the old songs for big bucks like Ray and Robby. Rather, it's because I still hang on to the naïve notion that we are all in this together, the Woodstock nation, sharing values and helping each other out. Do I mean sharing record royalties with the public? When you hit it big, yes, a portion.

I remember years ago, when I sat on the edge of the stage at Woodstock, watching wonderful drummer Mike Shrieve drive Santana into the stratosphere. I saw them play many times at the Fillmore in San Francisco, and on top of Carlos's extraordinary musicianship, his effusive spirit of love and giving back to the community remains unmatched.

I sent a donation to his Milagro Foundation because I really believed in the incredible work Carlos and his friends were doing by taking inner-city kids out into nature and teaching them about organic gardening and other sustainable practices. Carlos is this supposed crazy former hippie like me, who has formed a foundation that is so together, they receive major grants from large corporations. Carlos is Robin Hood personified and shortly after I sent my donation, he asked me to sit in with the band.

They were doing their yearly weeklong residence at the Joint in Vegas, a three-thousand-seater at the Hard Rock Hotel. I went to a rehearsal in the afternoon and witnessed ten world-class musicians working out. One of their covers was "Riders on the Storm," which Carlos wanted me to play on. It sounded great, but the feel was kind of like a salsa. "I hear this tune a little different," I said. "Approach it like it's a mysterious venture. All you have to do is breathe a little more."

That night, after working the crowd up into a frenzy, Carlos introduced me. "We have a guest tonight from my favorite band from the sixties . . . No, it's not the Rolling Stones . . . No, it's not Led Zeppelin . . . No, it's not Cream. I love all these bands, but . . ."

The crowd started yelling out names. "The Beatles!"

"No . . ."

This continued until everyone was shouting simultaneously. Then someone screamed, "*The Doors!*"

"THAT'S RIGHT!" Carlos said. "The most mystical, most mysterious band ever. Here's a musician who helped create that sound, John Densmore."

I walked out into a roar that Carlos had elicited from the audience, and I wondered how I was going to pull off this poetry that I'd planned. It was an incredibly flattering intro and I hoped I could deliver. "All right!" I shouted. "I'm going to do a Doors song, but first you've got to listen to a little poetry."

I dedicated the poem "Belly Song" by Etheridge Knight to Carlos. He did some wonderful guitar improv on it and also on an excerpt from Jim's "American Prayer" poem, which I recited while playing a hand drum. When the band started the intro to "Riders on the Storm," I stepped to the back of the stage and sat in on the drum set. It was an honor to jam with one of the world's greatest guitar players.

It was also an honor to support his Milagro Foundation that was helping so many kids find their way. I once read that billionaire Bill Gates, who has in recent years dedicated his life to giving back, said that properly administering his funds is harder than earning them. Author H.G. Barnett wrote, "Virtue rests in publicly disposing of wealth, not in its mere acquisition and accumulation."

When you consider that Gates is one of a group of three Americans who have more dough than sixty of the poorest countries' total worth, it makes you wonder, how does he carry that around? His shoulders must ache . . . or maybe he gets a lot of massages. Presently, he gives away a billion a year, so that's got to be an antidote to all that shoulder pain. Bill Gates recently said that inherited money is a terrible weight to lay on your kids. So he's giving away 95 percent of his loot, which means his kids will only get about two billion each. Not too shabby.

"How do you administer your funds?" Jerry asks me.

"I've established a scholarship fund at UCLA for African American students. They get their tuition every year and I get to meet them, which is very inspiring. That's one example. Documentary films are another way I give back. We don't make money. We lose money. Michael Moore is the only one who makes money on documentaries. But ours are primarily about the criminal justice system and how youth are incarcerated. The last one we did is called *Juvies* about Eastlake, the largest juvenile hall in the country. Eastlake in LA. It's mostly disproportionately minorities who are in prison, and we're giving them a voice."

Mark Wahlberg agreed to narrate the film because he said that he used to be a small-town hoodlum when he was a teenager . . . and if the laws had been as draconian as they are now, he's pretty sure he wouldn't be a movie star. He'd be in jail instead.

"Do you have a social philosophy that guides you today?" asks Jerry.

I'm glad he asked me that since Briggs, who doesn't know me at all, just suggested to the court that my philosophy was that of socialism, liberalism, and communism. What's next, terrorism?

"For me," I say, "after getting the brass ring by being a member of The Doors, it seems very natural to want to give back to those who inspired me when I was coming up. That's my philosophy."

When Jerry asks me to describe my musical career up to now, I tell him about my new group, Tribaljazz. "Not Tribal *Doors*," I accentuate for the jury. I go on to explain that I've played with the Flagstaff Symphony, joined by some Native American musicians. And Tribaljazz played the Skirball Cultural Center in Los Angeles, a gig I'd salivated over for years. I'd been to many summer evening concerts at this particular venue, a place that feels like a mini Hollywood Bowl, where I had played with The Doors.

But in my new group, no one onstage wears leather pants

and there are no lyrics. Jazz is an art form where the audience gets to participate by using their imaginations as they make up their own stories to the sounds. This art form challenges me since I have to use all of my inherent rhythmic skills to keep up with the young studs in my band, particularly Marcel Adjibi, Aziz Faye, and Najite Agindotan, three master African drummers who are about half my age. At first it was a task to translate their beats to a drum set, and we had a few tense moments when I was worried they wouldn't like my playing. I do have jazz sensibilities, but I'm known for rock drumming and Africa is the Motherland of rhythm.

But mutual respect was quick to come, as it was a relief to find out that these African musicians were also worried that I might not like *their* playing! Soon we were all smiling at each other, due to the *deep* pocket that we collectively laid down. I remember being in heaven at the Skirball that night, not longing for the good old days at the Hollywood Bowl, but rather being in the moment and not wishing to be anywhere else in the world.

I especially love how we began the evening with an empty stage and weaved our way through the audience like a N'awlins street parade. I got the idea to have the sax player start solo, up in the rafters behind the stage, and then the drums came rumbling in from the back of the auditorium. The "call to Mecca" chant from Art Ellis's soprano sax gave everyone chills, and then they turned their heads to see all the drummers dancing in from the back. Since the Skirball is primarily a Jewish cultural center and the audience was responding to an Arabic music form, it demonstrated the power of music and how it can heal cultural differences. This was so much better than trying to go back and recreate something that was gone.

For example, in the eighties I saw something new coming alive in the downtown LA loft district. Artists infiltrated the area east of Alameda, where the homeless were using the run-down warehouses as crash pads. With the cheap rents (not anymore!), a number of clubs and theaters sprang up, while an all-night café, Gorky's, sparked political discussions lasting till three a.m. The scene became so vibrant, I often found myself driving down the 10 freeway to the area, stuck in gridlock, looking for a hit of creativity. I've always loved the diversity of my hometown, knowing that you only have to travel on the freeway to get to a variety of places where the action is.

I found it at the Wallenboyd Theater, where transplanted New Yorker Scott Kelman ran the avant-garde scene. Scott was a West Coast version of Ellen Stewart, who ran La MaMa, New York's Lower East Side cutting-edge theater venue. Ellen launched the playwright Sam Shepard and Patti Smith, while Scott lent out creative working spaces to actors Whoopi Goldberg, Tim Robbins, and Helen Hunt. I played jazz there with Don Preston of Frank Zappa's Mothers of Invention and stumbled into writing music for Tim Robbins's company, the Actors Gang.

I had seen the French company Théâtre du Soleil during the 1984 Olympic Arts Festival, and Robbins wanted to do something similar. I told him that I knew exactly what they were up to, as they performed Shakespeare in French, wearing a Japanese kimono–type wardrobe, with two percussionists improvising behind the actors. It was wild. When we worked up *Methusalem* by Yvan Goll, I approached it like *Peter and the Wolf*, having a certain cymbal or drum representing different individual actors. When they spoke, I answered percussively and it really worked. After the run, while Tim was in

San Francisco doing the movie *Howard the Duck* (he wasn't famous yet), I received the *L.A. Weekly* Theater Award for Music. I wrote a letter to the paper saying the scene felt as vibrant as the sixties.

The thing is, after a peak like we had with The Doors, only another creative endeavor that pushes the envelope will feed me. Another good example was when Eddie Vedder, the extremely soulful lead singer of Pearl Jam, was on a solo tour and was coming to LA in a few days. We had originally connected when he inducted The Doors into the Rock & Roll Hall of Fame. Eddie liked the idea of just me and him, solo guitar and hand drum, doing our thing. We met backstage before he went on, and had a ten-minute rehearsal. That's all we needed. It was instantly simpatico and we worked up his beautiful song "The Long Road," from the *Dead Man Walking* soundtrack, and "Wishlist," one of my favorite Pearl Jam songs.

Eddie, even at his relatively young age, is an icon and his fans adore him. When he introduced me as someone who had taught him some things, I opened my heart to him even more. But really, it was a blessing to simply sit next to him and play music. The next day, the reviews said "The Long Road" had sounded mystical, which is how it felt to me. "Wishlist" turned into a sing-along, as we were feeling very kindred. I left the stage after that, remaining on the side to enjoy the rest of the set.

Toward the end of the show, I noticed a mic on a stand downstage. When I asked one of the crew who it was for, he said, "That mic is for anyone who wants to put on one of the long white jackets and jam." I'd noticed that all of Eddie's assistants wore outfits that made them look like scientists.

At this point, Eddie and his wonderful opening act, Glen

Hansard, the star of the Oscar-winning film *Once*, roared into a version of "Rockin' in the Free World" by my old next door Laurel Canyon neighbor, Neil Young. They were halfway through when I couldn't resist. I grabbed my drum, threw on a white jacket, which gave me the look of a mad scientist, and walked onstage. Besides the drumming, being a backup singer to one of the greatest songwriters in rock and roll was an honor.

For me, the process is the goal, which means the size of the audience is irrelevant to an artist, if he or she is truly in the moment. I see it like a dance, and whether the performers play solo or as members of a forty-piece orchestra, they represent one part of the equation while the audience represents the other part . . . no matter if the audience is one person or forty or fifty thousand people. So how will it go tonight? That's the exciting part. Will it be a waltz, a ballad, salsa? Will it be "pin drop" time or will the audience go crazy? For me, both reactions are equally valid. I remember when The Doors closed with "Light My Fire" and everyone got up from their seats to dance. Then we'd do "The End" as an encore, and the same people would file out quietly, as if they were exhausted and would take that song home and chew on it for a while.

Back here in the courtroom, Jerry gets down to business: "We've had opening statements, which are not evidence. So let's start the evidence. What or who were The Doors? How did they get started?"

I tell him about knowing Robby for a while and going to the meditation class where I met Ray, who was looking for higher consciousness. I leave out the "without the help of a usual toke" comment that Briggs had blurted about me during his opening statement. I explain that Ray knew Jim and we decided to form a band with the addition of Jim and Robby.

"Was there any kind of political persuasion to the music?" Jerry asks.

"The Vietnam War was heating up," I say, "and it was dividing the country. Kind of like today with Afghanistan. We were against the war. The seeds of the civil rights movement, the peace movement, and the women's movement were all planted in the sixties. We were steeped in that stuff and some of it came out subliminally in our music."

"Was there a social philosophy of the band?"

"Just that we were all together," I say. "We were a band of four brothers who were completely equal. We hoped we could sort of level the playing field for everyone else out there. It may have been a pipe dream, but we were trying to be socially conscious."

Court proceedings are called off for the rest of the day due to procedural red tape. I hold the swinging door open as the jury exits the courtroom, giving them a half smile. Verbal contact with a jury member is completely prohibited and so is any kind of communication with the judge. I leave the courthouse for the rest of the day and go home, exhausted, wondering what the hell I'm voluntarily putting myself through. If I continue to feel like this, I may actually be shaving off some of my time here on Planet Earth.

But before I drop off to sleep, I remember that even if I lose, it's worth it. Something inside of me says I have to stand up to my old bandmates, and although I am upset, my spirit feels empowered by going through the experience, as hard as it is.

* * *

On July 7, I awaken feeling somewhat groggy and out of sorts. Running through my head is the old Beatles lyric, *Woke up, got out of bed, dragged a comb across my head.* I put on my uptown duds and drive downtown to the courthouse, thinking about what my lawyer drummed into me at the beginning of this fiasco: "Be aware of everything you say, John . . . in public and in private."

This is because, now that the trial has begun, my words can (and will) get thrown back in my face. I greet Jerry at the door to the courtroom, we go in, and he says quietly, "It's showtime." He's referring to the fact that the judge, the jury, the clerks, and any observers all have their eyes on my attorney and me. I need to be aware of what I do, what I say, and the expression on my face at all times.

Jerry asks me to take the stand and we begin again. But first, he turns to the judge and says, "I want to advise the court that Admiral and Mrs. Morrison are with us today." Then he turns to me. "Good morning, Mr. Densmore."

"Good morning," I say.

"Yesterday when we left off, we were starting to talk about the business of The Doors. When you said that all things would be divided equally, how did that play out in the context of getting credit for music writing, lyric writing, and songwriting?"

"That was an amazing suggestion that Jim made," I say. "Not only did we split all the publishing money, which was unheard of, he also said, 'Let's just credit all the music and lyrics by The Doors.' It was unbelievable."

I remember Jim describing his life up until The Doors got launched as a bow being pulled back. As the band emerged, it finally let go. The pulling back, this incubation period, was sacred time. To me, it was holy and reminds me of when my son was in utero. I used to sing one song over and over outside his mother's belly, in the hopes that when he came out and heard the same song, he would feel at home. We wrote our songs back then with the same kind of hope, and we talked about how to nurse them into the world with enough care that, when they were born, the world would accept them. In the incomparable words of Leonard Cohen, *Just some Joseph looking for a manger.*

With a child (our songs) in gestation, we thought 24/7 about how to get this thing born. I'd drive down to Jim's rooftop apartment in Venice (he didn't have a car yet) and we'd cruise Hollywood engaged in a constant dialogue about the band.

"We need to write more original songs, Jim," I said one day, turning onto the 10 freeway heading toward Tinseltown.

"I love the blues," Jim said, pressing his body against the door to make room for me as I shifted into third gear in my Hillman Minx sedan. The car was so small, a passenger in the shotgun seat rubbed elbows with the driver. "But I can't play any instrument, so I remember these poems by thinking of a melody."

"Keep writing those words, man," I encouraged him. "When I heard 'Moonlight Drive,' I immediately heard little drumrolls every few bars imitating the ocean."

"Cool, I'll try and keep it coming. I've got stacks of notebooks full of poetry, which might turn out to be good lyrics. Hey, let's go to Pink's. I'm starved for a hot dog."

"They're great lyrics so far," I said. "Pink's it is."

Today, Jim's parents are in the courtroom and I hope they're proud of him for being so magnanimous. When Jerry directs me to discuss the dispute over Buick, I say, "Jim was out of town and this offer came through to use 'Light My

Fire,' which had been a giant hit a few years before. It was supposed to be 'Come on, Buick, Light My Fire.' And, you know, frankly, we were seduced by the money. Robby, Ray, and I all wanted to do it and we couldn't get ahold of Jim. So we said, 'Say yes.' But then he came back to town and blew up. I mean, he screamed at us. That was amazing because Robby had basically written 'Light My Fire' with a lot of our help. So it wasn't even Jim's song primarily. That's how much he cared . . . It wasn't even his song.

"He said, 'Ray, you're just a money-grubber. And Robby and John, you have no morals. Where is your integrity? What are we doing here? These lyrics mean stuff. It doesn't mean, you know, break on through to a new deodorant. This is our art.' Hearing him was shocking and I've never forgotten it. And since he's not here to defend himself, I'm doing it."

"Did he make any threats during that conversation?" Jerry asked.

"He did. He said, 'I'm going to call up some lawyers.' He called The Doors's attorney, Abe Somer, and asked for a list of lawyers so he could sue the rest of us."

Abraham Somer, who had been deposed in the months leading up to this trial, had some incredible credentials: Phi Beta Kappa graduate of the University of Southern California; senior class president; scholarship recipient; editor of the *USC Law Review*; and member of the Order of the Coif, the top 10 percent of a law school's graduating class. It doesn't get much better than that. During Abe's deposition some months prior, Lavely had asked him, "You do recall that Jim Morrison was extremely upset over the Buick Opel situation?"

Abe had said yes.

"And Mr. Morrison requested from you a list of attorneys, didn't he? And you wrote Mr. Morrison a letter in which you told Mr. Morrison you hoped he would work things out with his partners, didn't you?"

"Yes."

"And when you gave that advice to Mr. Morrison, you understood that this was confidential communication between you and he?"

"No," answered Abe. "I think everybody in the band knew what was going on. As I recall the incident, we all discussed the fact that I was going to recommend lawyers to Jim if he really wanted to pursue a dispute with his partners, and I wasn't going to be able to represent anybody. That's why I was recommending lawyers to him, hoping that it would pass over. There was no confidential communication between Jim Morrison and myself that was intended or kept secretive from other members of the band. Everyone was equal and open."

Back in the courtroom, in answer to Jerry's question, I tell the jury, "Jim said he'd go on television with a sledgehammer and smash the car so the public could see how he felt."

"What was the fallout?" asks Jerry. "It doesn't sound like such a big deal. But you call it the lowest point."

"In retrospect," I say, "we kind of undermined Jim's trust, this 'equal four parts' thing, you know, by going around his back. Granted, we couldn't get ahold of him because he was out of town. But the foundation of our band was equality. It was the cornerstone. It was the key to our success, and because of his suggestion, we put 200 percent into every song because we were all equal. And, you know, after going through these documents and seeing how document after document says, 'No commercials,' it was Jim getting that in there. And wow, we undermined the trust. We betrayed him."

"Did personal animosity result from this?" Jerry asks. "Did it affect how you dealt with one another?"

"Time made it better," I recall. "But looking back, I don't know if Jim ever got over it, even though we wrote more great music and functioned as a group."

At this point, Jerry asks the court to place its attention on Exhibit 5, a document called "The Amendment to Partnership Agreement of Doors Music Co." He asks me to validate the four signatures of the band members. I do, and he reads the document:

> No agreement, license, or other document respecting the partnership shall be binding upon the partnership unless signed by each and every member of the partnership.

Jerry adds that this paragraph had a management provision that said, in essence, that everything we did from there on in required unanimous agreement among all four partners. I reiterate that this amendment had resulted from the fallout of the Buick incident, stating that a document must be signed by all four people in the event of any and all music licensing.

"Is there any other reason that you can think of today," asks Jerry, "why the four of you entered into an amendment that required all of you not only to agree to a license but also required you all to sign a document for that license to be effective?"

"We wanted to further tighten the grip on control of licensing our songs," I answer.

Jerry instructs the court to turn to Exhibit 16, a document entitled "Administration Agreement," dated March 8, 1971. "This was the administration agreement entered into before Mr. Morrison went to Paris in 1971?" Jerry asks.

"It was," I say.

After Jerry asks me to establish the fact that Robert Greene had been a business manager for The Doors, he reads the following clause:

> *Whereas, Doors desire to authorize and appoint Greene the sole and exclusive administrator of the composition and Greene desires to accept said appointment . . .*

"What did you understand this agreement was intended to do?" asks Jerry.

"Jim was going off to Paris," I respond, "and we had to all sign when songs were used and that was going to be rather difficult because we had no fax machines back then. So we needed to have someone sign for us. That was what our business manager, Bob Greene, did for us. I'm positive that it was practically under penalty of death that he get oral agreements from the three of us and sign for us. Then he would talk to Jim on the phone in Paris and get his agreement."

Jerry reads more from that administration agreement:

> *. . . notwithstanding the foregoing, Greene shall not have the right to license or authorize the use of the composition, or any of them, in or in connection with radio or television commercials, it being understood that such license and authorization shall require the written consent and permission of all of the partners of The Doors.*

"Mr. Densmore," Jerry asks, "why was that 'notwithstanding' sentence included in there, if you know?"

Once again, I explain that it was about maintaining a tighter fist around the control of the songs being used for commercials. Jim was so worried after the Buick debacle that we specifically wrote in Bob Greene's contract that he could not authorize usage without all four of our signatures.

It was about that time, sitting at the witness stand, the judge to my right, the jury to my left, when it hits me. I really hadn't thought about all our old legal documents until this trial, but a bell goes off when I realize that Jim had insisted on a one-sentence amendment to our Doors Music Publishing Company agreement, saying everybody must sign or there would be no licensing of our songs to others. Then, before going to Paris, Jim had insisted again, more specifically, that Bob Greene would not have the right to okay our catalog to be used for radio or television commercials.

These realizations make the hairs stand up on the back of my neck. How did this language get into these documents? Someone made a point to spell this stuff out, and Jim's voice from the other side was deafening! *Rolling Stone* magazine, in the not-too-distant past, had called me a "brick wall" with regard to vetoing all solicitations for using Doors songs for ads, but our lead singer provided the cement between the bricks. It meant a lot to him, dead or alive. And so it means a lot to me.

The word man.

Young man . . . big dreams.

Our first SF ballroom gig: the Avalon.

Four lads in Venice, CA.

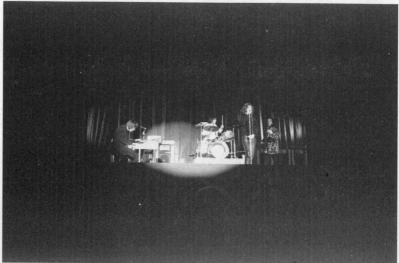

Driving . . .

The Lizard

King . . .

Paul Ferrara

That bright spotlight . . .

. . . was about to light our fire.

He didn't whip it out, Mr. Briggs.

"Just a little more and I'll truly be happy."

My nemesis . . .

. . . my teacher.

On the fence.

"Maybe I *am* a terrorist."

"He was the soul of the band and I want to honor my ancestor."

Chapter 9

TURNING A PROFIT

Crazy Horse
We hear what you say
One Earth, one Mother
One does not sell the Earth
The people walk upon
We are the land
How do we sell our Mother?
How do we sell the stars?
How do we sell the air? . . .
Possession a war that doesn't end . . .
Material fields, material harvest . . .
Crazy Horse
We hear what you say
We are the seventh generation
—John Trudell

I battle the relentless early morning traffic and honking of horns along the freeway route to the courthouse, recalling this beautiful poem. It was written by a friend, John Trudell, a Native American visionary activist and poet.

Now *there's* an elder, I muse, as I consider the Iroquois Nation, which is run by a council of grandmothers. If anyone ever wonders who pays for the latest wars, it's the poor, my friends, the poor, with their bodies as well as their pocketbooks. As Trudell says, "The third World War has already started. It's against the poor."

I understand that, in the larger scheme of things, whether or not The Doors's music is used in commercials will not address the more profound issues facing our world today. Likewise, I know that whether or not Ray and Robby are allowed to call themselves The Doors will not change the current state of society. I am under no illusions about either of those two things. But I do think that the conflict among the three of us is a profound metaphor for some of what ails society today.

From what I can see, there has to be something inherent in the human psyche that propels us toward the accumulation of wealth. Granted, this tendency may be a result of our emotional insecurities; but as statistics show, the gap between rich and poor is as large as ever, and I believe that what I call the "greed gene" is destroying our planet.

Stated quite simply, selfishness may allow a lucky small percentage to acquire more, but in the end, everyone is affected negatively because polluted air and water poison us all. Poverty in the inner cities leads to gang violence, while poverty around the world leads to religious fundamentalism and terrorism. Clearly, violence of all sorts is a direct result of poverty and the accompanying sense of hopelessness. Global warming, which does not discriminate between rich and poor, can be directly attributed to our unwillingness to change our energy policies, in large part because of the power and greed of our multibillion-dollar energy corporations. Still, the truth remains:

You can luxuriate in the stateroom on the Titanic, but if the ship goes down, we're all going down together.

Everybody knows that the boat is leaking
Everybody knows that the captain lied . . .

And everybody knows that it's now or never
Everybody knows . . .
—Leonard Cohen

So what does all this have to do with my lawsuit? I try to connect the dots as Briggs's characterization of me keeps repeating in my head: *These are the reasons why he didn't want the music used in commercials—because he equates, as the evidence will show, our system of government with greed.*

I park my car in the lot, pay the inflated fee, and head for the front doors to the courtroom. We were, dare I say it, a "radical" little garage band in Venice, California, back in the sixties . . . angry at the establishment for its lies and corruption, and now, my old bandmates, with the help of their very arrogant trial lawyers, are trying to paint me as anti-American.

The truth is that I'm just the opposite: I'm in love with this place I live, this country that isn't afraid to fast-track the challenge of ALL cultures on Planet Earth living together and trying to get along. Since when is it considered unpatriotic to question those in power for a failed foreign policy, or to confront the major corporations that abuse the environment? The famous words ring through my head: *Question authority*. The origin of this phrase is often attributed to Timothy Leary, but Benjamin Franklin was also quoted as saying: "It is the first responsibility of every citizen to question authority."

In my opinion, it is highly patriotic to question a society like ours that is so out of balance in its distribution of wealth. After all, this country was founded by colonists who, on December 16, 1773, decided to protest "taxation without representation."

Dressed as Mohawk Indians, a large group of citizens defied a perceived monopoly of the East India Company by boarding three ships in Boston Harbor and destroying hundreds of chests of tea by tossing them into the ocean. These are our roots, and I feel it is our responsibility to uphold these hard-won principles.

My own roots are under a freeway on-ramp. Literally. The home where I grew up is now under a cement slab that reads, *San Diego Freeway North*. At the time, the state gave my parents thirty grand and said, "You're outta here." There was no negotiating and no protesting the status quo in the fifties. Back then, Black people in the South were just mustering the courage to begin a movement that isn't over yet. So when I drove across the country in the early sixties and got hassled for being a male with long hair, I realized that this was just a taste of what African Americans endured every day. The Vietnam War jump-started the notion that democracy in action means getting out and expressing your disappointments as well as your admiration for your country.

As a kid, I often cruised through a beautiful canyon in the Los Angeles area, dreaming about living there someday. I knew the odds were against me, though, because I wasn't in love with any subject in school other than music, and at the time I thought a career in the arts was a total crapshoot. Still is. With a tight economy, it's even harder. What politicians don't understand is that the artists (along with the youth) carry the vision of what's next. Today, I feel so fortunate that

I've been living in that very canyon for twenty years. I walk the neighborhood some days, looking at the same beautiful trees, and I have to remind myself to look deeper and longer, as familiarity breeds boredom. I remember Jim wanting us to go to an island to rekindle our creativity and our vitality. It's true that vacations reinvigorate the soul, but we are a restless breed and we take the "pursuit of happiness" as a permanent mantra. As a result, we are always *pursuing* and hardly ever just *being*.

Le Ly Hayslip, the Vietnamese woman who wrote the book *When Heaven and Earth Changed Places*, which Oliver Stone turned into a movie, says that in Vietnam, people feel they are born happy and don't need to work toward it. Content to be planting rice, she believes it was only when she came to the States during the war that materialism crept into her psyche. To this day, many Vietnamese people don't understand why more US soldiers haven't come back so the people of Southeast Asia could forgive them. This extraordinary thinking comes from a culture of people who were just trying to defend against foreign occupation. Our American soldiers who fought in Vietnam, Iraq, and Afghanistan have extremely high suicide rates because of our aggression. Perhaps the restless soul needs to look deeper, to slow down and meditate. Myself included. Many of us have so much, but we still want more. *Just a little more and I'll truly be happy*, I tell myself. *Really. Just a little more*. And with time . . . just a little more. And then some more. It is just so sad when I look back that Jim had the correct and healthy impulse of going to a cave or an island to meditate on new songs. But then, I expect that the addiction that had already ensnared him would have played itself out the same on an island as it did in Paris.

I've been asked over and over again: if Jim had lived in a

time period like today, with our current knowledge of alcohol as a disease and so many substance abuse clinics and AA programs, would he have survived? I always say, "No, he was a kamikaze." But with the advent of Eric Clapton and now Eminem becoming clean and sober, I can see that it might have been possible. After all, if a guy as angry (and talented) as Eminem can title a new CD *Recovery*, maybe Jim could've made it. As I said at the conclusion of my first book, *Riders on the Storm*, my way is to try to glean something from these tragedies. Otherwise, I might find myself on the same road, and not see the signs that were left by these great, fallen artists.

I can hear Ray and Robby now, wishing I'd just shut up and be a musician and stop ranting on about politics. Who do I think I am? Sean Penn? George Clooney? No, I'm me, John Densmore, and I'm as responsible as the next guy for the state of the world, since we are all citizens of this country and of the world.

My internal musing ends as I enter the courtroom, nod to Jerry, and take my place back on the witness stand. My attorney draws the court's attention to a general partnership agreement among the three remaining Doors, signed on October 1, 1971, close to three months after Jim's death.

"When Jim died," Jerry says, "was there animosity among you and Ray and Robby?"

"Not at all," I answer.

"After Jim died," Jerry continues, "did Ray or Robby ever suggest to you that the way that you'd done business before should be changed in any way whatsoever? Did either of them say to you, 'Gee, you know, we used to make decisions this way when Jim was around, but let's change now'?"

"No, they didn't."

"So, it's October 1971, and you just signed a brand-new

partnership agreement with your two partners. You three also have a brand-new recording contract for five albums with Elektra. What happens next?"

"We recorded two albums without Jim," I recall, "and we toured. We collected $500,000 in advance for those two albums, called *Other Voices* and *Full Circle*. They did moderately well but nothing like the original Doors."

"Who did the vocals?" Jerry asks.

"Ray and Robby," I say. "I tried and it was rejected."

"The other guys vetoed your singing?"

"We all did," I say with a slight smile.

"Did you make a third, fourth, or fifth album?"

"No, we didn't make another album together at that time."

"You walked away from Elektra?" Jerry asks.

"Yes. We walked away from $750,000 in 1971 because we realized that without Jim, what were we doing? He was the soul of the band."

"So what happened next in the life of John Densmore?"

"Robby and I put a band together called the Butts Band, and we started recording."

"What kind of music did the Butts Band play?"

"Rock and roll."

"Did you ever consider, you and Robby, calling yourself The Doors?"

"No," I answer. "Never considered it. Sacred territory. And it was just the two of us. Although the Butts Band recorded a couple of albums, we were barely successful. Really, it was a small venture compared to our history."

Way back at the beginning, when we were still in the garage and Jim suggested that we split everything and each of us would retain 100 percent veto power, I didn't realize it was a historic moment for the band. Our unity and equality was cast in stone in that moment that still reverberates strongly within me, and will continue to be considered a historical act, long after we're all gone.

When Ray, Robby, and I got the news that Jim had gone over to the other side, it was another historic moment. We were rehearsing new songs, wondering if Jim was ever going to overcome his addiction and come back from Paris, when we got the devastating phone call. Jim would never be returning to Los Angeles or anywhere else for that matter. He was gone.

The rest of the day was surreal. The news didn't really register, we must have been in shock, but something told me we had just rounded a huge corner. Going back to rehearsing felt good, as we couldn't yet acknowledge the finality of it all or fully understand that nothing would ever be the same. There really was no question as to whether we could go on without Jim, although we asked the question anyway. But I soon discovered that that question was a no-brainer. The Doors without Jim was no band at all.

"Not the same level of success as The Doors?" Jerry asks.

"Definitely not," I answer.

"Did you consider," says Jerry, "that perhaps if you and Robby changed the name of your group to The Doors, you might enjoy a greater level of success?"

"Never considered it."

"Did you continue to perform from time to time with Robby?"

"I did. He created the Robby Krieger Band and I was an occasional guest."

"In that period of time until the beginning of the nineties, even though you didn't perform with Ray and Robby, did you continue to be friends?" Jerry asks.

"Friends and business partners. After Jim died, The Doors got bigger than ever and so we talked every few days amongst ourselves, our lawyers, and accountants and managers."

"How do you account for the fact that after Jim died and you stopped performing in 1973, that The Doors got even bigger than when you were performing?"

"I think it was the drumming," I quip. A giant laugh fills the courtroom, breaking through the otherwise formal atmosphere. A short and welcome relief.

"Could there have been any other reason?" asks Jerry.

"You know," I say, "it was about the genius of Jim Morrison and the magic of the four of us together, along with our careful orchestration of our business interests."

Jerry turns our attention to Exhibit 55, which is labeled, "Europe Tour 1997." When he asks me what that is, I tell him that Robby had originally asked Ray to go on tour with his band in 1997. They were playing some Doors songs and some jazz, but Ray got sick, so I substituted.

"What was the band called that was touring?" Jerry asks.

"The Robby Krieger Band," I answer.

"Why wasn't it called The Doors?"

Very crafty, Jerry, I think to myself, as I answer, "Because it was just two original Doors. The Doors were the four of us. And we never, never even discussed it. As I said, that was sacred territory you don't go into without all four parts."

Jerry presses, "Was it ever discussed that you and Mr. Krieger might call yourselves The Doors because you were two of the four original Doors?"

"Never."

"On this tour of the Robby Krieger Band with John Densmore, did you become aware that anybody referred to you as The Doors?"

"No."

"Did you hold yourselves out as The Doors?"

"Absolutely not."

Now, Jerry refers to Exhibit 56, a document from a booking agent that shows the layout of how ads for the Robby Krieger Band were meant to look. The lettering spelled out the name of the band and said, "with a special appearance by Ray Manzarek of The Doors." Another document was presented, one that also listed the name of the band, but this one said, "with a special appearance by John Densmore of The Doors."

"Do you have any problem at all," says Jerry, "with the description, 'Robby Krieger Band with special appearance by John Densmore of The Doors'?"

"No problem at all."

"And when Ray Manzarek was going to go on this tour, and it said, 'Robby Krieger Band with a special appearance by Ray Manzarek of The Doors,' did you have a problem with that?"

"No."

"Mr. Densmore," says Jerry, "was it The Doors that were performing?"

"No, it wasn't," I say.

"It was Robby Krieger's band and you, correct?"

"Correct." I let him know that these references, "of The Doors," indicated a founding member of the original band. "It was a way to identify us," I say. "It wasn't The Doors. We were founding members of 'The Doors.'"

"Do you have any problem at all with you and Robby being identified as 'of The Doors' as opposed to 'The Doors'?"

"No problem," I assure Jerry.

"Did Ray Manzarek ever indicate that he had any kind of a problem?"

"No."

Jerry asks one final question before we take a break: "Did Robby Krieger, in connection with this 1997 tour in Europe, ever even suggest that you call yourself The Doors?"

"No," I say.

It's time to stand up and stretch my legs for a few minutes. But when I make my exit, I deliberately take the scenic route to avoid the area of the hallway where the opposing lawyers are huddled. I'm heading for the men's room, going the long way because the menacing glances from the other side are not worth enduring. Hostile vibes are the norm here, which only increase on the rare occasions when the defendants are in attendance at the proceedings.

Their hostility seems to issue from the fact that the guys obviously resent my worldview. I can't understand it. We saw the Berlin Wall come down together and we watched the Cold War with Russia thaw. Now, it seems like the opposing attorneys are trying to put it back on ice. When will I remember that, from their point of view, winning is everything, at any price? Sacrifice your old bandmates . . . whatever.

After a short recess, I go back on the stand and Jerry asks me to clarify the events that occurred before the Buick offer. I tell him that we had okayed one commercial in England, for a tire company that wanted to license our song "Riders on the Storm." When Jerry asks me why I had allowed it, I say, "I guess I felt bad saying no all the time. That was the only time we permitted use of our music for a commercial, and I felt like I was betraying Jim so I gave my portion of the proceeds to charity."

"So," says Jerry, "I've got to ask the obvious question. Fifteen million to let Cadillac use a song. Why did you turn down so much money?"

Briggs stands up and says, "Objection. Asked and answered." He doesn't want to hear my answer, but the judge does, so he overrules the objection.

"They wanted us to advertise the Cadillac Escalade," I say, "that cost $66,000 and some change. But we didn't write songs for rich people only and it was our tradition not to do commercials. Jim was so against it and now that he's dead, he's my ancestor." My eyes fill with tears. "Like I said, he was the soul of the band and I want to honor my ancestor."

"At the time the Cadillac offer was presented to you," Jerry continues, "did anyone say you didn't have the right to veto it? Did they say, 'Majority rules, and the three of us are in favor. We don't really much care what you say'?"

Briggs objects again, but the judge overrules him again and I'm allowed to testify that Robby never said he was in favor of accepting the Cadillac offer. I also tell the court, "Our band was so protective of our logo after Jim died, we didn't even allow Oliver Stone to use it for the *Doors* film."

"Even though the movie was about the band?" asks Jerry.

"Precisely," I say, feeling like we are on a roll. It really couldn't be clearer.

"Will you turn, please, to Exhibit 83?" says Jerry. This is an article in *Billboard* magazine, the preeminent music business magazine, that begins:

Police Drummer Stewart Copeland and Cult vocalist Ian Astbury (singing the late Jim Morrison's parts) weren't just temporary additions to The Doors's lineup for last weekend's show in Fontana, Calif. As Doors keyboardist Ray Manzarek tells Billboard.com, "Stewart is drumming from here on out. Ian is singing from here on out. We're not doing a TV show. We're playing live music. This is the new Doors lineup for the 21st century."

"What was your reaction to seeing this article?" asks Jerry.

"I was hurt and angry," I say. "It looked to me like I was just publicly fired without a phone call."

"Prior to seeing this article," says Jerry, "had you understood from any source whatsoever that there was a new Doors lineup for the twenty-first century?"

"No."

"When Robby told you they wanted to go out and tour, you told him he had to do something to distinguish the name. Can you be more specific about that conversation?"

"I said they should use a modifier, a word or several words to make it real clear. For example, 'The New Doors.' 'The Windows.' 'The Hinges.' It takes four doors to make a sedan, so call yourselves 'The Coupes featuring Ray Manzarek and Robby Krieger of The Doors.' That's all right. Just make it real clear that there's a difference."

Jerry asks again, "Did you have any problem if they identified themselves as 'of The Doors'?"

"No."

"When you told Mr. Krieger he had to call his band something different from the original band and he couldn't use the logo, did he agree?"

"He agreed."

Jerry begins his wrap-up of my direct examination with the following question, as he points to Exhibit 183: "The band in this ad is identified as it says: 'Witness rock and roll history. The Doors.' Then underneath it says: '21st Century Live.' But the band is identified as Ray Manzarek, Robby Krieger, Ian Astbury, Stewart Copeland. And this is an ad for a performance that was going to be at the Universal Amphitheatre in Los Angeles?"

"Yes."

"Did either Ray or Robby tell you they'd decided to call themselves The Doors?"

"No," I say.

"When you talked to Robby about using a modifier for the name The Doors, is this what you had in mind, that it would say '21st Century' in small print under 'The Doors'?"

"Absolutely not. This infuriated me. I couldn't believe that the modifier '21st Century' was about a tenth the size of the word 'Doors.' And the word 'Live' under it implied it was a '21st Century Live Tour' starring this band, The Doors."

"You testified earlier," Jerry goes on, "that at about this time, you started to receive some phone calls from people. Would you elaborate on those?"

I explain, "A father in my son's class called me and said, 'Can you get me tickets to see you play?' I said, 'But I'm not playing.' I received several of those calls."

"Did you have a conversation with Robby Krieger in which you expressed your concerns about what was happening and what this band was being called?"

"Most definitely."

"Tell us about the earliest conversation you had with him where you expressed your concerns about what you had learned or seen."

I explain that I asked Robby what he was doing using the logo. I let him know that it was not clear that this was a new band and the lettering for "21st Century" was so small, you needed reading glasses to see it.

"And what was Robby's response?" Jerry asks.

"Something like, 'We've got to do it this way if we want to play big concerts.' He added that this was the way they *were* doing it. I told him how manipulative it was, and they were also using the front cover of our second album, *Strange Days*, in the background of this picture. You know why? Because it's the only cover I'm not on. All the rest of them have all four of us. So this is the only one they could kind of sneak back there as propaganda that it was the old classic Doors band."

Ray and Robby want the old fame thing back again (big bucks, stretch limos, never enough attention, and crowds hounding us), but I felt relieved that we didn't have The Doors's version of Beatlemania all the time. When we were off the road, I was glad that we could function as normal people and go about our business. I used the time to discover what other artists were creating. There were just so many talented people expressing themselves in unique ways and I was always happy to be a part of something new. I still am.

For example, years after Jim was gone, I met Johnny Depp at an Allen Ginsberg memorial in 1997. It was an incredible all-day-and-night event that was chock-full of talent. I did my hand drumming while reciting Jim's poetry, and Johnny went on after me. As we passed each other backstage, he said I was a hard act to follow. That felt good! And then he did a wonderful reading of notes from renowned gonzo journalist Hunter S. Thompson. But I noticed that some fans who made it backstage practically followed Depp into the bathroom when he went to relieve himself. "Does that happen much, Johnny?" I asked.

"All the time," was his sad response.

Years later, he narrated our documentary film *When You're Strange*, which garnered a Grammy and ultimately aired on PBS's *American Masters*.

While The Doors were on the road, all of us did occasionally pick the fruits that were offered, the fringe benefits that came along with that kind of notoriety. And, of course, Jim, the handsome lead singer, managed to garner most of the flowers. But that was then.

"Let me ask you, Mr. Densmore," says Jerry, bringing me back to the present in an attempt to clarify what I believe is already crystal clear, "is it your desire to stop Ray Manzarek and Robby Krieger from performing Doors music live in public today?"

"Absolutely not," I say.

"Is it your desire to stop Ray and Robby from performing and identifying themselves as founders of The Doors?"

"No."

"Do you have any objection," Jerry asks, "to Ray and Robby touring and advertising themselves the same way you and Robby did when you went to Europe in 1997?"

"I have nothing against that."

"And I have no further questions."

Chapter 10

CROSS

"Yesterday," William Briggs says to me, "you discussed your last telephone conversation with Jim Morrison."

Opposing counsel has risen from his table, buttoned his suit jacket with great deliberation, and now he saunters up to the podium as if he is about to make a killing. Litigators call what I am about to undergo a "cross," as in cross-examination. I was left with a good feeling before lunch today when Jerry finished his direct. I thought we'd made some clear points, but now I brace myself for trickery, as if I have a bull's-eye on my back.

"You told the jury that you had a love/hate relationship with Jim," Briggs says.

"A love for his artistry and sadness over his self-destruction."

"It was a hatred, wasn't it?" he presses.

"Hate is a form of love," I say. "If you're angry with someone who's hurting themselves, it's called tough love."

"The fact is," says Briggs, "you didn't want Jim Morrison to return, did you?"

"I beg your pardon?" is all I can say to such an absurd projection.

"When Mr. Morrison went to Paris," Mr. Briggs continues, "he called and said, 'Hey, how's "L.A. Woman" going?' He indicated that he wanted to come back, but you didn't want him to, did you?"

"I was worried about his drinking, trying to figure out whether he was still going down or if he'd turned the corner."

"You didn't want to get back onstage and perform with Mr. Morrison again, did you, sir?" says Briggs.

"I would rather he lived and we didn't get to do another tour or another album," I answer. "I only wanted to get back onstage with him if he improved his health."

"Mr. Densmore, you've just testified that you and Robby Krieger had a conversation about his and Ray's use of the modifier 'Doors of the 21st Century.' You told Robby, 'It's okay for you to use that.' Do you recall that?"

"For one concert. I didn't know they were going to do the entire world."

"Did you say, sir, to Mr. Krieger, 'You can only use "The Doors of the 21st Century" for a one-off concert?'"

"I assumed they were only doing a few gigs."

"So you assumed, but you did not tell him that, did you?"

"No."

"And did you also tell him in this conversation that the font size has to be the same as 'The Doors'?"

"I did. I said, 'You're manipulating the modifier—never in my wildest dreams did I imagine you would make the modifier smaller and "The Doors" real big. I assumed they'd at least be the same size.'"

"You said that The Doors made substantial income from licensing songs to movies." I guess Briggs has reached a dead end with his last mode of questioning and now he's taking a sudden turn onto a side street. Better watch out for whiplash.

"That's correct," I tell him.

"How much did The Doors make for licensing their catalog to Francis Ford Coppola in *Apocalypse Now?*"

"Somewhere around $100,000," I say.

"When Oliver Stone made the movie *The Doors*, how much of a fee did he pay for use of the catalog?"

"Millions."

"How many millions?"

"A few."

"Two? Three?"

"Somewhere around there." Briggs is really annoying me. Where the fuck is he going with this? Okay, so we made a lot of dough. Am I supposed to feel guilty about earning money legitimately?

"When some of the songs from your catalog were used in the movie *Forrest Gump*, how much of a fee did you receive?"

"Several million," I say.

"Two or three?"

"Three or four," I tell him.

Briggs wants big numbers so I'm giving them to him, not mentioning that it was divided four ways after we paid our managers and agents the requisite 25 percent. What is he up to?

"How much were you paid for *Monsters, Inc.?*"

"About a million or a million and a half." Not me, personally, but I let it go without trying to explain.

"So that's a lot of money," Briggs says.

"Yes, it is."

"But not as much as fifteen million, is it?"

Jerry objects to this question as argumentative and the judge upholds the objection. But now I see where Briggs is trying to lead me. I guess he thinks I'm not rich enough. Since we only got about eight and a half million (gross) for our licensing, he seems to be suggesting that I should have compromised Jim's prophetic lyrics to "Break on Through" for a gas-guzzling, global-warming Sherman tank called a Cadillac Escalade so we could get all the way up to fifteen million dollars! That makes a lot of sense.

Briggs works around Jerry's objection by saying, "I mean you never received an offer for any song in The Doors's catalog as great as what Cadillac wanted to offer . . . not just to you, but to the estates and my clients, for that catalog or for one song. Isn't that correct?"

"No," I say. "You're not considering the effect of having a song or two or three in a film. The effect on the catalog itself, besides the front money, is tremendous."

"Well, sir," he says, "do you know how much money was earned by you, Robby, Ray, and the estates as a result of allowing Francis Ford Coppola to use 'The End' in *Apocalypse Now*?"

"I don't know specifically. But I do recall my commitment to give 10 percent to charity. And every time we got a song in one of these movies, I noticed my hand would shake when I wrote out the check for the 10 percent."

Briggs frowns and says to the judge, "Move to strike everything after 'I don't know specifically.'"

The court complies.

Briggs continues, "Do you know how much money you, Robby, Ray, and the estates made as a result of the effect of The Doors's catalog being used in the movie *The Doors*?"

"Millions and millions of dollars," I say.

"How many millions?"

"Five, give or take."

"That's not fifteen million, is it?"

Jerry's cocounsel, the Morrison estate's attorney Jeff Forer, objects.

Jerry adds, "When? What year? What dollars?"

The judge sustains the objection and Briggs narrows down his question: "Do you know how much money The Doors earned as a result of using the catalog portions thereof in *Forrest Gump*?"

"Several million dollars besides the front money."

"Okay," says Briggs. "Can you sit here and tell us whether or not, as a result of licensing some of the music for *Forrest Gump*, you, Robby, Ray, and the estates earned fifteen million dollars as a result of the licensing?"

I expect it was more than fifteen million if you consider the effect on our catalog. But Briggs is looking for fifteen million up front. "Five to ten million," I say.

"Can you tell us whether or not the effect on the catalog of using the songs in *Monsters, Inc.* approximated fifteen million dollars?"

"No. I couldn't tell you." I take a deep breath and try to collect myself. I can't believe I volunteered for this harassment, where you're instructed to answer the question only, and not elaborate. I work hard to stifle an urge to scream out, *Yes, Mr. Briggs, we made less money by not doing the Cadillac ad, but the meaning of our songs was not raped!* I consider that a good compromise, but I guess I'm the only one.

Now Briggs changes his direction again: "Did Jim Morrison die on July 3, 1971?"

"Correct."

"And you believe he's dead?" says Briggs. "I mean, there's no confusion that Mr. Morrison has passed away?"

"I saw him destroy himself."

"Was there ever a unanimous decision made by Ray, Robby, and let's even throw in the estates for a moment, to appoint you protector of the legacy of The Doors?"

When my team objects as argumentative and the judge sustains it, Briggs tries again: "Yesterday, didn't you testify that you were going to assume the mantle of protector of The Doors because Jim Morrison is no longer around to do it? Wasn't that your testimony, sir?"

"*Assume the mantle?* What does that mean?"

"Well, didn't you testify, 'Jim Morrison is dead and I'm going to be the one to stand up to protect my ancestor's legacy'? Weren't those your words in this courtroom to this jury?"

"I think they were. And the estate is here and is also doing that. I didn't meet Admiral Morrison until this lawsuit, but it's been a gift, a healing, because he commanded eight battleships during the Vietnam War. We were against it, his own son wrote a song against it, and now he's here standing up for his son's legacy along with me. So I don't feel so alone. I don't feel like the sole, or whatever you call it, protector."

Wow . . . where did that outburst come from? Sure felt good, and they didn't even try to stop me.

"What I mean is," Briggs says, "as you put it yesterday when Mr. Mandel asked you why you're bringing this lawsuit. You said you wanted to protect the legacy of The Doors."

"That's true."

Briggs motions to a copy of my book, *Riders on the Storm*, which is in front of me. "Please turn to page 207," he says. "Let's read along:

I was relieved when we got permission to have the limousines driven out to the bottom of the steps of the planes.

It furthered our isolation from the public (and the real world), but avoided any possibility of a scene from you in a public place. Remember the time in Minneapolis/St. Paul airport when you [Jim] were asked for an autograph?

"Could you make it to Jill?" the fan said, pointing to his very shy girlfriend hiding behind him.

"I won't read the next sentence," Briggs says. "That was an embarrassing moment for you, wasn't it, sir?"

"Yes."

"Is this the legacy you're attempting to protect in this courtroom?"

"I'm trying to protect Jim's words and music. This is a hint of whatever was inside of him eating him alive. It's sad."

"Sir, don't you consider it sad when somebody who is idolized tells a shy girl in an airport asking for an autograph, 'You'd eat your own shit, wouldn't you?'"

"Thought you weren't going to say that, Mr. Briggs," I admonish. The jury and the gallery let out a big laugh. I'm not amused. I wonder if Ray and Robby would approve of their lawyer implying that Jim's self-destructive qualities overshadowed his talent. But they're not here to see their lawyer trashing The Doors's legacy.

My inquisitor drones on, "You're going to call forty-seven witnesses to protect this legacy, so I need you to understand why we're here. There are plenty of quotes like that one in your book, we can go page after page in excess of three hundred pages. You went on a lecture circuit with this book and talked about incidents like this."

"*Plenty of quotes like that* is an exaggeration," I tell him. "I can give you a couple of lines about the reason why I'm trying to protect the legacy."

"Shall we go to page 212?" says Briggs, ignoring my offer. He reads from my book:

As the audience filed in at seven o'clock and the open-
ing act began their set, my anger toward Jim intensified.
His unpredictability was affecting the live performances
more and more, and it was making me nuts! Why did
he want to ruin everything we'd created? I wondered as
I took my usual peek at the crowd. Maybe it was a last,
desperate attempt to fight the possession that was taking
place. The vulnerable shy college kid with his back to the
audience was long gone. The Lizard King had won and
Jim couldn't breathe with his new skin on. "There's a
point beyond which we cannot return. That is the point
that must be reached," Kafka once wrote. Morrison had
finally reached it. He had become the cockroach. He had
metamorphosed into—

"Metamorphosized," I interrupt.

"*Into a monster that could still charm*," Briggs finishes the sentence that I wrote. "Mr. Morrison had become a monster, right?"

"When he was drunk. We were really great live. It was only the last bit that got really bad live."

"The point that the jury needs to understand," says Briggs, "is what legacy you're here to protect."

I am quick to answer, "The reason I include some of the bad stuff in my book is to show that people have dark sides, and Jim's got too dark. We're all human. The legacy I want people to get is the brilliance of . . ." Without thinking, I suddenly break out into song:

Drivin' down your freeways
Midnight alleys roam
Cops in cars, the topless bars
Never saw a woman
So alone, so alone . . .
L.A. Woman, you're my woman

"You can see why I'm the drummer," I add.

Without cracking a smile, Briggs says, "Can you please go to page 299 where you say: 'For thirteen years I've been trying to crawl out from your—our—shadow and find who I was, who I am, who I can be, besides John Densmore of The Doors.' That's what you were attempting to do when you wrote this book, weren't you, sir?"

"I also wrote in this book," I remind him, "that 'of The Doors' is permanently etched on my forehead and I'm proud of it. I want to expand my artistry into writing and other music as well as this wonderful background." Is this man trying to suggest that lifelong unwavering allegiance to the corps is permanent, that I'm not allowed to expand my artistic horizons?

"And that wonderful background included the music that was created?" he asks.

"Yes."

Now he picks up the pace of his questions, tossing them at me like hot potatoes: "You wrote music so people would listen to it? You played music so that people would enjoy it? You recorded music so that people would buy those recordings?"

I answer affirmatively to all of the questions.

"But you can't control who buys and listens to your music, can you?"

"No," I reply quickly, hypnotized as if at a tent revival.

"And your music can be played on radio stations listened to by Republicans?"

"I hope so."

"Democrats?"

"Yes."

"God-fearing people?"

"You bet."

"People who go out and buy expensive cars?"

"The whole gamut."

"You really can't control who listens to your music or who buys it."

"The records we make, no. But the licensing we can control."

"But you understand that when you and Robby and Ray and Jim were recording your music, even people who used drugs would buy your music. Right?"

"I don't know who used drugs and who didn't."

"But you understood that some of the concertgoers at Doors concerts were perhaps in there taking tokes?"

Now he's really starting to piss me off. "You use that word implying that I took a toke—"

"No, I'm not implying that," he interrupts.

"—before going into meditation."

"No. That's not what I mean, sir," Briggs says. "Not you. I'm talking about people in the audience that listen to your music. People that came to enjoy The Doors's music."

"I don't control what the audience does. It's their choice."

"So if this lawsuit is about protecting the integrity of the music and you understand that even people who use drugs may listen to the music, what is it about Cadillac that you find so offensive?"

Whoa! I'm certainly not on drugs right now and I can't follow this logic. "Sorry," I say, "what does Cadillac have to do with drugs?"

"Yesterday, you testified that you were attempting to protect the integrity of your music. And this is one of the reasons why you don't want to give a commercial license to someone like Cadillac. I think the jury would like to understand what is it about Cadillac that you find so offensive?"

Now he has asked a question that goes to the heart of the matter. I am happy to give the following answer: "I define art as having a gift in it that people receive even if you pay for a ticket to a movie theater or buy a CD. It doesn't affect the gift. If you turn the art into an entire commodity, you're degrading the art. And that's the gift. The gift has something to do with humanity and being a human being. What it is to see a painting or hear music."

"Don't you turn music into a commodity when you record it on a digitally remastered CD and sell it in a store?" Mr. Briggs asks.

"When you license your music for a commercial," I explain, "you've turned it into a total commodity. Tom Waits said, 'You just sold your audience. Those lyrics mean, oh, it's a jingle now. And that's the sound of coins in your pocket.'"

"Do you think Paul McCartney thinks of his music as a jingle?" Briggs asks.

"It's the artist's choice to do what he wants with his catalog."

But not always. The late Michael Jackson's estate, not Paul McCartney or Ringo Starr, now owns these Beatles songs. You better believe Paul was pissed that people were selling his babies when he didn't own them.

"Do you think that Mick Jagger thinks of his music as a jingle?" Briggs asks.

"I don't know."

"Do you think that Steve Nicks thinks of his music as a jingle?"

"That's a woman, *Stevie* Nicks," I say, as the entire courtroom lets out another big laugh. "Fleetwood Mac. Woman singer." This guy should have taken a crash course in rock history before he stood up in court and tried to cross-examine me about my world.

He apologizes and asks me, "You've heard popular rock music used in commercials today, haven't you, sir? And you know it's one of the avenues through which artists get greater exposure for their music. Isn't that true?"

"I guess Bruce Springsteen and The Doors are the only ones left standing. Some music is priceless."

"So you put The Doors's music up there with Beethoven, Picasso?"

"I'm sorry," I say, "I sound like I have some helium upstairs."

Apparently, Briggs is finished with me "for now," as he turns to the judge and says, "Your Honor, I'd like to reserve any further cross-examination for my case in chief . . ."

His "case in chief" is where he gets to argue the countersuit the guys filed against me. This is where he will really try to cut me up. I can hardly wait. For now, I'm relieved to leave the witness stand, and I step down as Jerry calls Robby Krieger to the stand. But he isn't here. He's in South America (an entire continent that The Doors never played), charading his latest band as The Doors.

We turn to a video of Robby's deposition instead, to the part where Jerry asked him if he remembered tearing up posters with our manager, Danny Sugerman, which promoted his band as The Doors. Robby recalled that Danny tore up the posters, not him, but the point was made that the touring band that featured Robby and had Ray as a guest was not The Doors. And that Robby was aware of the false advertising.

Later in the deposition, Robby said that he hadn't liked the idea of the Cadillac offer at first, because of what had happened with Buick. He said he was on the fence because doing commercials was not our policy. But he admitted that the large fee involved had sparked his interest and so had Ray's complaints that he needed more money.

It came out that Robby and I had offered Ray a loan of close to a million dollars. When Jerry asked Robby if he thought I was sincere in my offer, Robby failed to mention that I had come up with the idea in the first place, only saying that he had no idea what I was thinking. In the end, however, Ray never accepted the money because he and Robby had started playing gigs and getting paid. The upshot was that Robby's testimony showed that I cared enough about Ray's situation to offer help . . . but not enough to go against my own principles.

When the video presentation is over, it's time to go home. I head for the men's room, and as fate would have it, Mr. William Briggs is standing at the urinal. I make for a stall even though I only have to "splash me boots." I take my time as I hear Briggs wash up and exit. I leave the stall and, glancing at the urinals, see a little red rubber insert with wire netting that says, *Say NO to Drugs*. Maybe there *is* a connection between drugs and Cadillac. Somebody could make some serious dough by creating a larger version of this insert as the Escalade's new floor mats . . . a little message from General Motors not to get high while you're at the wheel.

Chapter 11

TOM & GEORGE & BOB

It's the weekend and I need a break from all this linear thought lawyers seem to love. Music will be just the cure, so I'm on my way to the Forum in Inglewood, California, to see Tom Petty's band. I love their music and I especially love Tom's dedication to his fans. He has a ceiling on his ticket prices and allows no VIP section in the front for execs who don't really care about the music. He once said, "I don't want the real fans in the nosebleed section." This evening will be a good antidote to the pressure I've been under during this trial.

I take my seat just as Jackson Browne, who is opening for Tom, starts his set. Now *there's* a guy whose integrity sits directly on his shoulders for everybody to see. He is known for his philanthropy, but to me, that word has an arrogant ring to it. The Greek translation of "philanthropy" is literally "loving people," but I'd rather call someone an altruist with deep pockets. Jackson Browne is one of the best examples of the true definition of "philanthropy," "an *active* effort to promote human welfare." Most people would agree that helping others gives us the greatest satisfaction—it's in our nature—but most of us were just educated wrong. Jackson has a PhD in this area. His heart is so open, you can almost see his caring nature running through his veins.

In the audience, I find myself sitting next to Jim Ladd, the legendary Los Angeles rock disc jockey, who is an old friend. When he tells me he's going to introduce Petty, I get an idea. You see, Tom's latest album is called *The Last DJ*, and the title cut is about Jim Ladd, the very man beside me. The song tells a story about how, as a result of a corporate take-over of a radio station, the disc jockeys were ordered to stick to the dictated playlist. But "the last DJ" wouldn't toe the line. And in real life, that was exactly what Ladd did. When the corporate heads threatened to fire him if he wouldn't play the music *they* wanted him to play, he said, "Fine, and I'll take my fans with me." The station backed down and soon he was the only "free-form" DJ left . . . doing his thing, playing what-ever he felt like in the moment.

"Hey Jim, what if I introduce *you* before you intro Tom?" I say, with a mischievous grin.

His eyes light up. During intermission, we go backstage and run the idea by the promoter. It's a go. I'm standing in the wings, waiting for my cue to walk out in front of fourteen thousand Petty fans already frothing at the mouth. They're stamping their feet and making a lot of noise. The reason: they *know* Tom cares about them. There is another song on the new album, "Money Becomes King," which is also one of the reasons I'm here. It's about some dedicated fans who become disillusioned with their hero because he starts doing light beer commercials and can't remember his original lyrics.

This particular song reminds me of an interview the Who's Pete Townshend did in *Rolling Stone*, where he was challenged by reporter Chris Heath for licensing his songs for various commercials:

> *Heath: There are a few interesting uses of the Who's catalog at the moment. I thought it was strange that you let them use "Bargain" in the Nissan car ad, given that the song is so very much not about that.*

> *Townshend: Yeah, but not many people know that [laughs].*

> *Heath: Well, correct me if I'm interpreting it wrong, but the song is saying that you are prepared to give yourself up for enlightenment or spiritual satisfaction and that this bargain is the best you've ever had.*

> *Townshend: That's right. Yeah.*

> *Heath. Which is about as antimaterialistic a message as one could think of.*

> *Townshend: [Mock-snarling] So, what's your point?*

> *Heath: My point is that it is now being used to sell shiny new motorcars.*

> *Townshend: I still don't get your point—you haven't completed the argument.*

> *Heath: Well, I'll complete it, then. The suggestion of the ad is that one might buy a super new Nissan car that is the best one for the finest price, and that's the bargain.*

Townshend: Well, that's their suggestion, isn't it? For about ten years I really resisted any kind of licensing because Roger Daltrey [lead singer of the Who] had got so upset when somebody had used "Pinball Wizard" for a bank thing. Who *fans will often think,* This is my song, it belongs to me, it reminds me of the first time that I kissed Susie, and you can't sell it. *And the fact is that I can and I will and I have. I don't give a fuck about the first time you kissed Susie.*

Heath: But surely you care about some of the deep, personal meanings in the songs?

Townshend: If they've arrived, then the message is there. The licensing of "Bargain" to Nissan—it was an obvious shallow misreading of the song. It was so obvious that I felt anybody who loved the song would dismiss it out of hand. And the only argument that they could have about the whole thing was with me, and as long as I'm not ready to enter the argument, we don't argue. Well, I'm not ready to argue about it. It's my song. I do what the fuck I like with it.

The Who may have more fans than Tom Petty, but they can't be as dedicated as this crowd, which swells to a roar when I'm introduced. It's flattering, but I know it comes from the fact that, besides admiring me, they now know that, like them, I'm a Petty fan. As Morrison wrote, "Music inflames temperament."

This crowd is on fire as I say, "Hello! I'm here to introduce the man who will bring out the band. Some call him the Last DJ!" They go nuts as I bow to Mr. Ladd and make my exit.

After Petty is introduced by Jim, while he rocks the house, I think about a number of artists who portray the other side of Pete Townshend's argument—the ones who side with my belief that art is a gift that shouldn't be treated as a commodity. Tom Waits (recently inducted into the Rock & Roll Hall of Fame), for example, sent a very poetic letter to the editor following the publication of my article in the *Nation*:

Thank you for your eloquent "rant" by John Densmore of The Doors on the subject of artists allowing their songs to be used in commercials. I spoke out whenever possible on the topic even before the Frito-Lay case (Waits v. Frito-Lay), where they used a sound-alike version of my song "Step Right Up" so convincingly that I thought it was me. Ultimately, after much trial and tribulation, we prevailed and the court determined that my voice is my property.

Songs carry emotional information and some transport us back to a poignant time, place, or event in our lives. It's no wonder a corporation would want to hitch a ride on the spell these songs cast and encourage you to buy soft drinks, underwear, or automobiles while you're in the trance. Artists who take money for ads poison and pervert their songs. It reduces them to the level of a jingle, a word that describes the sound of change in your pocket, which is what your songs become. Remember, when you sell your songs for commercials, you are selling your audience as well.

When I was a kid, if I saw an artist I admired doing a commercial, I'd think, Too bad, he must really need the money. *But now it's so pervasive. It's a virus. Artists are lining up to do ads. The money and exposure are too tantalizing for most artists to decline. Corporations are hoping to hijack a culture's memories for their product. They want an artist's audience, credibility, good will, and the energy the songs have gathered as well as given over the years. They suck the life and meaning from the songs and impregnate them with promises of a better life with their product.*

Eventually, artists will be going onstage like race-car drivers covered in hundreds of logos sewn to their costumes. John, stay pure. Your credibility, your integrity, and your honor are things no company should be able to buy.

The loyalty of the fans tonight is palpable as they demand several encores from Tom Petty's band. My mind flashes back to the early days that every band goes through, struggling to get a toehold in an ever-increasingly difficult industry. I'm not saying that *no* rock songs should ever be sold as commercials. Certainly, a new group that is out there struggling to pay the rent could get some help hawking stuff. But once they get a toehold on success, I think they should drop the soundtrack to TV ads or they'll get stuck. Lewis Hyde, in his seminal book *The Gift*, says that a work of art needs to have a gift component or it will only be a commodity. He writes: "Even if we have paid a fee at the door of the museum or concert hall, when we are touched by a work of art something comes to us which has nothing to do with the price." Hyde concludes, "It may be possible to destroy a work of art by converting it into a pure commodity . . . I do not maintain that art cannot be bought and sold; I do maintain that the gift portion of the work places a constraint upon our merchandising."

Then there's another point of view, proposed by Tom Petty's bandmate from the Traveling Wilburys, and possibly the greatest songwriter of the twentieth century, Bob Dylan. I first met him in Malibu years ago when I was visiting friends. I went for a walk and I saw "the man" jogging down the street in a sweat suit. When he stopped and asked me for directions, I thought to myself, *I know that craggy voice.* "Are you Bob Dylan?" I said.

He backed away.

"I'm The Doors's drummer," I quickly told him.

Then he held out his hand. Months later, backstage at the Rock & Roll Hall of Fame, there was that guy again, sauntering around in the wings wearing motorcycle boots, leather pants, and a hoodie. It was hard to tell who he was, but I remembered the body language as he motioned for me to join him.

"Hey," I said, pleased that Dylan had recognized *me*, "I saw you jogging!"

A tech guy standing nearby overheard us and his reaction attested to the fact that Dylan was in disguise. "Are you guys into jogging?" he asked us. He wanted to talk about the latest running shoes or something like that. Dylan and I took a few steps away.

"Did you get my book?" I asked him.

He said he had, and that he liked it very much. I thought I could die happy at that moment. It had taken me a year to acquire his approval to use some of his lyrics in my memoir. His agents had said he would never approve because where I placed them in the text implied drug references. But great artists seem to write universally, allowing the reader to have his or her own individual interpretation. I persevered, finally getting through to Dylan when Paul Rothchild (The Doors's record producer) provided access.

At the time, Billy Joel was asking me for four hundred bucks for his lyrics from "Goodnight Saigon." Dylan said fifty bucks was fine for his. I called Joel's people back and told them how reasonable Dylan had been, but they still wouldn't budge. Billy Joel had had an expensive divorce.

Physically getting the book to Bob as a thank you was quite a challenge as well. My Malibu friends had done construction on his home, so since I knew where he lived, I went over to his house to hopefully put the finished book in his mailbox. Two rather rough-looking bikers sauntered up to my car and I rolled the window down. "I have a book for Bob I want to give him," I said.

"Bob who?" one of them snarled.

"Bob Dylan, of course," I said.

"Never heard of him," the man barked.

I'd seen some heavy security in my day, but these guys were ridiculous. They pretended not only that Dylan didn't live there, but also that they'd never even heard of him. "We'll take the book off your hands if you like, but whoever he is, he doesn't live here," the other biker said.

I pulled the book back inside the car and said, "Naw."

They revved their motors and zoomed back into the compound. As I drove away, I thought of a friend who knew Dylan's ex-wife. I figured maybe that would prove to be an inroad. It was.

Now, backstage at the Rock & Roll Hall of Fame, I told Mr. Zimmerman (Dylan's real name), "I saw you play recently and you were great." Then I blurted, "I never saw you in the old days because I'd heard how you trashed your songs." As soon as I said it, I wondered where the fuck that audacious statement had come from.

"Trashed?!" Bob said.

"Well, what I mean," I stumbled, trying to recover, "is that you changed the melodies so much, the audience had a contest to guess which song you were singing. The point is, you were great the other night!" I took my foot out of my mouth as Ray walked up in awe.

"Nice to meet you," he gushed to Mr. Dylan.

Months later, I heard that Dylan had become a little more articulate in his live shows. Somebody *had* to say something. In retrospect, though, I think Bob was trying not to repeat himself, looking for freshness, as Jim was when he suggested we go to that island and start all over. The muse is elusive, and she doesn't like staleness. She will disappear at the drop of a drumstick. True artists such as Dylan and Morrison are chameleons, reinventing themselves every so often.

So when Dylan later let one of his songs be used for a bank ad in Canada, I tried to ignore it. Then he did a Victoria's Secret commercial, which I also tried to ignore, but Dylan was IN the commercial! There were several close-ups of his face intercut with a nubile model writhing around in underwear. Let me quote Leslie Bennetts, former contributing editor of *Vanity Fair*, who critiqued Dylan's ad in the *Los Angeles Times*:

> . . . *the distasteful spectacle of a geezer sexually fixated on a girl young enough to be his granddaughter. When the man who wrote "Forever Young" starts leering at jailbait during prime time, the result looks like a recruiting tool for a pedophilia advocacy group.*

Hey, maybe he was trying to date the model. As composer Randy Newman wrote, "It's lonely at the top."

Bennetts continued:

> . . . *when he's shilling for bras and panties . . . Can we be surprised that an old guy is cashing in too? These days it's all about merchandising. Now, there's a legacy to pass on to the next generation.*

Ms. Bennetts's comments are quite harsh, but they obviously come from disappointment. Back in the sixties, when Dylan was called the "spokesman of his generation," he felt trapped and got obsessed with not conforming to people's expectations. He was totally contrary (and still is) in his interviews about his art and would continue deflecting the idea that he has all the answers. Don't put Dylan in a box. He gets claustrophobic very easily.

It's been a number of years since the Victoria's Secret ad happened, and my respect for Bob has deepened again. A four-CD release of his songs for Amnesty International reminded me that the breadth of his work is staggering.

The Tom Petty show ends and Jim Ladd and I head to the dressing room to pay our respects. Tom is very gracious and there's a kindred vibe in the air. I remember reading about Petty having the same reaction as I did when I heard "Good Vibrations" (a metaphoric song for the sixties by the Beach Boys) selling Orange Crush soda pop. I was crushed. Whatever "gift" I felt I received about the message of love in the counterculture had been doused with yellow dye #5. My flower power was wilting and almost dead from the onslaught of inorganic commerce and pesticides. One of Jim Morrison's gifts was to write lyrics that seemed to have universal meaning, though everyone got something a little different from the words. But I'm sure his intention wasn't to "Love Me Two Times" because I just took Viagra.

Tom Petty, Jim Ladd, and I say our goodbyes and I hit the road. As I get into my Prius, I remember another letter I received in response to my *Nation* article:

> It makes me want to puke when I hear Jimi Hendrix selling Pontiacs. I can't believe Hendrix would ever have signed off on that, but Hendrix like Morrison died way too young, and evidently his heirs inherited only his rights, not his ideals. Morrison was luckier, and more prescient. And believe me, the fans do care.

I pull into my garage and just sit there for a few minutes. I can't stop ruminating on all this. The line in the sand I've drawn has turned into a wall. But I've got other "ancestors" rooting for me who "broke on through to the other side." It's public knowledge that George Harrison wasn't too thrilled to see Beatles songs used for commercials. Although we met only a few times quite briefly, George Harrison and I followed strikingly similar tracks. It is uncanny how our lives were strangely parallel and synchronistic, even from across the Atlantic.

He was in a famous rock and roll band, as was I. He was cautious about that bright spotlight on the front men (Lennon and McCartney for him, Morrison for me), staying in the background with his meticulous guitar lines, me with my drum fills. We both viewed fame as *maya* (illusion), a Sanskrit word meaning something not to be taken too seriously, only getting a little singed by the edge of that shaft of light on the lead singer.

I first met George at a small Hollywood party during the release of the Beatles's *White Album*. We were at the hilltop Hollywood pad of Alan Pariser, a promoter/groupie who couldn't get enough of rock and roll celebrities. I'd heard that the Beatles were going to be there, so up the narrow snake trails my Morgan crawled, huffing and puffing its way out of the sea of twinkling lights below on Sunset Boulevard. Entering the dark living room, there was George sitting with a small group of folks, and I was so intimidated, I couldn't even look into his eyes, those eyes that penetrated from his photographs as if he were looking right through the viewer.

After getting myself a drink, I sat down across from the star and noticed a stack of *White Albums* in the corner. His strikingly beautiful wife Pattie asked me if I'd heard it. The record hadn't been released yet, so my answer was no. She bathed me with her gorgeous gap-toothed grin and said it was quite good. She was clearly proud of her man. My small talk was getting even smaller than my one-word answer to her question, so I quickly slipped out and slinked back down the hill. My confidence hadn't caught up yet with The Doors's growing record sales.

And yet, the similarities in our lives were obvious. In our youths, for example, both George's and my dad gave us flack about our hair, George with his greased-back Teddy Boy look of the early sixties, and me later emulating Harrison's mop-top shag around '64. I got A's in music and barely passed the rest of my courses, while George excelled in art and failed the rest. The Liverpool Institute High School for Boys decided to hold Harrison back for one year because of his poor performance, and George elected *not* to tell his parents. When I failed sociology in college, I didn't show my report card to my dad, because the repercussions would have been him coercing me to get a job or go into the army. When George quit school, his dad, Harry Sr., insisted that his son accept an apprenticeship as an electrician, a trade that the young man hated. My parents eventually found out about my inferior grades and I quickly got dishpan hands from a six-nights-a-week restaurant job that was forced on me. I switched to folding shirts in a 120-degree Chinese Laundromat because how could I play drums with wrinkled hands?

When I attended a meditation class with my friend Robby Krieger, Jim was living the Jack Kerouac bohemian lifestyle on a rooftop in Venice, while the Beatles had just named themselves after the (Beat) generation of poets who were "on the road." Around this time I was experimenting with LSD, which I found quite blissful. At least I had the good sense to trip in nature, so I could relate to Harrison's description of his acid excursions: ". . . there was a God, and I could see him in every blade of grass."

Actually, I thought *I* was God for a few minutes there . . . I guess my ego was a bit larger than George's, but on LSD, the vibrancy of the yellow coming off the acacia tree outside my Topanga bachelor pad was almost too much to bear. The Beatles guitarist said that LSD had "changed me, and there was no way back to what I was before." As I wrote in *Riders on the Storm* about my ingesting LSD, "A crack had appeared in the façade of reality, and I had peered through . . . Nothing had changed, yet everything had."

George again: "It was like opening the door, really, and before, you didn't even know there was a door there." I thought that now, with the direct experience of another reality, I could tolerate this one more easily.

A final word on psychedelics from the quiet Beatle: "It just opened up this whole other consciousness, even if it was down to, as Aldous Huxley said, the wonderful folds in his gray flannel trousers."

It is once again synchronistic that we took *our* name from Huxley's *Doors of Perception*. Having had our fires lit by psychedelics, we were all looking for a less shattering route for our nervous systems, like Eastern religion and mysticism. The Beatles and The (future) Doors were poring over Paramahansa Yogananda's *Autobiography of a Yogi*. Jim didn't actually take up meditation, but he came with us to one meeting and said that Maharishi had something special in his eyes. In any event, at the threshold where the West was being exposed to the East, The Doors were born. But like the Beatles, The Doors had no idea how famous we would become. At that time, I told my mom that if we had a hit album, not just a single, we might be able to make a living and last maybe a decade. Apparently, George didn't fantasize his group going through the roof, either. He just hoped that they could make enough money for him "to open a little business."

During a 1968 meeting with Derek Taylor, our new press agent who'd promoted the Beatles to worldwide notoriety, a surprising thing happened. We were sitting in the Sunset Boulevard offices of our *Oceans 11*–type managers, who suggested we hire the handsome, erudite PR man from England. Derek had a clipping he wanted to show us. I got up off the plush Vegas-like couch and took the *Los Angeles Times* article from him on the "boys," from the Brit with the ascot. It told of the lads being informed of the death of their manager, Brian Epstein, by Maharishi at a retreat in India. "Far out," was our reaction to the *temporarily* secret ritual of Transcendental Meditation we'd stumbled upon a couple of years back, now subject to mass exposure via the Beatles. Hindu chanting was to become a household practice. And so, my second reaction wasn't so secular. I realized that meditation could bring a balance to the drug-induced sixties.

Another related landmark on my road-less-traveled with George was Ravi Shankar. The Doors had recorded their first demo with Dick Bock, Shankar's record producer, so early exposure to raga music seeped into our first couple of albums. If Indian musicians could play fifteen or twenty minutes per tune, so could we. "The End," complete with sitar-like guitar and a Hindu climax, was ten minutes long! Outrageous for the traditional three-minute AM rock radio format. Later, Francis Ford Coppola would resurrect the beautiful raga-tuned song as a contrast to visuals of the Vietnam War in his epic *Apocalypse Now*. Meanwhile, George's Shankar influence was steeping Fab Four tunes into exotic teas with sitar ingredients. Both bands started donning Nehru jackets, beads, and paisley shirts . . . except Morrison. He would wear a simple strand of Indian nuggets over a T-shirt, but down below was black leather, Dionysus balancing all of us "peace and love" advocates.

Early on, Robby and I studied at Shankar's Kinnara School of Music on Fairfax Avenue in Los Angeles. There, we crammed sitar and tabla lessons into a couple of four-week blocks, in between Doors road tours. Still paralleling my growth, George went to India for six weeks, learning some basics from Ravi that are normally taught to a music disciple over a period of years. Back in merry old England, George convinced the other lads to pack in the idea of playing live, as thunderous adulation overshadowed the very sound they were trying to put out. In the studio, however, the lead guitarist's influence was so strong, it seem like *all* the Fab Four's new tunes had been dipped in curry sauce.

The pressure of fame came down on both of our bands,

straining group relations to the breaking point. Harrison told a dictatorial McCartney he was "full of shit," and for a little while he quit the band. As for me, I once threw my drumsticks down on the floor during the recording of our third album, and in frustration I said, "I quit!" I was sick of Jim's destructive behavior. I returned the next day and the guys quietly accepted their drummer back. After all, this was my musical family.

I certainly see similarities in what George said about parenting his then nine-year-old son Dhani. When *my* nine-year-old boy needed discipline, I found myself flashing back to how my dad would have handled a particular incident. "With a child around I can realize what it was like to be my father," Harrison said. "At the same time, you can relive certain aspects of being a child . . . It somehow completes this generation thing."

The second time I met George, I was a little more at ease. The Doors had made a couple of respectable albums and maybe the guitarist had even heard them. He was taking a look at Elektra's recording studios when we were working on *The Soft Parade*, our first and only album experimenting with horns and strings. "It looks like the sessions for *Sgt. Pepper*," Harrison said with a smile. He was commenting on the sea of string players filling up the recording booth. It was just that. We were trying to emulate the biggest group in the world as Jim sang, "*Come on, come on, come on, come on / Now touch me, babe*," with the musical support of the Lonely Hearts Club Band.

Along with the other parallels, the Beatles were our mentors in terms of their integrity toward the songs they had written. "The history of the Beatles was that we tried to be tasteful with our records and ourselves," said the guitarist. "We could have made millions of extra dollars [doing commercials], but we thought it would belittle our image or our songs." In my case, there were obscene offers to "sell out," but in the spirit of George and Jim, I've held out. George Harrison once said about communicating with the dead, "It would be real handy if we could talk to John about our business decisions. It would be a lot easier if John was around to get things resolved."

Speaking of séances, I've been talking *a lot* to my British spiritual brother since his passing on November 29, 2001. George and I had met one final time, at Ringo's party at Bar One in Los Angeles in 1990. I was about to leave when George popped in and said, "I hear there's a photo opportunity here!" I noticed that Harrison was chain-smoking, and the great session drummer Jim Keltner remarked to me that the Beatles guitarist couldn't quit. Ringo introduced me to George and I said, "We've got much in common, we should talk."

He sensed my impending exit, though, and he said, "But not now."

"Right," was my response, which I've regretted since George's final exit. Part of me is pissed that he checked out so early, at fifty-eight years old. I still find it difficult to acknowledge that George Harrison isn't walking around on the planet, 'cause we need people like him. You'd think he could have whipped ciggies with the discipline he displayed meditating and practicing sitar, but the tobacco companies are *adding* nicotine to make up for decreasing sales. Time has healed this disappointment, as it did with Morrison. I was so angry with Jim's self-destruction when he died, it took me years to start grieving. Now, in hindsight, his early demise seems to be part of a larger plan.

I wrote the following note to George when I learned he had been attacked by an intruder:

Jan. 15, 2000

Dear George,

It's John Densmore, drummer for The Doors. We met briefly several years ago at a press party for Ringo's band in Hollywood. I said we should talk, but it was too loud, and we agreed to have that conversation "next time."

It is shocking and terrible what happened to you, and it's made me reach out to connect now. When you guys started, you were mentors to me. Our paths have had such similar routes: I met Maharishi a year or two before you got into it, I was in Ravi's Kinnara school studying tablas, Derek Taylor was our press agent, and Jonathan Clyde looked after us when we were in England.

So . . . I just wanted to reach out at a vulnerable time when you might be questioning your karma, and wanted to say you have my utmost admiration.

Sincerely,
John Densmore

P.S. I asked a Guatemalan shaman friend of mine to send you some healing energy.

Harrison once said of his connection to Lennon, "We saw beyond each other's physical bodies, you know . . . If you can't feel the spirit of some friend who's been close, then what chance have you got of feeling the spirit of Christ or Buddha or whoever else you may be interested in?"

These days, George has been on my mind. *The Tibetan Book of the Dead* says that the deceased can't get to where they're supposed to go without the encouraging thoughts of us over here. I sent "good vibes" for the required thirty days, and now George seems to be a spiritual ally for the duration. He is definitely with me and his photo sits beside my laptop, his eyes staring directly ahead as if he were saying, *Tell the truth.* He quoted Bob Dylan's lyrics when Lennon was shot:

> *If your memory serves you well*
> *We're going to meet again . . .*

"I believe that," commented Harrison.

Ditto to you, George.

Recently, a fan letter alerted me to a very sad situation. George Harrison's song "Taxman" was used as a commercial for tax accountants, right around the time he died. The song was obviously written as a protest against high taxation:

> *Let me tell you how it will be*
> *There's one for you, nineteen for me*
> *'Cause I'm the taxman . . .*

George clearly wasn't resting in peace. Rather, he was being picked over by scavengers. I emailed my friend Jonathan Clyde who works for Apple Corps Ltd., the Beatles's company. He confirmed that up until the *White Album*, the boys had sold their publishing so they were exposed to any use of those songs the publisher wanted. Knowing George, this info would probably have washed off his back like water off a duck, but I feel compelled to get a broom and sweep those ravens and crows off his resting place. They'll come back, but I'll come back too.

I realize it's time to get off my butt and get into the house. Thank God the heirs of Dylan's deceased pal Johnny Cash had the sensibility *not* to okay the classic song "Ring of Fire" for an ad to cure hemorrhoids. May Johnny's burning sphincter rest in peace.

Chapter 12

ALLY(S)

During this phase of the trial, I am being bolstered by several luminaries who have volunteered to step up to the plate (the witness stand). I recall a book called *The Teachings of Don Juan*, written by Carlos Castaneda, in which he talks about the need for an "ally," or a spiritual helper. Since Ray and Robby no longer qualify, I've turned to some other musical brothers who seem to care about musical integrity.

I started by writing a letter to an old friend, Neil Young, who lived next door to me in Laurel Canyon a long time ago, although I hadn't seen or spoken to him since the sixties:

Dear Neil,

I hope this doesn't give you an acid flashback, but it's John Densmore. Gosh, you've done OK since the Buffalo Springfield. I've done OK too. Unfortunately, as you might have read, my relationship with my old band has deteriorated. Along with Jim Morrison's estate, I'm suing Ray and Robby for using the name The Doors, which, on paper, they have no right to do. They have countersued me for an amount many times the value of my entire net worth. The main basis for their complaint is that I vetoed the use of our songs for ads. The main one is Cadillac, which you might have seen with Led Zeppelin.

Thanks to Jim's generosity (and insecurity about how to write a song), he suggested we split everything, publishing included. We are all loaded, have nice houses and several groovy cars (probably not as many as you, but . . .). I vetoed the ad, thinking our original intent should be kept pure (if we were broke, that might be different). I wrote an article in the Nation magazine (eventually syndicated in the London Guardian and Rolling Stone) on this subject. Tom Waits wrote a very interesting letter to the editor in response.

That famous session drummer that you use, Jim Keltner, called me when Ray and Robby were on Jay Leno with the "Jimitator" (Ian Astbury). Stewart Copeland was sitting behind The Doors's logo on his bass drum, as he blasted into "Light My Fire." Keltner said, "Stewart is a wonderful drummer, but he isn't The Doors's drummer, and Ray and Robby shouldn't be playing those songs!" (They eventually parted ways with Stewart.) They certainly should be allowed to play. I just insist on the name being changed ("former members of The Doors" is fine with me). I bumped into Randy Newman and he said, "I hope you win that lawsuit." Bonnie Raitt wanted to join in, but she's in Europe until the end of June. A mutual friend said Bono expressed solidarity with me, but he's in Ireland.

I wish the trial was in Greendale [the title of Neil's last CD], but it's in LA . . . Any chance you might want to testify as an expert and express your opinion on how *songs should keep their integrity? I'm humming "This Note's for You."*

If this makes you uncomfortable, forget it. This unfortunate occasion has at least forced me to make long-overdue contact. I can't believe you're still writing important stuff! Prolific dude. We have much in common: enjoyed playing music with Eddie Vedder; and a sensibility of trying to hang on to the values we grew up with on the Sunset Strip!

John Densmore

P.S. Of course it's the eleventh hour, and I need your response ASAP. Thanks for even considering . . .

Elliot Roberts, Neil's manager, quickly called and said Neil enjoyed my letter very much and would testify, if his schedule permitted. He certainly didn't have a problem with being uncomfortable . . . A year later, Neil released *Living with War*, an album rant against the preemptive strike in Iraq. For that, some critics called him a traitor and terrorist sympathizer. Shades of things to come for Yours Truly.

I wrote a letter, similar to the one I sent Neil Young, to Randy Newman, asking if he wanted to join the party . . . perhaps perform "It's Money That I Love" for the jury. Newman called and said that he'd already done "I Love L.A." for the Lakers, so if I wanted a before (Neil) and an after (himself) thing . . . he was up for it. Quite funny, but it turned out that it wasn't necessary for either of them to testify. Their solidarity felt great, though.

Now that the weekend is over, Stewart Copeland is on the

witness stand, much to the chagrin of the other side. A few moments earlier, before the jury entered the courtroom, they filed a motion to exclude from evidence the memo that Stewart wrote to Ray and Robby stating his opinions about the name of the new band. It was overruled. I imagine Briggs was upset about this, but he is not the man who stands up to question Copeland. He must have sufficiently embarrassed himself with the Stevie Nicks gender-bending statement to allow a young pinch hitter from his firm, Paul Lukacs, to argue this in his place. This guy is supposedly knowledgeable about rock and roll as he strides up to home plate to address the judge.

"When you actually look at what's in Exhibit 85 [Copeland's memo]," says Lukacs, "it's of no evidentiary value."

If that's true, I think to myself, *then why are you trying so hard to have it excluded?*

Lukacs goes on, "If this was written by Mr. Copeland, then this is at most Mr. Copeland's own private, personal, amusing opinions. When you look through this, there are nine points mentioned. By magic, eight of those points are the major incidents and points in this litigation. And we're somehow supposed to believe that in September of '02, Mr. Copeland sat down and very succinctly, very precisely, in an almost lawyerly manner, hit on eight points which are the full basis of this litigation. When you take the potential for prejudice or confusing the jury, and the very mysterious circumstances of the letter, it certainly should be stricken from evidence."

Jerry takes his turn and says, "Well, Your Honor, it certainly comes as no surprise that they want to keep out what's probably the single most important piece of paper in this case. To suggest that there's some impropriety with respect to how it was prepared is ridiculous. What's important here is that every single one of these people that received it has lied about seeing it. There's going to be testimony about with whom it was discussed and the fact that it was sent out. I think it goes to credibility."

The judge agrees with Jerry, allows the memo into evidence, and he calls in the jury.

Jerry then approaches Stewart on the witness stand: "Mr. Copeland, in front of you is a three-ring binder. Can you turn, please, to Exhibit 85? Hopefully, that is a memo from September 15. Did you prepare this memo to Ray, Robby, Ian, and Tom Vitorino, their new manager?"

"I did," says Copeland.

"When you prepared this memo on September 15, 2002," says Jerry, "did you cause it to be transmitted to the addressees?"

"Yes, I did."

"And subsequent to your sending or emailing or transmitting of the memo, did you thereafter have conversations with one or more of the recipients about the subject of the memo?"

"Yes," says Copeland, "I talked to Ray and to Tom."

"And did each of them acknowledge to you that they had receipt of the memo?"

"Yes."

"When you had your subsequent conversations with Ray and Tom about the memo, did you discuss the various points in the memo?"

"With Tom, I discussed all of the points at great length, before sending the memo and after sending the memo. With Ray, I wasn't able to get much of a conversation out of him. But I did get a confirmation that he had got it. He commented on one of the points, which confirmed to me that we were talking about the same document."

"Subsequently," Jerry says, "did you also, independent of going through the memo, discuss the various items in the memo with Ray, Robby, Tom, Ian, or any of them at various rehearsals?"

"Yes. All these points had been discussed very vaguely during all of the rehearsals that came up in conversation. That's why I wrote this list down—to clarify, if need be, that these are things we need to figure out."

Jerry takes a seat and Briggs stands up for the cross, approaches the witness stand, and asks, "Did you personally mail the memo to Ray Manzarek?"

"No. My assistant did all of that."

"Were you present when your assistant purportedly faxed the document to Ray Manzarek?" asks Briggs.

"No."

"Are you familiar with how fax machines work?"

"Yeah," says Stewart. "Not as good as my assistant, which is why I have an assistant, but kind of."

"Did you see what's referred to as a fax confirmation sheet that the document had been faxed to Ray Manzarek?"

"No. That's not my normal practice with my assistant. I do ask her, 'Did you send all of my stuff?' And she says yes."

"Did you see a fax confirmation with respect to Robby Krieger?"

"No."

"Did you see a fax confirmation with respect to Tom Vitorino?"

"No."

I guess Briggs isn't getting what he wants right now. Copeland just told him that he gets confirmations from his assistant, but Briggs insists on asking the exact same questions over again, naming each recipient. He gets the same answers from Stewart, which reminds me of the definition of insanity: doing the same thing over and over and expecting different results.

Briggs finally moves on: "Now, when you had your conversation with Ray Manzarek, did Ray say, 'I have in front of me the September 15, 2002, memo?'"

"That's not the sort of conversation we had, no. Shall I describe it for you?"

"Let me ask the questions, sir," barks Briggs. Stewart must have hit a nerve. After all, we can't have a witness going off and telling the truth. It has to be massaged in the right direction. After Briggs acknowledges to the jury that my attorney will go through the memo thoroughly with Stewart later, he asks him if Ray told him that he received the fax.

"Ray said, 'Uh-huh, yes,'" says Copeland.

I have to stop myself from laughing out loud during the next exchange:

"He said, 'Uh-huh,'" Briggs repeats. "You took the 'uh-huh' . . ."

"As a yes. He's a taciturn man. He's not voluble," explains Stewart.

"You're sure the 'uh-huh' wasn't a 'huh-uh'?"

"Positive," says Stewart.

"Could you interpret the 'uh-huhs' and the 'huh-uhs'?"

"Yes. Certainly in this case."

"There was a definite 'uh-huh'?" Briggs says.

Stewart answers yes again. Wasn't that a doo-wop rap?

"And you're positive," Briggs has another go, "that he was referring to this particular memo even though he didn't verbalize that to you?"

"Yes," says Stewart. "What we were going to do about the Morrison estate and John Densmore was very much on my mind. My understanding of the way bands work is if you create what's essentially a brand—the name of a group—that the people who created it have an interest in it and you can't just shine them off. I was very concerned about how to deal with the other owners of this trademark. It's a simple matter. As The Doors, it's a big-ticket item. As the solo efforts of the names of the individuals, it's not. And so this was something that we talked about quite a bit."

Briggs's attempt at evisceration has obviously failed, and now Jerry takes over by getting Stewart Copeland's background. A five-time Grammy Award–winning film composer and member of the Rock & Roll Hall of Fame, Copeland was in the original Police with Sting as lead singer. I saw their magnificent reunion tour in 2007 at the Hollywood Bowl, and I have to say, if I'd been asked to fill Stewart's shoes, or rather pick up his drumsticks, I couldn't have done it. No one could. His drumming is so creative and uniquely perfect for the Police, it fits as tight as the golf gloves he wears when he's playing.

He tells Jerry, "About a year or two ago, when Ray and Robby started touring again with The Doors or thinking about it, I got a call from them as an invitation to play. When The Doors were famous, I was sixteen. Exactly the age of a Doors fan. So here I am as an adult getting to play this music with these guys. I couldn't believe it. And so I was very enthusiastic about the whole thing.

"I did ask them, 'What is the position of the Morrison estate and John Densmore about this?' I felt very uncomfortable sitting on the drum stool of somebody that I regard very highly. I was very concerned about that relationship and I was assured, 'There was a bad relationship. But it's worked out, don't worry about it.'"

Jerry draws the court's attention to the memorandum dated September 15, 2002, and he asks Stewart about it.

Stewart says, "I never realized what was going on until the first Harley-Davidson concert. We were at the press conference, microphones in front of us, pictures being taken, just about to play the show. 'And so what's in the future?' someone asks. And I hear Manzarek say, 'Lots of shows. We're going for it. This is The New Doors of the 21st Century.' It was kind of news to me. And then there's a press conference at the House of Blues where I learned more about what the plans were going to be, which I hadn't learned directly from Mr. Manzarek."

"Is that what prompted this memo?"

"No. This is just a comment about, *Can't we have band meetings to decide what's going on? Can't I get straight answers rather than hearing it in front of the microphone?* There was conversation that, I think it was Mr. Densmore had refused to sell 'Break on Through' to Cadillac. And they turned down lots of money. Once again, at the press conference I'm sitting there with Ray and he said, 'You'll never see The Doors in a car commercial.' But there we were, sitting in front of a gigantic poster: *Harley-Davidson presents The Doors.* It was a little thing that I would use to nudge my fellow musicians. Joking, teasing point. 'Come on, Ray, get off your high horse.'"

"When he said that," says Jerry, "did you understand he was being serious or that he was being . . ."

"No," says Stewart, "he was deadly serious. I was very rarely able to get a laugh out of Mr. Manzarek."

"Did he say it in a way that he was proud that the music wouldn't be used?"

"Yes. Very proud," says Stewart. "Absolutely vehement. I think he was being congratulated by a journalist. 'We've seen other bands in there. But never The Doors.' 'Are you ever going to [do a car commercial]?' asks a reporter. He said, 'No, you'll never see it.' In fact, the Cadillac commercial came out with a song called 'Break Through.' They took out the 'on.' Then they used a Led Zeppelin track instead. Another legendary band name."

It turns out, by the way, that when Trent Reznor, Oscar winner for the soundtrack to *The Social Network* and lead singer for Nine Inch Nails, was interviewed about Led Zeppelin okaying their song for Cadillac, he said, "Now every time I heard that fuckin' song, I think of a car."

By the time Copeland leaves the witness stand, his testimony looms huge. It calls Ray's and Robby's credibility into question and demonstrates that other musicians, not just me, had concerns about using The Doors's name. Now, to build on a good foundation, Jerry calls another ally, Anthony De-Curtis, to the stand, a writer for *Rolling Stone* magazine who has also contributed articles to the *New York Times*. A coeditor of the third edition of *The Rolling Stone Illustrated History of Rock & Roll* and *The Rolling Stone Album Guide*, DeCurtis was a critic for *All Things Considered* on National Public Radio, covering culture, music, and movies. For a year, he was editorial director for VH1.

Jerry begins with a simple question: "What is your opinion of The Doors touring?"

"As I'm sure we all know," says DeCurtis, "Jim Morrison died in 1971. If you lose as iconic a figure as that . . . somebody who gets put on the covers of magazines and is regularly the subject of books, if you put together a version of that band without that individual, how legitimate can it be?"

"What was your opinion about that?" asks Jerry.

"Essentially," says DeCurtis, "that it was not legitimate.

Those guys are perfectly welcome to perform their own music. But the idea of The Doors without Jim Morrison . . . there's a handful of people in the history of popular music . . . You can't have the Rolling Stones without Mick Jagger. You can't have Nirvana without Kurt Cobain. Or Police without Sting. You can't have U2 without Bono. And you can't have The Doors without Jim Morrison.

"Once you see the name The Doors and that very, very identifiable logo, you're in a whole other league of what you can ask for. The Doors have become a kind of rite of passage for people who are interested in rock and roll. As you grow up and get interested in this music, they're one of the bands that you have to learn about and find out about. Stewart Copeland was just in here. He would probably agree with this. You can't find another kind of young, good-looking singer and substitute that person for Sting and call it the Police. That's the band that he was in because Sting has a kind of importance in that regard as well. I think this falls into that category of the absence of Jim Morrison that trumps the other concerns. If somebody doesn't know the difference between Jim Morrison and Ian Astbury, to me, that's a problem. And something that I think potentially could damage the kind of stature that this band deserves and has earned."

"Let me change subjects for a minute," says Jerry. "Do you have an opinion about the use of rock and roll music in television or radio commercials?"

"My feeling is that people should avoid doing it. It can damage the stature of their work. I think we've all had that moment where you're riding in the car and that great song comes on but it's really a commercial. There's such a letdown to that . . . it's not the whole story. But I think that feeling cheapens the song and the emotions that you attach to it. Over time, that erodes the regard people have for that music."

"Like Carly Simon and 'Anticipation,'" says Jerry.

"Becomes a ketchup ad," agrees DeCurtis. "At this magazine, *Tracks*, we just did a big story about Jimi Hendrix's estate selling his songs for ads. The fans are very upset. This guy is an artist. He shouldn't be treated like that. But in *Apocalypse Now*, you have a situation where a major American director is making a major movie about one of the most important issues in American foreign policy and history, using The Doors's music to open that film. One of the most dramatic things you'll see. It was like hanging a painting in a museum, like something that takes a song and gives it a whole new life. Apart from the fact that soldiers in Vietnam listened to The Doors. There was something about their music that helped them understand and get through the difficulty of that situation. That could never have happened if 'The End' had been in an Oscar Mayer wiener commercial."

I'm trying not to smile as DeCurtis continues, "The Doors's music means something. To put it in this other context is to devalue something very valuable that many, many artists strive for. This band is in the Rock & Roll Hall of Fame. This band doesn't need to do a lot to stay on people's minds. They're taken seriously. Morrison is somebody who strove his whole life for recognition as a writer. To trample on that and diminish it is a big, big mistake."

Jerry says he has nothing further and Briggs takes up the cross: "I want to pick up on a thread of something you just said. You said music would lose its long-term significance if it were used in commercials. That's your testimony, right?"

"Yes," says DeCurtis.

"You've heard of Beethoven?" asks Briggs.

"I've heard of Beethoven."

"What about Bach?"

"I've heard of Bach as well."

"Mozart?"

"Yes."

"Would you consider them great musicians?"

"Of course."

"Would you consider some of their music some of the most classical music in the world?"

Briggs is showing his musical ignorance again. The music is classical by definition. I think he means "classic," but DeCurtis lets it slide by saying, "Yes."

"Has any of their music lost significance because they've been used in commercials?"

"There's nobody to protect their music. Anybody can use it who wants to."

"That's not my question," says Briggs, trying to snare DeCurtis in his sticky web of confusion. "My question is, has their music lost significance because it's been used in a commercial?"

"No. Their significance is fully established."

"And you just testified that The Doors's music is fully established, right?"

"To the degree that something as recent as The Doors music could be fully established, yes."

My next witness will further DeCurtis's argument. Nigel Williamson, a thin, distinguished-looking Brit with a ponytail, is called to the stand on my behalf.

Chapter 13

THE "L" WORD

"I'd like to go through an article you wrote in the British Airways magazine a little bit and review some passages," Jerry tells Nigel Williamson. "You say, 'The Doors were one of the most extraordinarily potent bands the world has ever seen.' That's quite a statement."

"They were quite a band, Mr. Mandel," says Nigel, who has just arrived from London. I've read some of this man's journalistic pieces and I think he's very smart. Of course, Mr. Lukacs, second batter for the defense, just tried to get rid of him, arguing that he presented no special knowledge that would qualify him to take up jury time. But the judge disagreed, stating unequivocally, "He has extensive experience."

At Jerry's prompts, Nigel tells the jury he's been a writer and a journalist for the past twenty years, specializing in music for the last ten. Prior to being political correspondent for the *Times* of London, he worked for the British Labour Party as editor in chief of their publications department, alongside Labour leader Neil Kinnock and a young, promising, as-yet-unknown politician named Tony Blair.

A highly respected music critic, Mr. Williamson interviewed countless groups, from the Rolling Stones to Led Zeppelin, and he wrote several books, one called *Neil Young: Journey through the Past*, and another called *The Rough Guide to Bob Dylan*. Associate editor of the very popular *Uncut* magazine in the UK, he has a weekly column in *Billboard*, an American music trade publication. Does that kind of experience sound moot, Mr. Lukacs? It sounds more like special knowledge and special expertise to me.

"In your article," Jerry goes on, "you say that Mr. Morrison has been elevated to the highest echelon of popular culture. What do you mean by that?"

"He's one of those iconic figures," says Williamson, "whose influence has continued to grow long after his death and long after the music he was making. We could go into the reasons for that, but I think it's undeniable. The Doors are, certainly in Europe I would suggest, as popular today as they probably were in the late sixties, which is extraordinary for a band that hasn't really existed in that original form for thirty-four years now.

"My two sons, for example, who are in their midtwenties, are huge fans of The Doors, which is strange if you think about it. When I was their age, there was no way I listened to the music that my father listened to forty years earlier. And yet there's something about this music, and I think particularly about the poetry and the vision of Jim Morrison, that continues to reverberate down the decades."

"You say in your article, in the last sentence of this paragraph: 'But let's not kid ourselves. This isn't The Doors. Because The Doors were Jim Morrison.' Why do you say that?"

"I believe that the musical vision and the power of The Doors came specifically from Jim Morrison. I'm not denying the contribution the other three musicians in the group made. But I think without Jim Morrison there would not have been a group as we know The Doors to have been. The music would not have existed in that shape or form."

After Jerry establishes that Nigel knows of Ian Astbury, he asks, "Could you explain a little bit about who he is?"

"He was the singer, I guess he still is," says Nigel. "My understanding is he hasn't left his other group, the Cult. They may come back at some point. He's been the singer with this goth metal group called the Cult best part of twenty years."

Jerry asks Williamson to explain the following excerpt from his article:

All of these years on, Morrison remains implacable. And so the current incarnation is nothing more than a Doors tribute band—which just happens to include two of the original band members playing tribute to their own long-lost youth . . .

"It comes back to the discussion earlier about tribute bands, Bootleg Beatles and Counterfeit Stones," says Williamson. "This incarnation of The Doors is in a similar category. However, there is one significant difference . . . the guitarist and the keyboard player, Mr. Krieger and Mr. Manzarek, both were part of that original lineup. Which I agree gives it a certain twist.

"Nevertheless, without the iconic front man, the Jim Morrison figure, the Mick Jagger figure if we're talking the Counterfeit Stones, or the Lennon and McCartney figures if we're talking the Bootleg Beatles, without those figures, I think they are nothing more than tribute bands."

"In your mind," asks Jerry, "can two of them continue on as The Doors?"

"In my mind, no."

"Have there been other bands where singers and musicians have been replaced?"

"Yes, there have. One thinks of a band like Fleetwood Mac. They've gone through a number of different incarnations with different personnel. If you think about it, Fleetwood Mac takes its name from the drummer and the bass player. Mick Fleetwood was the drummer in that group. John McVie was the bass player. They are the constants in the group, so they're a slightly different situation. I can't think of a major group that has done what The Doors are doing in this incarnation."

Jerry reads aloud two more paragraphs from Williamson's article:

It makes you rather respect those who have resisted telephone number deals to rehash their past. Pink Floyd have been offered millions to get back together but have sensibly refused. [They did later appear in a benefit for Live 8.]

Another example might be Brian Wilson from here in Los Angeles. The man who wrote all the Beach Boys songs. Now, he is touring at the moment. He's played some very, very successful concerts in the UK playing old Beach Boys songs, Pet Sounds *and* Smile. *If anybody has the right to use the name Beach Boys, you would have thought he has that right. He hasn't done so out of respect for the former members of the group, including two of his brothers who both died. And he is playing Beach Boys songs but calling himself Brian Wilson . . .*

"How about the Beatles?" says Jerry. "Anybody tried to regroup those Beatles?"

"No. I don't think any of them ever would. You could imagine the situation where the two surviving Beatles, Paul McCartney and Ringo Starr, could round up a couple of young hopefuls. John Lennon has two sons who are musicians. George Harrison has a son, Dhani, who is a guitar player. I don't think they would ever even contemplate that in a million years."

Jerry reads more from Nigel's article:

It's called charisma. As meticulously as you may perfect the moves and copy the vocal inflections, it's a quality that cannot be reproduced. Good luck to Ian Astbury. He's going to need it. But however good he proves to be in the role, the band he's leading still isn't The Doors.

"What do you mean by that?"

"I genuinely don't wish Ian any ill," says Nigel. "It's an enormous, unenviable task to try to fill Jim Morrison's shoes, which is, after all, what he's trying to do. But he never will be Jim Morrison, however good he is. In fact, when I did the deposition prior to this court appearance, there was some discussion about: was I suggesting that Ian Astbury wasn't a good singer? I was trying to get across that it was irrelevant whether I thought he was a good singer . . . My simple contention is, because he's not Jim Morrison, the band he's singing with is not The Doors. You could get any kind of fantastic singer to take his place. You could get Mick Jagger. You could get anybody. It's not an issue of how good they are in the job. It's simply the fact that they are an impostor."

Now, Paul Lukacs from the defense picks up the bat and takes a swing at the erudite Mr. Williamson: "Would it be correct to state, sir, that you don't have any specialized knowledge of The Doors?"

"No, it wouldn't," says Nigel. "I bought those records and I saw the band in the 1960s. I've been listening to them ever since. They remain an important part of my life."

"Have you ever written any books about The Doors?"

"No, I haven't. Although you never know after this experience," muses Nigel. "There could be a book in it."

Very funny, Nigel, I think to myself, *but can you please wait until I get this book out first?*

Lukacs says, "My question, sir, is why are you more qualified to talk about the use of The Doors's name than someone who has reviewed the underlying evidence?"

"I have followed The Doors's career for thirty-five-plus years," says Nigel. "And I work as a professional music journalist interviewing musicians and writing about bands who have disbanded and got back together. It isn't *me* that regards myself as an expert. It's the people who employ me. I get asked again and again by national newspapers and magazines to write on these subjects."

"Have you reviewed any tape, videotape or audiotape of the Doors of the 21st Century concert?" asks Lukacs.

"No."

"Wouldn't this jury, after hearing any such evidence, be in a better position than you to opine about the quality of those performances?"

"It has nothing to do with the quality of the performances," says Nigel. "It's absolutely irrelevant."

I have a hard time suppressing my laughter as Lukacs asks, "When you say it's irrelevant as to whether or not Ian

JOHN DENSMORE

Astbury is a good singer, doesn't that show that you have a closed mind on this issue?"

"Not at all. It's not the issue under discussion. The issue under discussion is simply that he's not Jim Morrison. Therefore, the band that he's singing with is not The Doors. He could be a better singer than Jim Morrison—it still wouldn't change my view."

I'm impressed with how these Brits can kick ass. Apparently so is Lukacs, who takes the testimony in a new direction, asking Nigel to read a sentence from his article out loud.

"'The whole idea of Ian Astbury dressing up in Jim Morrison's leather trousers and mimicking him is thoroughly distasteful.'"

"Sir," says Lukacs, "do you have any factual knowledge that Ian Astbury is in any way attempting to mimic Jim Morrison?"

"He's singing his songs," Nigel answers. "What more do you want?"

"Well, if I start singing 'Light My Fire,' am I going to confuse anybody, sir?"

"If you stood up onstage and called yourself The Doors of the 21st Century, quite possibly."

I can hardly believe I paid a ton of money for this trial, which is turning out to be a stand-up night at the Comedy Store.

Seemingly unperturbed, Lukacs continues to amuse me by asking, "When you make the reference to Jim Morrison's leather trousers, are you saying that Mr. Astbury wears leather trousers onstage?"

"Not specifically. Although he certainly did wear leather trousers with the Cult. But no, I certainly didn't mean to suggest that he's raided Jim Morrison's old wardrobe and is wearing his leather trousers. Figure of speech."

194

"What opinion, if any," asks Lukacs, "did you have of Raymond Manzarek's autobiography?"

"It's nine years or so since I've read it. But my general impression was that the tone was a little bit sour."

Lukacs jumps on that: "In your deposition, when I asked you this question, didn't you say 'a thoroughly enjoyable read'?"

"Yeah, enjoyable read."

"There's no contradiction there in your mind?"

"No."

"Were you the editor in chief of a British magazine called *New Socialist?*"

"Yes, I was," says Nigel.

"Have you written for the *Guardian* newspaper?"

"Yes, I have."

Lukacs opens a can of worms by asking, "Would it be correct to state that the *Guardian* is one of the more left-wing daily newspapers in the United Kingdom?"

Despite Jerry's objection as irrelevant, the court allows it and Nigel says, "The *Guardian* is a liberal newspaper, yes."

The "L" word has been officially introduced into the courtroom. And gosh, the *Guardian* syndicated my *Nation* article, so what does that make me? Is Mr. Lukacs prompting Mr. Williamson to do some courtroom remodeling, as in painting the gallery "red"? Or at least pink, as in "pinko"? He asks, "Did you write a book about the British Social Democratic party?"

"Yes, I did."

"After you are done here in the US, to what countries are you traveling?"

Nigel says he is traveling to Mexico and then Cuba . . . . where the other side probably assumes he's gonna hang out

with Fidel. I hope the Latino jurors will see through this ridiculous BS.

Lukacs continues, "You mentioned several bands or several people affiliated with bands who went on tour and did
not use the band's name. Do you have any knowledge as to
whether or not Brian Wilson has the legal right to call himself the Beach Boys when he performs?"

"I don't know the legal position, no," says Nigel.

"Do you have any knowledge as to whether or not Mr.
Plant or Mr. Page [from Led Zeppelin] have the legal right?"

"My understanding is yes, they do."

"What is your understanding based on?" asks Lukacs.

"Interviews with both of them," he says. That sounds to
me like a slam dunk.

"So is it your position that when an iconic member of a
band leaves, that band cannot legally call itself by the name it
had when the iconic member was participating in the band?"

"It's not a legal question at all," Nigel says.

"Do you characterize it as a moral question?" asks Lukacs.

"It's high-flown words to throw around. I think it's a question of dignity quite honestly, Mr. Lukacs."

"Isn't it true that you accept the general proposition that
a band can sometimes have greater success after a lineup
change?"

"Yes, Fleetwood Mac is the one example you could cite."

Lukacs now directs the court to an exhibit of one of The
Doors of the 21st Century's ads. "Is there anything in this advertisement that leads you to believe that this is advertising
anything other than Ray Manzarek, Robby Krieger, Ian Astbury, and Stewart Copeland playing a night of Doors songs?"

Nigel answers thoughtfully, "I've made two observations
on seeing this for the first time. One is the use of the lettering

around the words 'The Doors,' which is remarkably similar to the logo the band used on their early albums. The second is the prominence of the words in relation to the rest of the name. I mean, you could hardly read '21st Century.' When the Bootleg Beatles played the Albert Hall, they did not put 'Bootleg' in tiny lettering and 'The Beatles' in huge lettering."

The defense seems to need a rest, and they turn the questioning back to my trusted barrister.

"I just want to clarify one thing, Mr. Williamson," Jerry says. "When you're in Cuba, is that pleasure or work?"

"It's work . . . I've written a lot about Cuban music over the last decade. I wrote the liner notes for *Buena Vista Social Club*, which won a Grammy Award and has sold eight million copies. I'm going to meet some of the same musicians who are still alive who played on that record."

The documentary to which Nigel is referring, produced by Ry Cooder and directed by Wim Wenders, was released to great critical acclaim and received an Academy Award nomination in 2000 for Best Documentary Feature.

"I have no further questions," declares Jerry, dismissing Nigel from the stand.

I thank him silently. In one neat sweep, my attorney has splattered Lukacs's new red paint job with a high-gloss white sheen. Against this backdrop, while the red-baiting lawyers look embarrassed, Mr. Forer calls his client, George Stephen Morrison, to the stand. Jim's dad. I watch as my "new father figure" is sworn in by his attorney. It is quickly established that Admiral Morrison is eighty-six and has been married to his wife Clara, who is in the courtroom, for sixty-two years.

"Do you have any children?" Forer asks.

Admiral Morrison says, "I have two children. One child died. I had three children. Two left. James Douglas was the oldest son. I have a daughter named Anne Robin and a third son, Andrew Lee."

God, this is painful. It feels like I'm witnessing the "legalization" of Jim's death. The death of my musical brother. Admiral Morrison isn't showing any emotion but I bet way down, he's hurting. He explains that Anne and Andrew are in the courtroom and that he has three grandchildren and three great-grandchildren. After attending the Naval Academy in Florida, he became a commissioner in the navy.

"I was ordered to a ship called *Pruitt*," Mr. Morrison says, "a mine force in the Pacific fleet which was headquartered in Pearl Harbor."

"You were there when Pearl Harbor was bombed?" asks Forer.

"Yes," Mr. Morrison says. "We were at extensive overhaul at the time in the ship. Our armament was all ashore. So basically we were spectators. But we were there."

"Spectators while the bombs were falling?" asks Forer.

"True." Then, in response to a question about his history with the navy, the Admiral says, "I served on a number of ships and squadrons as a pilot and then as a commanding officer of a carrier and of other fleet units. And I served on a number of staffs all around, both ashore and afloat, in London, in the Naval Forces in Europe, and with Carrier Division in the Pacific, and in other places like that. Also in Washington."

"Did you have some action in Vietnam, sir?"

"In Vietnam I was there at the beginning . . . commanding the *Bon Richard*, which is an aircraft carrier. That was a long war. And I later came back again on the staff of a Carrier Division command."

"Sir, what was your rank?" asks Forer.

"I started out as an ensign, and I finished thirty-eight years in the navy as a rear admiral."

How ironic that the antics and popularity of his deceased son's songs against the war created obstacles to the rear admiral getting promoted to full admiral. And yet, here he stands, supporting my case against turning Jim's creations into cheap commercialism.

At this point, the judge suggests we take a lunch break, giving the usual admonishments about not discussing or forming or expressing any opinions about the case. I take a seat next to the Admiral in the rooftop cafeteria, feeling slightly intimidated to be sitting next to Jim's father. He hardly eats as I try to strike up a conversation with him.

"Now I see why you're so thin," I tell him as he chews on a piece of apple.

"I don't eat much until dinner. Then I have a couple of martinis and a steak," he says with a twinkle in his eye.

It's impossible not to like this guy, but having a rear admiral for a dad would be difficult for any sixties kid. Still, I'm feeling extremely appreciative of Jim's parents for showing up to this courtroom drama. Joining us is Jim's sister Anne, who is very friendly as she jokes that Jim must have teased us as much as he did his siblings. She's right.

When lunch is over, we all trudge down from the rooftop cafeteria to the fourth floor, where the Admiral's short but sweet testimony wraps up.

"Sir," says Forer, getting straight to the heart of the matter, "do you feel that The Doors's partnership has been damaged by anything that the new band with Ray Manzarek, Robby Krieger, and Ian Astbury has done?"

"I believe it was damage to the partnership to have them go on the circuit as The Doors."

"Why is that, sir?"

"Because to me," the Admiral says, "The Doors have always been a group of four young men that came together rather uniquely, all with great talent, but they somehow managed to synchronize and put them in one voice as indicated by the fact that they didn't have their names on special as the vocalist or the writer of the song and one wrote the music. It was The Doors as a group. And they made a great body of music because of this unique combination. And it carried over into the business side because they decided that they were one and you didn't do anything separately. And then when I found out that the group was on the tour, just two of them and calling themselves The Doors, I thought that was wrong."

"Do you oppose Ray Manzarek and Robby Krieger performing concerts in which they use the name The Doors in any part of their band name?"

"Yes," he states.

"Do you oppose Ray Manzarek and Robby Krieger performing concerts in which they do not use the name The Doors?" asks Mr. Morrison's attorney.

"Oh, no. Not at all. They're great musicians."

"And they have the right to perform?"

"Absolutely."

"But not as The Doors?"

"That's correct."

"Nothing further," says Forer.

It appears that Mr. Briggs has mustered enough psychological insight to realize that crossing the eighty-six-year-old Morrison might backfire, so he leaves him alone and skips doing a cross-examination. George Stephen Morrison is excused.

You just don't fuck with the Admiral.

Chapter 14

ROBBY

When Robby takes the stand, this is the first time I've seen him and Ray in the courtroom while I've been doing the downtown shuffle for many weeks of testimony. It appears that Briggs is on to his "case in chief," which requires both Ray's and Robby's presence at the trial. It's about time they showed their faces, but seeing them here is like that strange feeling of going to a twenty-year high school reunion and staring at familiar faces stuck on older bodies.

In the early days, I looked up to Robby. He was quiet, so I thought he knew something, and when he finally spoke up, what he said had weight. After a couple of incidents where Jim displayed obnoxious behavior and I asked Robby what he thought, he said Jim was capable of anything, including stardom. Years later, when Ray tried to dominate the press, I asked Robby if Ray had changed or if he had always been such a control freak. He said that Ray had always been that way. In fact, Ray had hired Danny Sugerman, our manager, on the side in order to promote himself. No wonder all the interviews went to Ray.

When Ray and Robby went off to do the Ray & Robby Show, stealing The Doors's name, they abruptly dumped Sugerman. A wounded Danny reached out to me and I responded, having learned to appreciate the kid from the mail room who worked his way in an uphill climb to running our career. Unfortunately, Danny's substance abuse caught up with him and his health prognosis grew dim.

Toward the end, Danny continued going to AA meetings, carrying a breathing machine in tow. The pushy kid had turned into a noble elder. Just before his death, he and his wife threw an unstated "goodbye" party, which was extremely poignant, but Ray and Robby were not invited. I had the good fortune to sit with Danny just before he broke on through, and gave one of the eulogies after his crossing. At least Robby had the depth to show up and say some touching words.

Here is the text of my eulogy:

I had the luck of good timing to be with Danny a few hours before he died. It was a blessing, because he [and Fawn Hall] have become teachers of how to make this fearful crossing that we all have to make, and do it with such courage and dignity.

He was off chemo, all drugs that day. He seemed weak, but really clear. The Tibetans believe that this transition is best made as conscious as possible. He was supposed to have some painkillers the next day, but he chose to leave that day. He knew his time was just about up. I told him that I'd made contact with everyone I knew on the other side, and they were ready for him. We talked about Fawn [although in the past, I'd had major disagreements with Ms. Hall about her politics]. There's no greater example of living the lyrics "Stand by Your Man" than Fawn Hall. Awe-inspiring.

We talked about how I'd gone to see his brother Joe a few days before . . . for my annual ear cleaning, and Danny tried to find the words to express how much gratitude he had for Joe, who supported him emotionally as a brother, as well as guiding him through years of medical troubles. The love was palpable.

We talked about how every time I pulled a gray hair out of my head, I got twenty more, and here was Danny, fifty years old, being chemo'd and radiated for years, lying on his death bed, and his hair was perfect! I looked like Colonel Sanders now, and he did not have one single gray hair.

Danny was a closet Buddhist. The Tibetans believe that when the deceased first go, they need us over here, to help them get to where they're supposed to go, by thinking of them for thirty days . . . positive thoughts, or candles lit . . . and then I think they reciprocate, after they have arrived, as guardian angels for us.

And from the feeling in this room, Danny is well on his way. I want to leave you with a line from the Pulitzer Prize–winning Irish poet Galway Kinnell, which goes: "The wages of dying is love."

In other words, we mortals have to die, so the payment for having to go through this is love. "The wages of dying is love," and there is so much love for Danny here in this space, he's going to have a smooth journey. It is an honor to be a part of this community.

The first question Briggs asks his client is about how far back Robby and I go. We actually hung out in our formative teenage years when we experimented with then-legal psychedelics and lusted after girls. While Robby tells Briggs how close we were, I remember us running around town, trying to "find ourselves." As the band got famous and Jim's self-destructive behavior escalated, we shouldered each other through the maze . . . or rather the purple haze.

During that time, as I recall it, Ray had Dorothy, whom he married, Robby and I had each other, and Jim had the bottle, along with a number of so-called friends who hung around the "star," encouraging his drug and alcohol abuse.

"Sir," says Briggs, "how long have you known Mr. Densmore?"

"Since high school," Robby answers.

"It goes way back?"

"Yeah."

"More than forty years?"

"Well, that sounds like a lot of years," says Robby, "but it could be."

"And you and Mr. Densmore were good friends?"

"Yeah, we were."

"Very good friends?" asks Briggs.

"Yeah, at one time."

"Who introduced you to Ray Manzarek?"

"John Densmore."

"Who introduced you to Jim Morrison?"

"John."

"So you have your friend of more than forty years," summarizes Briggs, "who introduced you to all of your bandmates, and all four of you went to the top of your profession. Do you want to be involved in this lawsuit, sir?"

"No," Robby answers, "I never had a desire to be in this lawsuit. In fact, I think it's ridiculous that this thing actually has come to trial, to tell you the truth. To me, it's three sixty-year-old rock stars arguing about the size of lettering and what you can call yourselves. I mean, to me it's a waste of time and money and never should have happened."

Boy, do I ever agree with my former bandmate. This is a waste of time and money, so I wonder why Ray and Robby's barristers played such hardball throughout the various settlement conferences. I know that Robby is not a confrontational guy, but I wish he'd stood up during those early meetings and offered to reduce the size of the damned lettering. All of this could have been completely avoided.

"Did you and Mr. Densmore ever have any discussions about the font size of 'The Doors,' the name itself, being so large and the font size of '21st Century'?" asks Briggs.

"He was unhappy that 'of the 21st Century' was smaller than 'The Doors.'"

"What did you say when he expressed his unhappiness with the font size?"

"I said, 'You're probably right about that, and I'll try to make it bigger next time.'"

"And did you try to make it bigger next time?"

"I think I forgot about it," says Robby, "to tell you the truth. Never got around to it."

And he's wondering why we're in this mess.

At this point, Jerry takes his turn: "Would you say that even until this lawsuit was filed, you considered John to be one of your very closest friends in the world?"

"I would say so," Robby responds. "I mean, because of this lawsuit, no. But to tell you the truth, after The Doors, John and I were in a group called the Butts Band. And after that, we went our separate ways and haven't been that close for many years. But I still consider him a good friend, you know."

"Good enough to tour with you in Europe in 1997 and 1998, right? 'Robby Krieger and John Densmore of The Doors,' right?" says Jerry.

"I'm not sure what it was called, but—"

Jerry interrupts, "And one year it was 'The Robby Krieger Band, with musical guest star John Densmore,' right?"

Robby agrees.

"And one year Manzarek was supposed to be the guest star, but he got sick and you called John and asked if he would fill in, right?"

"Right."

"And in 1997," says Jerry, "it was 'The Robby Krieger Band, with guest star John Densmore'?"

"That sounds right."

"And in 1998, you and John Densmore had a multiple-city tour in Europe, where you were billed as 'Robby Krieger with John Densmore of The Doors,' right?"

"Yeah."

"Did Mr. Manzarek complain at all that you guys were billed as 'Robby Krieger with John Densmore of The Doors'?" asks Jerry.

"No."

"Did John Densmore object that you called yourself 'Robby Krieger with John Densmore of The Doors'?"

Once again, Robby says, "No."

This makes me want to say, *Sorry, Robby, but why didn't you call yourselves "Whatever! starring Robby Krieger and Ray Manzarek of The Doors"? We're all fine with "of The Doors."* But then, the lure of the big venues and the big bucks was just too much, and Robby knew that the big dough would only come if he eliminated that one little word—"of"—which meant so much.

But how much does it really mean? Without the huge money and venues, Ray can still get his retail therapy by shopping and Robby can still eat an expensive meal at Spago. Yet the addiction to money in this culture is as strong as heroin. In fact, when the culture dictates that more $ will make you happy, it's a real mind-blower to imagine that not everyone wants more of this powerful entity. The greed heads, I mean corporate heads, haven't learned the lesson of George Harrison. His song "Living in the Material World" (which is also the title of Martin Scorsese's film doc about him) says that when George got all that dough from being a Beatle, he still felt a void, that something was missing, that money didn't provide all the answers to a complete life.

Jerry interrupts my thoughts by asking Robby, "You certainly understood that Mr. Manzarek was in favor of the Cadillac commercial?"

"Right," answers Robby.

"Mr. Densmore was not in favor of the Cadillac commercial, as it was presented?"

"Right."

"And you were on the fence?"

"Right."

"You never told anybody that you were in favor of the Cadillac commercial, did you?" Jerry asks.

Robby says, "Correct."

"I want to be clear about your recent experiences in talking with people. You were on the fence about Cadillac at the time the proposal was presented, right? But now, with hindsight, you look at it and you say to yourself that it might not have been such a bad thing to do?"

"Right."

"And John respected your opinion at the time, didn't

he?" Jerry says. "And you respected John's opinion at the time, didn't you?"

"Yes."

Jerry smiles and says, "Twenty-twenty hindsight is a wonderful thing, isn't it?"

"Sure is."

So why did Ray's and Robby's representatives state somewhere along the line that no billionaire would ever turn down the Cadillac commercial? Is this the new standard? *I guess I'll never make the grade*, I think to myself as Jerry moves on to the next issue.

"There are rather prominent artists today who don't allow their music to be used in commercials, aren't there?"

"I suppose there still are," Robby says reluctantly, and Jerry names various artists who have taken a stand against commercializing their music, including Bruce Springsteen, Neil Young, Jackson Browne, and Bonnie Raitt. When he gets to John Mellencamp, the truth is that he recently crossed over the "commercial" line by selling a song to Chevrolet. The *Los Angeles Times* quoted him as saying,

> *The bottom line is, I'm a songwriter, and I want people to hear my songs. I'm not saying it's right. I'm not suggesting it for anybody else. This is just what I did this time to reinvent myself and stay in business. Sometimes I get sad about it, really. I still don't think that people should sell their songs for advertising.*

"The Beatles," says Jerry, "when they owned their own catalog, didn't allow it, did they?"

Robby isn't sure about that.

Jerry goes on, "You have been very selective in where

your music can be used, haven't you? You want it to be associated with what you think is a quality movie, a piece of art? As well as something that might enhance the catalog as well?"

"Yes."

"And that's what happened—*Apocalypse Now* had a tremendous effect on your catalog, didn't it?"

"I'm not sure what effect it had," Robby says. "I'm sure it was good, though."

Jerry asks Robby if licensing our music to the movies *The Doors*, *Forrest Gump*, and *Monsters, Inc.* had a big impact on our catalog and Robby says that it did.

"Didn't you just get offered $500,000 to let your song 'People Are Strange' be used in a movie being shot this Christmas with Keanu Reeves?"

"I'm not sure of the amount, but—"

"A pretty big sum of money," Jerry rephrases his question, "whatever it was?"

"Yeah."

"You pick and choose those opportunities that you think are best for you and your business?"

"Of course," says Robby. "Yeah."

"You don't take them all, do you?"

"No, not all."

"And if it was a crummy movie, but they offered you five million, you still wouldn't take the five million if you thought the movie was crummy, would you?"

"That's true."

"I want to ask you a question," says Jerry, about to return to the ever-tantalizing issue of sexploitation—the perennial question of Jim's alleged lewd behavior in Miami that has been discussed ad nauseam ever since he was falsely arrested back on December 9, 1967. "I don't mean to embarrass anybody by this question, and please don't take it that way, but it was something that was said in the opening statement of this case. And I think you're the only one here or in the world who can answer this question. When you were onstage in Miami on that fateful concert that ultimately resulted in Mr. Morrison's arrest, did he engage in oral copulation with you on the stage?"

Briggs jumps to his feet. "Objection. Misstates what I said in the opening statement."

The court overrules the objection.

Robby answers, "No, he didn't."

"You're absolutely certain about that, aren't you?" says Jerry.

"I think I would have known if that happened, yes."

Laughter issues from the courtroom. Now that this very important issue is resolved, back to the business at hand.

"The three of you got together to try to resolve the dispute surrounding the band name and the font usage?"

"With lawyers," says Robby.

"You mean that Mr. Densmore actually tried to work this out with you before a lawsuit was filed? A meeting with you and Ray and John and lawyers?"

"Right," says Robby. "You were there."

"How long did it take, that attempt?"

"A couple hours," Robby recalls.

"How many hours?"

"A couple."

"Actually," says Jerry, "that meeting took place the entire day, didn't it?"

"Was it that long? I tried to blot it out of my mind."

"And in the meeting that you're talking about were you, Mr. Densmore, Mr. Lavely, and me, right? In the meeting where the discussion was had, it was just the four of us and a mediator, isn't that right?"

"That's true, probably."

"And we spent a whole day trying to fix this little mess so that people wouldn't have to be here today, didn't we?" says Jerry.

"Yes, we did."

"And you believe that everybody was sincere in that attempt?"

Mr. Briggs objects to the question. The judge allows it.

"I hope so," Robby answers.

"And even after this lawsuit started, there were more attempts to resolve this without having to be here this day, wasn't there?"

"Yes, there were. Unsuccessfully," Robby says.

"We actually spent two full days in this very courtroom trying to resolve this, didn't we?"

"That's true."

"And Mr. Densmore was here for every minute of those attempts, wasn't he?"

"Yes, he was."

"As were you?"

"Yeah.

"You understand," says Jerry, "don't you, that there are three lawsuits that are being tried here in this courtroom today? One of them is a lawsuit filed by Mr. Densmore against you and Mr. Manzarek with regard to who has the right to use the name The Doors. You understand that?"

"Yes."

"There's another lawsuit filed on behalf of Admiral and Mrs. Morrison, and Corky and Penny Courson [Jim's parents-in-law], against you and Mr. Manzarek, also with respect to the right to use the name, among other things. You understand that, don't you?"

"Yeah."

"Did you ever talk to the Morrisons or the Coursons about the right to use the name The Doors?"

When Robby says no, Jerry tells him, "Now, there's a third lawsuit, which is you and Mr. Manzarek suing Mr. Densmore . . . for, among other things, not agreeing to allow the Cadillac commercial that *you* also didn't agree to. Is that right?"

"That I was on the fence about," Robby says.

"You never told anybody that you agreed to do it, correct?"

"That's true."

"And you told people, in fact, that you were on the fence, and you weren't voting in favor of it, right?"

"No," says Robby.

"What did you tell them?" asks Jerry.

"I didn't say I was *not* voting for it. I didn't say I *was* voting for it."

"You just stood on the fence?"

"Right."

"But you're suing—"

"And my feet hurt," Robby cuts in.

No one laughs at his attempt at humor.

Jerry carries on, "And you're suing Mr. Densmore nonetheless?"

"That's right."

Now we have a little tag-team cross-examination as Mr. Forer, the lawyer for Jim's estate, approaches Robby. "Mr. Krieger," he begins, "did the Morrisons ever tell you that they were going to sue you because you didn't approve the Cadillac deal?"

"No, they didn't."

"Did you ever hear from anybody," Forer asks, "that the Morrisons or the Coursons or their representatives were going to sue John Densmore because he did not approve of the Cadillac ad?"

"No."

At this point, Jerry stands up, points to an exhibit of the Doors logo, and says, "You made those little baby changes for John when you moved the lines on the O's from diagonal to straight up and down. And you changed 'The' up there from Wavy Gravy [font] to something else, right?"

"That's right."

"But otherwise," Jerry says, "that's the Doors logo, isn't it?"

"Well, yeah, you could say that."

"And this one," Jerry goes on, "which you say you're now using, in fact you're *not* using, because this DVD just came out, didn't it?"

Robby stumbles over his words, "Well, yeah, but this was—it was, you know, made like almost a year ago, so—"

"You mean it was shot almost a year ago?" Jerry says.

"Right. Exactly."

"But it wasn't printed and published a year ago. It was printed and published thirty days ago."

"Well, how do you know that?" Robby asks.

"Wasn't it?" Jerry replies.

"I don't know."

"By a company called Image, right here in the San Fernando Valley, isn't that right?"

"Well, anyway," Robby says, clearly trying to avoid the question, "if what you're trying to say is that people are going to buy that and think it's The Doors and not The Doors of the 21st Century, then I think you're wrong."

"What I'm trying to say is, ten minutes ago you told the people in the jury box that this is the logo that you're now using, and it isn't, is it?"

Briggs tries to save his client by objecting vehemently that my attorney is misstating testimony and being argumentative. The judge overrules it all. Robby is required to answer a question that just caught him lying.

"I was sadly mistaken," he says.

"So it appears," Jerry responds. "You said, Mr. Krieger, that you thought the whole logo issue was unimportant and meaningless. When Mr. Densmore asked you or suggested or requested, whatever word you want, that the Doors logo not be used by your new band, why didn't you just say, 'Okay, it's unimportant, it's meaningless. We'll pick another one'?"

"I thought we did, and, you know, things get confused, and I'm sorry that we didn't. It ended up not being changed, and it wasn't meant to be a slight to Mr. Densmore. In my case, it was just an oversight that, you know, because of my belief that it wasn't that important, I let it slide."

"Is there a time when you said, 'Let's don't use the Doors logo anymore'?"

"I believe that we did decide not to use the Doors logo at one time, yeah."

"Sometime in the last six months?"

"Probably earlier than that."

"I have nothing further, Your Honor."

Robby leaves the stand and we recess for the day. I make my way to my car, reeling from having watched my former bandmate and former best friend testify against me. I'm relieved that this day is over, but it seems that Ray and Robby's countersuit will allow their attorneys to call me back to the witness stand tomorrow for a cross-examination.

Chapter 15

RED BULL

"Do you dislike Mr. Manzarek?" asks Mr. Briggs.

I'm in the witness box, feeling cornered by Briggs, and I have to admit, his first question surprises me. From my point of view, what we are doing here is not the slightest bit personal. It's about honoring what is sacred and real. "I love Ray Manzarek as a brother," I answer, "and Robby too. I mean, how could I not? We created magic in a garage. This lawsuit is not about my view of Ray Manzarek. It's about a partnership among Ray, Robby, myself, and the estates, and some property of that partnership was stolen. I didn't ask for damages, as in Ray and Robby's countersuit, which is more money than all of us ever have earned in our entire lives, trying to terrorize my family by wiping us out."

Originally, when I started this mess, I told my wife that we might lose a bunch of money, but our house would be fine. Now, in bad moments, I entertain the worst-case scenario: that I have to pay the forty million ransom and all the attorneys' fees. Let's see, my lawyer is around three hundred an hour and their dudes are four hundred fifty and six hundred an hour. Those are the big guns, and they always have two attorneys present. That adds up to more than a thousand an hour for my former and generally absentee bandmates. If I have to pick up that tab, well, I can consider myself royally fucked. I would lose everything, but I do my best to keep my nightmares to myself.

"All I ask," I say, "is that the money that was earned by the stolen property, the name and the logo, be returned to the partnership and distributed to all four of us. That's what it's about."

"Let's talk about performances, sir," says Briggs. I stare at him for a moment to get my bearings. I guess Mr. B. doesn't like my summary because he's doing one of his abrupt subject changes that leave me somewhat breathless. "You understand that to go and perform a two-hour set is hard work?"

"I'm doing that tonight at the LA County Museum," I respond. "Free jazz concerts. Hard work."

"To get up there and perform and give it all you've got is strenuous work for a person? To rehearse, to get up onstage, to perform before an audience, is hard work?"

I agree with him again.

"You understand that Mr. Manzarek is in his sixties?"

"And I understand I'm only a few months behind that decade."

"And Mr. Krieger is right up there with you. Right?"

"A year behind me."

"Okay. Does it get any easier to perform a two-hour set the older you get?"

"Well, hopefully you don't have to show off technically as much and you can place the right note in the perfect spot and it's as powerful as a big flourish—"

"But it doesn't get easier, does it?"

"In some ways, yes," I say, "and in some ways, no."

"What about the traveling, sir? Does that get any easier when you travel from city to city to put on a two-hour set? Is that easier?"

"The European tour they just did was booked way before this trial, and they could have been here, but they chose to go to Europe." I'd like to add that they flew first class, but I know Briggs will jump all over me.

"That's not my question, sir. My question is simply whether or not it gets any easier as you get older to travel from city to city, away from your family, to perform a two-hour set."

"Depends on your relationship with your family," I say.

"For you, sir, does it get easier?"

"No."

"It's hard?"

"It depends. Maybe my family would come with me."

I'm having some trouble understanding William Briggs's logic on this one. Is he suggesting that since Ray and Robby are old, I should let them steal the name and logo and travel all over the world, staying at Four Seasons hotels, all paid for with assets that don't belong to them?

"Sir," Mr. Briggs blusters, "If I told you right now that you could go out and perform with Mr. Manzarek and Mr. Densmore—"

"*I'm* Mr. Densmore."

"I'm sorry. Mr. Krieger. Would you do it?"

"If Jim Morrison showed up," I say with great enthusiasm, "I'd be there in a New York minute." Several chuckles issue from the gallery.

"But we know that can't happen, so would you do it?"

"I'm on another track right now," I tell him. "I played

with Jim. I don't want to do the songs with someone approx-
imating Jim."

Briggs sits down and my own lawyer is allowed to bolster
me with a few questions before he sends me back into the
ring.

"Are you a communist?" Jerry asks.

"Absolutely not."

"Are you opposed to people making money?"

"It's a free country. People can make as much money as
they want."

"You like to make money, don't you?"

"I like it, sure."

"You made a lot of money from The Doors, even in the
last two years, haven't you?"

"True."

"And you're going to continue to make a whole bunch of
money, aren't you?" Jerry says.

"Probably."

"Are you proud of the article that you wrote in the *Nation*? That it was republished in *Rolling Stone*?"

"Yes."

"Are you proud to be among people like Bruce Springsteen, who's taken a stand on this?"

Briggs objects, citing lack of foundation, but the judge
allows it and Jerry lists several musicians, including Bonnie
Raitt, Jackson Browne, and Tom Waits, who have not succumbed to commercialism.

"Are you embarrassed by your association with these people?" Jerry asks me.

"No," I answer, adding R.E.M. to the roster. "The list
goes on."

"Did you ever sue Mr. Manzarek," asks Jerry, "because he

vetoed a commercial by Texas Gas using or wanting to use 'Light My Fire'?"

"No."

"Did you sue Mr. Manzarek because he vetoed the idea of letting Muriel Cigars use 'Light My Fire' for a commercial?"

"No."

"Did Admiral and Mrs. Morrison or their lawyers ever pick up the phone and say to you, 'John, we're going to sue you because of Cadillac'?"

"No."

Jerry initiates a new subject: "Are you familiar today with this compact disc, *Myth and Reality: The Spoken Word History?*"

"I am now, due to this trial, yeah," I say.

Jerry is referring to a CD that Ray put out on his own a few years ago, in which he waxes eloquent on his personal version of our career. The CD has liner notes in which Ray describes his take on the Buick Opel incident:

> It's a good song and a good car in a thirty-second commercial. You get rock 'n' roll on a nationally televised commercial. That hadn't been done before. So we said, yeah, let's go ahead and do it. Two days later Jim came back and said, "Don't do it . . . no! . . . [Y]eah, that's a neat little car, there's nothing wrong with that. But don't go to bed with those guys. Once they get you in bed, they're gonna screw you in some hole you don't want to be screwed in. Let's not do this. I've got a bad feeling about this."

In the same liner notes, Ray goes on to say that the sale never happened, adding, "The Doors all had veto power. If one guy didn't want to do something it wasn't done, that's the way it's always worked with The Doors."

"Mr. Densmore," says Jerry, after citing these notes, "is that your understanding too?"

"Totally."

"Thank you, Your Honor."

Could anything be clearer? Here we have Ray, on his own CD, stating Jim's vehement opposition to "selling out." He also stated that we all have veto power. And yet, Ray continues to say that the "veto idea" is a myth. His foot is inserted so far back in his mouth, it must have gotten stuck.

I'm ready for a break, but first, Mr. Forer, the estate lawyer, has one more subject on his mind. He steps up to the witness stand and says, "Turn your attention to Exhibit 387, Mr. Densmore. There's some handwriting on that document. Is that your handwriting?"

"Yes, it is."

"And have you seen this advertisement before?"

"Yes, I have. This is a fax I sent to Lou Reisman, another estate lawyer, and I wrote a note that said, 'Apparently your client's deceased son is going to perform as well as me, John Densmore.'"

"Now, whose picture is that?"

"Jim Morrison, a very famous photograph taken by Paul Ferrara, our photographer."

"Now, who's playing on February 7, 2003?"

"Well, I didn't and Jim didn't."

"But The Doors are?" Forer asks.

"That's what it says."

"Is that picture of Mr. Morrison an album cover of some sort?"

"Could be."

I was saddened that Ray and Robby had refused to take down Jim's fifty-foot picture at their concerts, when his parents, his in-laws, his sister, and his brother begged them to do so. It took a lawsuit, this one, to hopefully get them to stop the manipulation of Jim's image as an endorsement.

"This looks like an advertisement from sales of tickets, doesn't it?" says Forer.

"Yes."

"What site was that on?"

"I got this off of the House of Blues website and sent it to the estate."

The judge calls a lunch break and my stomach is growling. Too bad the choices are so limited. Besides the rooftop cafeteria, the only reasonable place to eat is across the plaza in the cafeteria at the Hall of Records. Every day (today is no exception), my crew and I head down the escalator, walk through the parking lot, and go to the cafeteria. I notice that Ray, Robby, and company head across the street to the most expensive restaurant in the area, where the defense attorneys go every day.

Jerry pokes me in the shoulder. He wants me to know that one of the jurors is standing behind us. I have to make sure I only talk about the weather, because if a juror hears one word about this case being discussed between my lawyer and me, there exists the possibility of a mistrial. In fact, I've been living in what I call "mistrial paranoia" ever since we started.

Jerry and I and our friends pay for our food and look for a table "far from the madding crowd" so we can talk in peace. Just yesterday, during the afternoon break, I headed for the snack shack, trying to buy some energy via a Tiger's Milk candy bar. Yet just as I entered the area, I saw Judge Alarcon paying the cashier for something he had bought. Our eyes met but he quickly looked away. I knew not to take it personally. If William Briggs or any of his cohorts saw the judge and me having any kind of communication, he would scream "mistrial" at the top of his lungs. I follow the rules, though it's a pretty weird feeling being here every day and taking care not to look in certain people's eyes.

I try to relax and eat lunch with Jerry, his wife, and my good friend Sam Joseph. I need my strength since Mr. Briggs gets to "cross the cross" now. In other words, he gets to try to refute what Jerry and Forer got me to say. Or maybe he's just gonna beat the shit out of me.

When I go back and take the stand, Briggs has pumped himself up with a few swigs of his Red Bull energy drink. He does this each day after lunch, and as the sugar kicks in, he goes on a caffeinated, escalating rant. Today I am the recipient as he begins by saying, "February 4, 2003, is the date that you filed your very first complaint in this action."

"Sounds correct," I say.

"So you filed your complaint against Mr. Manzarek and Mr. Krieger four days before they made their appearance at the Universal Amphitheatre. Sound about right to you?"

"Sounds about right."

"Before you filed your complaint against Mr. Manzarek and Mr. Krieger, did you go to them with a copy of the complaint and say, 'Hey, guys, I've got this complaint here. I'm about to file it. I *will* file it unless you change the name of your group'? Did you do that, sir?"

Jerry tries to save me by objecting as irrelevant but the judge overrules him.

I say, "I had continuous dialogue, trying to get them to change it. They didn't and I had to sue."

"That's not my question," Briggs responds loudly. He paces up and down the aisle in front of the jury, toward me and then away from me. When he turns and heads back in my direction, he points a finger at me. "My question is quite specific. Did you go to Ray and Robby with a copy of the complaint before you filed it on February 3 and say to them, 'Here is my complaint. Here are all my allegations in this complaint. Look at it, read it, consider what you're doing. And unless you change to meet my demands, I will file this complaint against you'? Did you do that?"

"I talked to them about all the allegations, and it wasn't getting anywhere, so I filed."

The Red Bull is really working and Briggs begins yelling at me, "Sir, my question is quite specific! Did you provide them a copy of the complaint before you filed it?"

"I had my attorneys send it to them."

Briggs is in a crescendo now, getting even louder. He should have been drinking Rock Star, another caffeinated energy drink that hadn't come out on the market yet. "Did you file—provide Mr. Manzarek or Mr. Krieger with a copy of the complaint before it was filed in this action?"

"No," I say, wincing because the high decibel level of his voice is hurting my ears.

"Did you read the allegations in your complaint to Mr. Manzarek?" he thunders.

"You're going to give me tinnitus again. Can you take it down a little?" I ask.

"I'll take it down a little," he concedes. "Did you read the allegations in your complaint to Mr. Manzarek and Mr. Krieger before you filed this action against them?"

"Well, over the phone?"

"Yes."

"It would take a few hours. No."

"Did you sit down in a room with them," says Briggs, "and go over, page by page, the allegations in the complaint against Mr. Manzarek and Mr. Krieger?"

Jerry objects and the court sustains it. Now Briggs is unhappy and wants a sidebar, a little huddle in the corner of the courtroom with the judge and the other lawyers. Alarcon, however, is not willing to budge, stating that Briggs's line of questioning is repetitive. He denies Briggs his sidebar, which alienates the man in a big way. Jerry has done his best to prepare me over the last months for personal attacks that might have nothing to do with the case, but even so, I am not ready for what comes next.

"Sir, I'm truly happy that you recently were able to license one of the songs, 'People Are Strange,' I believe it was, to the Keanu Reeves movie. You approved that, right?"

"Yes."

"That was five hundred thousand dollars, right?"

"Yes."

"What percent of fifteen million dollars is five hundred thousand?"

Forer objects to the question as argumentative. When the judge sustains the objection, forcing Briggs to take another tack, he becomes as stealthy as a terrorist, as if he just slipped a sack over my head when I wasn't looking.

"Mr. Densmore," he begins, "I can appreciate the fact that you told this jury you're not a communist."

"Thank you," I say.

Briggs pauses, which puts me on alert. Whenever things get slow on his watch, this man is generally winding up to smack me one. "But let me ask you this question," he says. "You understand that in approximately one month, we're about to have a three-year anniversary of a horrendous event in this country, don't you?"

"Sorry," I say, genuinely confused, "I can't track this one. You'll have to help me."

"Does the date September 11 have any meaning for you?"

Forer objects, questioning relevance, but the judge decides that for the sake of clarification, he will overrule, since he hasn't heard the question yet.

"Are you asking, does September 11 mean anything to me?" I say.

"Yes."

"Yeah. Tragedy for our country."

"It was a horrible tragedy for our country, wasn't it?" says Briggs.

"Yes."

"A lot of people lost their lives after it, didn't they?"

Forer objects again, the judge sustains the objection, but now, with the proverbial sack still over my head, Briggs quickly begins a series of verbal punches to my body.

"Sir," he says, "since your political beliefs have been touted in that article, the *Nation*, and Mr. Mandel asked you whether or not you were a communist, I want to ask you whether or not you're a supporter of Al Qaeda."

A giant gasp comes from the jury and the gallery.

Jerry murmurs, "Oh, come on," while Forer objects as argumentative and ridiculous. The judge sustains the objection.

And yet Briggs seems set on finishing his interrogation—I mean questioning. He removes a verbal pistol, a hidden handgun, from his inside jacket pocket, and starts to whip me unconscious with it: "Well, sir, a day after the event, did you tell Robby Krieger and Ray Manzarek, 'We got what we deserved'?"

Mr. Forer objects.

"SUSTAINED!" the judge says dramatically.

My wife, who is in court today, starts crying and storms out of the courtroom.

But Briggs isn't quite finished. He says, "Those were your sentiments, weren't they, sir?"

The judge intervenes, admonishing Mr. Briggs that he has sustained the objections and it's time to move on to something else. I'm so dazed from being thrown in the "brig" by Briggs, I can't hear the judge suggesting we take an early lunch.

I sit motionless at the witness stand for several minutes, finally looking up to see that everyone has gone. As I make my way out of the courtroom, my friend Sam grabs my arm to steady me. We step out into the cold marble hallway and there on a bench sits Robby Krieger. I head toward him with a vengeance, but he makes a preemptive strike since he can see my rage.

"You said it, you said it," he blurts out defensively.

"Don't do it!" Sam barks into my ear. "Don't reply." He hustles me toward the bathroom, where I stumble in and try to collect myself. I stare at my face in the mirror, stunned at the extremes that people will go to when they don't have a case. The truth of the matter is that, after the Twin Towers went down, Robby and I had a long phone discussion about the implication of the attacks. Somewhere during that conversation, I said something like, "Maybe as a country we should look at why this happened."

I'm in agreement with Dr. Cornel West, the Princeton scholar who famously said that 9/11 made Americans a "blues nation," and that we could benefit from the knowledge that Black people as a "blues people" have carried for a long time. I had told Robby, "We're so rich compared to the rest of the world, there's a message in this. It's a wake-up call."

I splash some water on my face. I guess all's fair in love and war, and to Robby, this is war.

"You were there when Pearl Harbor was bombed?"
Rear Admiral Steve Morrison, Jim, and Clara.

Four parts = more than the SUM.

"I felt like a bow being pulled back for twenty-two years."

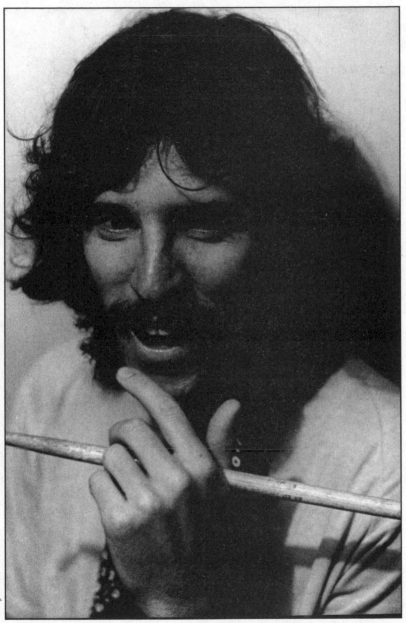

Henry Diltz

Rider on the storm (Red Bull whipped).

"Four-way veto power . . . 'in case things got weird.'"

Receiving Jim's last phone call.

Ride the king's highway, baby.

TO CALL
POLICE
USE THIS
TELEPHONE

There's danger on the edge of town.

Hero of the Doors documentary *When You're Strange*.

Paul Ferrara

"Sometimes darkness gets so close, it's almost visible and downright palpable."

Jerry Hopkins

The late, great Taylor Hawkins helped Robby and I honor the late, great Ray Manzarek, February 12, 2016.

Reunion at the Los Angeles County Museum of Art, December 5, 2013.

This is not the end.

"Our raft was seaworthy only for a short crossing."

Chapter 16

SLEEPLESS IN SANTA MONICA

It's one a.m., my head hit the pillow hours ago, but my brain won't lie down with the rest of me. After a light dinner (I had no appetite), I kissed my wife good night at about ten p.m. Although she was still disturbed by the day's courtroom proceedings, she fell asleep instantly. I'm not so lucky. I'm wide awake, staring at the ceiling for the last three hours, and I can't stop obsessing about my day inside the torture chamber.

Trying not to wake my wife, I get up carefully and wander into the kitchen. I just can't seem to wrap my mind around the fact that the extraordinary creative road that Jim, Ray, Robby, and I traveled together could end up like this: estrangement.

I'm just too raw to reach across the aisle, because right now it feels like the Grand Canyon. I wonder if I'll ever be able to bury the hatchet, and it really bothers me that so many of our fans want closure and can't understand what's really happening among us. Well, the fact is that The Doors, the US version of the British Fab Four, died in a bathtub in

Paris in 1971. Earlier on, as difficult as everything had become with Jim's impending self-destruction, when we got together to write new songs, all of our problems outside of the music seemed to slip away. Rehearsing was the arena where Jim was consistently straight and his demise faded into the background for the moment. He so respected the incubation state of creating new ideas.

Not that Jim wasn't in trouble, even back then. On Sundays, when we were off, he would go to bars, get drunk, and crash his car. It was as if something started really early in Jim, got channeled into creativity temporarily, but was bound to get him one way or another.

I don't know if Jim is up there resting in peace or not, but down here, we're fighting like cats and dogs over his entrails. I hope he's getting a big laugh out of it. As for me, I just can't feel any sense of closure with Ray and Robby because they're acting like nothing has changed. I feel betrayed and, for whatever reason, they're attacking me in an intensely personal way over a business disagreement. When we were tight and traveling and making amazing music together, I never would have predicted this, and I expect they wouldn't have either.

I heat water to brew up some Sleepytime tea, which I know won't cut through the rage I'm feeling. *You guys essentially called me a communist, and you know full well that I'm anything but that!* I want to yell at the kitchen wall. Come to think of it, Dr. Martin Luther King Jr. wasn't a communist either, even though he was tagged as one by J. Edgar Hoover. After a few minutes, these emotions subside into what's really underneath—sadness and deep disappointment. How did bullshit politics get into this hassle? It obviously emerged in the internal huddles among the defense lawyers. When did they come up with the implication that I was an ally of terrorists and was funding them? They know that isn't true and the mere suggestion of such a thing goes beyond the pale, even in the context of a lawsuit.

The teakettle whistles and I turn it off quickly, loath to wake up the household in the middle of the night. My mind is wound up and it won't settle down as I ponder the fact that communism, as it was practiced in the past, consisted of two tiers: the "haves" within the party, and the "have-nots" who were outside the party. And now, here we are again, looking at a large disparity in income in our society.

I pour the boiling water into a cup and drop in a tea bag to steep. I wonder if the guys would agree with me that societies are more successful and prosperous, not to mention less violent, when there is less of a gap between rich and poor. They used to agree with me about all of these things, but that was before Jim died, when we were all on the same page about so much of life.

I recall my old Cal State professor Edmund Carpenter, who assigned the book *Understanding Media: The Extensions of Man* as our textbook. Marshall McLuhan, a fixture in media discourse from the sixties until he died in 1980, planted the concept of an upcoming global village into my psyche back when I was still in school. Since then, I really did think we were all in this together, our own League of Nations, which makes Ray's and Robby's attacks against me incredibly shocking. I can't believe that my former bandmates would turn on me like that, changing the Greenpeace spotlight on me to red . . . with a dash of "funding terrorists" for seasoning.

The tea is ready and I take a sip. The heat from the cup feels good in my hands while I ponder the ways in which we have built walls to keep the poor at bay, as in our gated communities and our jails. Are we going back to feudalism but nobody's noticed yet? If we eliminate the people in the middle, the middle class, where will we find the glue to arbitrate between the lower and upper classes? At this point in time, the financial disparities between the haves and the have-nots in this country are at their most extreme since the Great Depression. I take another sip of tea, savoring the minty flavor. I want to shout at Ray and Robby, *You and your reps are probably thinking I'm talking income redistribution, but that's SOCIALISM! I'm not a socialist! Have you guys turned into Republicans?*

I really need to go to bed because I'm telling myself some crazy shit, and I want the guys to listen up. Have they forgotten that Western powers (including the United States and Britain) essentially created many of the countries in the Middle East solely to ensure a steady flow of oil? Do they know that most, if not all, of these countries are led by dictators who encourage great inequality of wealth between the ruling class and the masses? Don't they understand that our propping up of these regimes causes resentments?

"Dervish at the Door" by Rūmī

A dervish knocked at a house
to ask for a piece of dry bread,
or moist, it didn't matter.

"This is not a bakery," said the owner.
"Might you have a bit of gristle then?"
"Does this look like a butcher shop?"
"A little flour?"
"Do you hear a grinding stone?"

"Some water?"
"This is not a well."

Whatever the dervish asked for,
the man made some tired joke;
and refused to give him anything . . .

"You haggle and make jokes
to keep what you own for yourself.

You have forgotten the One
who doesn't care about ownership,
who doesn't try to turn a profit
from every human exchange."
(Translated by Colman Barks)

I stand up and start pacing as my thoughts refuse to slow down. I really believe it's a smart move for people to study their "enemies." If we'd truly studied the history of the Vietnamese, I don't think we'd ever have gone into that war. I also believe, at the risk of sounding partial to Muslims, that we could learn from the way they deal with money. I'm not talking about the fanatics here. I'm referring to the millions of regular citizens who worship Allah and believe that *riba* (loaning money at high interest rates) is *haram*. No, not harem. *Haram*. It means "forbidden."

In case you're wondering, no, we don't have to give up our credit cards. That isn't what I'm suggesting. Many Muslims interpret the law in a different way. They say that using a credit card is acceptable if the cardholder never pays any interest by clearing the balance each month. "Pay as you go." That's something people could use in this country.

We all know that owing money is not a good thing. And yet, both Ronald Reagan and George W. Bush, in the not-so-distant past, cut taxes for the rich while running up huge deficits. The truth is that, until just recently, we Americans believed that we were *numero uno*, omnipotent and all-powerful, but in my opinion, we are in denial, convinced that we are immune from repercussions. After all, we have "our" God on our side. So much so that He is stamped indelibly on our legal tender: In (our) God We Trust.

And yet, there's nothing like an economic collapse to make you question your religion, which for some is the Almighty $$$. But it just isn't worth what it used to be. I guess Ray and Robby are becoming more conservative these days, and I expect they're rattling their sabers at my line of thought. What if I told them that the Buddhist mind thinks that one should care not only for the human family, but for all sentient beings, right down to the tiniest ant?

I can hear you, Ray, thinking, *We're not responsible for the entire human family, for God's sake, John! Go ahead . . . let your liberal heart bleed all over everything until there's nothing left to give.*

I check the digital clock on the stove. It's nearly two a.m., the perfect hour to be pondering the fact that, as a race, I believe we are collectively headed toward vegetarianism, even though we still have two teeth left in our mouths for flesh-tearing. When someone asks me if I'm a vegetarian, I say, "I am a vegetarian, but only when I don't eat meat." My point is that when a person amasses a certain amount of money, enough, say, to live off the interest alone, it ought to be time to think more about altruism and less about flesh-tearing . . . but it's not that easy.

Just like those two teeth in our mouths, hoarding is in the

blood, a kind of security taken to the max or a preemptive strike. Didn't Jesus say something like, "My giving is boundless"? I have to admit, my accountant doesn't agree with this philosophy. I've met the accountant who Ray and Robby are using for their new band and I'm absolutely certain that he wants them to keep those flesh-tearing teeth as long as possible.

I pour myself a second cup of tea and think about the late Robert F. Kennedy, who summed up our financial problems in a remarkable speech that is one of the best I ever heard. This is an excerpt:

> We will find neither national purpose nor personal satisfaction in a mere continuation of economic progress, in an endless amassing of worldly goods. We cannot measure national spirit by the Dow Jones Average, nor national achievement by the gross national product. For the gross national product includes air pollution and ambulances to clear our highways from carnage. It counts special locks on our doors, and jails for the people who break them. The gross national product includes the destruction of the redwoods, and the death of Lake Superior. It grows with the production of napalm and missiles and nuclear warheads. It includes the broadcasting of television programs which glorify violence to sell goods to our children.

When RFK was assassinated, I knew in my gut that a visionary had fallen. He really understood the dangers of where we were headed as a society. Sometimes I think that I should vote Republican because I'd be saving myself some money. But I'm one of those Democrats who votes against his wallet, not because I'm crazy, but because I want to level the playing field a little. It seems like the playing field is so slanted these days, folks without duct tape on their shoes are in danger of falling off it.

I sit at the table, sip some more tea, and reminisce about my college days. I was an anthropology major, and while I may not have been the best of students, I was heavily influenced by reading about the first people of the Northwest and studying some of their customs. They were revolutionaries although they didn't know it, because they simply did what came naturally to them. Or maybe they behaved in ways that were tried and true, since they had been tested over time.

To twenty-first-century folks like us, some of their customs may seem outrageous, particularly one tradition called "potlatch," practiced by the Haida tribe. A big party lasting for days, this ritual was put on by a member of the tribe who aspired to raise his status by giving away some or even *all* of his assets. In this tribe, rank and philanthropy were always linked. Therefore, no one could elevate his or her position without demonstrating generosity. So, even though the US government passed a mind-boggling bill back in 1884 outlawing the practice of potlatch (fearing for the future of capitalism), Warren Buffett and Angelina Jolie are on the right track.

Yes, Warren Buffett, the third-richest man in the world, has pledged to give away 85 percent of his fortune, and Brad Pitt and Angelina Jolie are tithing one-third of their dough. In the same spirit, the potlatch tribes gave gifts to "make a name for themselves," which was commensurate with the amount of their giving. According to Lewis Hyde's book *The Gift*, some of the names "givers" received were:

- *Whose Property Is Eaten in Feasts*
- *Satiating*
- *Always Giving Blankets While Walking*

In other words, the more of your fortune that you distributed, the higher you ranked in the Haida tribe, who called the festivities "killing wealth." As our front man Jim's old hero Friedrich Nietzsche said, "One hundred people started the Renaissance. If you could get me one hundred people, we could move in an entirely new direction."

Here is another beautiful quote from Lewis Hyde:

> Gratitude is labor undertaken by the soul to effect the transformation after a gift has been received. Passing the gift along is the act of gratitude that finishes the labor.

Is this too much tribal wisdom for Ray and Robby? I'm not suggesting we go back and live in the rainforest with the Pygmies, but they do have some knowledge we just might be able to use, as did the Native Americans before we unceremoniously wiped them out. *Wait a minute*, someone might think. *Since we already wiped out the Native Americans, what do we have to worry about? They're not coming after us.*

The point is that we could learn from these people instead of outlawing their traditions. When you destroy the rituals and symbols that hold a culture together, you are destroying the heart and soul of that culture. Just maybe we're on shaky ground around here because we've practically committed genocide against the very people who actually have some of the answers.

I have to turn off this rant in my brain and get some sleep or I'll be delirious in the morning. So much for Sleepytime tea. It's time to pop an Excedrin PM that knocks me out and leaves me with a hangover. I just need some sleep. I take the pill and quietly slide under the covers beside my wife. I'm back on the pillow, starting to fade, counting sheep, counting sheiks . . . and I keep coming back to the thought that I just can't believe Ray and Robby would go this far.

I guess it's not so surprising when you consider the current climate in our country. The hysteria involved in "getting those terrorists" has reached a level where the feds are bugging any and all phone calls between the US and the Middle East. Our intelligence agents are snooping on American soldiers' private lives, even after the real terrorists have stopped using technology. There is even a vicarious "Listen to tape #7 for some good phone sex" going around the eavesdroppers' tent.

My last thought before passing under "sleep's dark and silent gate" (thanks for the line, Jackson Browne) is that, probably right now, some private investigator is out back, snooping on my personal life, rifling through my trash.

Chapter 17

BACKLASH

First thing Monday morning, the judge calls in the attorneys without the jurors present. There is backlash from Friday (how could there not be?) and Mr. Forer is deeply offended by what he calls "the antics of Mr. Briggs." He says, "I cannot believe the things he has dredged up and paraded in front of the jury, not only on Friday, but all during the trial. I don't appreciate the Al Qaeda reference. I don't appreciate the 9/11 reference. I don't appreciate a lot of things that he's been doing, and I don't appreciate the way he spins his little pointer while Mr. Mandel is talking to the witness . . . or kicks back and yawns loudly so the jury gets distracted from what's going on. That may be okay tactics if we're in some really strange universe, but I think this is particularly offensive. It continues on and on and on, on a daily basis. There's some strange thing or out-of-line thing that goes on, and I just think the man should be admonished. I just don't know if this is the way to practice law."

Mr. Briggs retaliates, "Your Honor, let me respond, if I may, and I'll respond to the Al Qaeda reference. Mr. Mandel opened the door to that with respect to whether or not Mr. Densmore was a communist, and he talked about the *Nation* article. I didn't display the entire *Nation* article and some of the beliefs that are espoused in that article by Mr. Densmore, but to say the politically correct term, is 'antiestablishment,' that's putting it mildly, okay? We understand that it was his political beliefs—it may well have been his political beliefs that motivated him to say no to Cadillac.

"And if he's exercising business judgment," Briggs continues, and starts stumbling over his own words, "if he's bringing his political beliefs in, and Mr. Mandel opened it up, in your best verdict, weren't you offering this, using your, exercising your best judgment, well, if he brought his political beliefs into it, whether dealing with Al Qaeda, the *Nation* article, antiestablishment, I think the jury is entitled to hear all that, because it's relevant to the determination of whether or not he exercised sound business judgment or not and denied or turned down that offer in bad faith because that is our case, Your Honor, and I think I'm entitled to ask that type of question and even other questions that may come up."

That's quite a mouthful.

Jerry weighs in: "Your Honor, I didn't open this issue about whether John was a communist. I think that Mr. Briggs has a memory failure from the first week of this trial of the opening statement of the questions of Mr. Densmore, where he is the one who opened this whole issue. I think that counsel for the defendant has gone over the top, and the degree to which people are defended is measured by their own personal standards. But I find it offensive, I know Mr. Forer does, and I don't know that there's any more to say about it."

Judge Alarcon looks thoughtful. "That's a tough thing," he finally says. "I already ruled . . . that it's definitely not admissible, and I don't think I heard anything to change the ruling."

I take a long, deep breath. I just spent an entire weekend as an outpatient, licking my wounds, trying to breathe deeply and get my center back. My paranoia has only been exacerbated by the recent news that Secretary of Defense Donald Rumsfeld okayed phone tapping. Now that these trial transcripts are public domain, fanatics could have a field day surfing the web for Al Qaeda references and coming up with my name. Who knows? I could end up in the real Abu Ghraib prison.

I return my attention to the court. Judge Alarcon informed the jury when the trial first began that they could submit written questions to him in order to clarify any matters they were pondering. Briggs's distasteful comments must have sparked some questions, because the judge says, "I think I've read all the questions that the jury gave me. But I was just handed another question that gave me enough concern to have the jurors go into the jury room before it was read. I think this has to do with some things that came out on Friday. The first question is, 'What organizations are you involved with?' The second one is, 'Are you with the ELF or know about them?' I thought that this is the type of questions that counsel should be alerted to before they are asked or if they are asked."

"Somehow," says Jerry, "I suspected we'd get to this place after Friday."

I'm glad for the backlash against the opposing lawyers, but I suppose they can claim a degree of success since some in the jury are presently wondering if I'm involved with radical groups.

This is ironic since I'm very careful that I invest in only

socially responsible causes, rather than those "radical/terrorist" charities that they have accused me of supporting. One of my favorite causes is the Liberty Hill Foundation, whose motto is "Change. Not Charity." They focus on my home-town, because sadly, Los Angeles has the sharpest economic divide in the nation—the fourth-worst in the world, right after Calcutta. My point is that everyone who can should loosen up those purse strings. But Ray is interpreting this as my supporting radical groups. I suppose I shouldn't take it personally since I read a newspaper in which Ray called Judge Alarcon "pinky." Maybe he's soliciting for a gig as a Fox News anchorman.

Jerry takes a short break to remind me that there is still some pink on the walls, and that I should simply be hon-est and speak from the heart as I answer the jurors' latest questions. That's fine with me; I have nothing to hide and I don't want anyone to think I'm avoiding anything, even though the questions themselves are incriminating. So why am I starting to sweat profusely? All I have to do is answer the questions. The judge calls in the jury to hear my answers.

"I'm kind of glad these questions were asked," I say, once the twelve and the two substitutes are seated, "because I was doing a sound check for my performance with Tribaljazz at the Los Angeles County Museum of Art when apparently I was accused of being an anarchist, whatever that is . . . Before I answer this, I'd like to say I don't think this case is about my politics. It's about whether people sign contracts and adhere to them. But what is ELF? I don't know who they are. I think they're some real radical violent group. I'm involved with the Sierra Club, Heal the Bay, Rainforest Action Network. Sev-eral other environmental groups. Let me just tell a little story that might clarify this.

"The Rainforest Action Network tries to save trees. Bonnie Raitt, a well-known singer, and I purposely committed nonviolent civil disobedience against a company in Chicago that cut down old-growth trees. Those are the thousand-year-old trees. And, you know, I think we need a few of those left as an example of the magnificence of growing old. And the Rainforest Action Network encouraged us to do this.

"We called the police the night before we did this, and we said, 'In the tradition of Martin Luther King, we are *nonviolent* protesters. First Amendment rights. And we're going to trespass because we want to make a point about this company cutting down these trees. We are not like—I think they were called anarchists in Genoa—these WTO protesters, fringe radical groups that do cause violence. We are not like that. 'Would you please be peace officers and not hit us with bats, and we'll just put our hands out to be arrested?' And they said, 'We will.' And they did. It was very peaceful, thank God, and fortunately, the company stopped cutting old-growth trees. So there was a little step there. I hope that kind of illuminates what I'm up to. I am *totally* against any kind of violence. Does that do it?"

"I think that answers the question," says the judge. "Does counsel have additional follow-up questions? Mr. Mandel?"

"No, Your Honor."

"Mr. Forer?"

"No, Your Honor."

"Mr. Briggs?"

"No, Your Honor."

I thought for sure that Briggs would have some kind of comeback. Well, good night and good luck, John. I seem to have stopped the fringe speculation for the moment. The judge calls a recess and I stand up to leave the courtroom, waiting until I can see where Ray and Robby are headed so I can go in the opposite direction.

When the room is clear, I take the elevator to the ground floor and walk outside for a breather. I take some comfort in recalling my experience with Bonnie Raitt, a budding elder. At barely two hundred years old, our culture is still in its adolescent stage compared to the rest of the world, where elders are looked up to. It's slim pickings here, but at least there are a few among us, compared to the sixties, when we were coming up. Seasoned mentors were nonexistent back then. I'm talking *real* elders, the type who look after the youth going through Latima.

Latima, you say? This is a term used by the Gisu people in Uganda for that period when kids are between the ages of fourteen and twenty-seven and the mature people of the tribe keep an eye on them. Interesting that it goes all the way up to age twenty-seven . . . the very age when the singer of our band checked out, along with Janis and Jimi. They all died at twenty-seven and the Gisu must know something, because I think twenty-seven is pivotal. I mean, there's a *big* difference between twenty-two and twenty-seven. At twenty-two you feel immortal. By twenty-seven you sense that life is moving so fast, you just might consider getting married and having kids.

So what makes an elder? Michael Meade, author, mythologist, and one of the leaders of the men's movement in the eighties, said, "Everybody gets older, not everybody gets elder." What happens to a society where the admired people are merely rich and famous, not necessarily noble or honorable? Michael Meade also said:

If young people saw older people acting courageously, calling BS when it arises, pointing out injustice, taking stances, holding those stances . . . it would be much more encouraging for the youth and they would begin to realize, maybe I do want to enter this world and live a long time, because they could see their elders acting it out, and therefore aspire to a long life as well . . .

Teacher and Greek philosopher Nikos Kazantzakis wrote:

True teachers use themselves as bridges over which they invite their students to cross; then having facilitated their crossing, joyfully collapse, encouraging them to create bridges of their own.

Maybe the moment you truly start considering others as well as yourself and your family, you're becoming an elder. If you can think of your actions as having the effect of concentric circles, like dropping a pebble in a lake and seeing the reverberations, then maybe you'll be more scrupulous about where you cast your next pebble.

In the light of the past Enron and WorldCom financial scandals, as well as the more recent Wall Street meltdown, it seems like our CEOs are not good role models for younger executives. They are hardly teaching the younger set to conduct business with any kind of moral restraint. In the words of Paul Krugman, Nobel Prize–winning economist and *New York Times* op-ed columnist:

Now, as each day seems to bring a new business scandal, we can see the theory's fatal flaw: a system that lavishly rewards executives for success tempts those executives, who control much of the information available to outsiders, to fabricate the appearance of success . . . Unless you

go to jail—and does anyone think any of our modern male-
factors of great wealth will actually do time?—dishonesty
is, hands down, the best policy.

Actually, some of them did pay a price and went to jail,
but they were few and far between. I certainly don't want Ray
and Robby to "do time," but it is unjust that they try to continue to use The Doors's name and logo in South America.
Can't they just be wise elders and do the right thing?

Bonnie Raitt, a great teacher and guide, is the epitome
of an elder. She is the right kind of mentor, a positive one,
since she is committed to giving back, staying connected to
the street, and not becoming insulated by her success or her
notoriety. I think we need more people who are willing to use
their celebrity status to push for positive change . . . people
we can feed off of, aspire to be like, get energy from . . . especially people like me who grew up in the sixties and had
leaders who deceived us and undermined our sense of self by
being poor examples of how to function with integrity. When
we realized we'd been duped into an unjust war (Vietnam),
we decided "not to trust anyone over thirty." So how were
we supposed to *live* past the age of thirty? Jim didn't make it
to that number. Neither did Kurt Cobain and a host of other
talented artists.

Elders should be wise about death. They know more
dead people! And coming from my generation, there are a
lot of corpses around. As Neil Young (who in my opinion is
an elder) reflected on the casualties of the sixties, "*It's better
to burn out than to fade away.*" It was a continuation of the
lament with which Allen Ginsberg started his most famous
poem, "Howl": *I saw the best minds of my generation destroyed
by madness . . .*

So along with Jim, my musical compadres have been dropping out all around me. Bonnie Raitt, however, is still very much with us. I got involved with her when she was upset over a "dinosaur" corporation (Boise Cascade) continuing to use the obsolete method of cutting old-growth forests for lumber. In all Native American cultures, you honor the elders, the grandmothers and grandfathers, but we've cut down most of them in the redwood family. When I decided to lock arms with Bonnie in the Chicago protest, I knew it was going to result in a visit to jail. This would be my second bust, the first for police harassment for having long hair in Reno back in 1965.

It all began with a pal of Dick Cheney's who had a non-profit organization, Frontiers of Freedom, funded by Exxon and Philip Morris. It seems that they persuaded the IRS to look into the 501(c)3 status of the Rainforest Action Network, the group that put on our protest. Frontiers of Freedom was implying that people who break the law, even peacefully, should forfeit their nonprofit status. One wonders what that would do to the NAACP. Our goal, under the umbrella of RAN, was to differentiate ourselves from those violent protesters in Genoa ("the men in black") that the defense lawyers just tried to convince the jury I was aligned with.

When we got to the protest site, the corporation had barricaded the building with yellow tape and called up several police divisions. Now there were hundreds of cops there who had not received our phone call asking them not to beat us up. Everyone's fear escalated, mine included, but Bonnie was still down for the "action," a plan to step under the tape and sit down as we held our hands behind our backs for cuffing.

When the time came, however, trepidation crept into the veins of several members of our party, and they refused to step under that tape. A priest in a brown robe, for example, disappeared, and a rabbi, who looked so beautiful in his full-on white outfit complete with yarmulke, bailed on the protest. I calmed my fear by thinking of a poem from the *Panchatantra*, old Indian stories for children:

> *Better with the learned dwell,*
> *Even though it be in hell*
> *Than with vulgar spirits roam*
> *Palaces that gods call home.*
> (Translation by Arthur Ryder)

When I walked the perimeter of the small group that was left, I spotted the police captain to whom we had spoken earlier. He had said that if we kept the numbers down, everyone could go to the "nice" jail. With the group narrowed down to me, Bonnie, Julia "Butterfly" Hill, and a few board members of RAN, including founder Randy Hayes and future founder of Code Pink, Jodie Evans, there were just ten of us. Maybe they would go easy on us, I hoped, when it was time for us to step up and sit down.

I took a deep breath, stepped under the ominous yellow ribbon, and sat down on the ground beside Bonnie, our hands obediently placed behind our backs. In moments, the police ascended upon us to take us to jail. When I got cuffed, I told the arresting officer that I was a musician and would he be kind enough to make the bonds loose? Was I ever relieved when he responded with a sweet note, "I like your music!" Can you believe that?! Fame does have its perks. While Ray and Robby get nice tables at nice restaurants, I get the nice jail!

Being hustled into the police van escalated everyone's

blood pressure, but organizer Randy Hayes lightened the situation with his outrageous humor: "How do you guys like the Irish limo [paddy wagon]?" Bonnie's beautiful vibe, haloed by her bright red hair, got her the shotgun seat (I don't think there's anybody who doesn't love this woman), and we sat in the seats behind her. The ride in the police van was scary but the tension was completely defused at the station, where they quickly took off our handcuffs, offered us bottled water, and asked for autographs. A very cushy bust. At least we had the courage to do it and not be intimidated by the feds. It was interesting to note that while I was being handcuffed and taken away in a paddy wagon, thousands of fans were flocking to Paris to commemorate Jim's passing . . . it all seemed fitting, sort of like a sixties flashback.

The point is that even though it involved getting arrested, I was thrilled to hang out with Bonnie Raitt, a true elder who has been on the road for the oppressed (trees included) for many years and speaks eloquently on their behalf. I feel like a beginner at this, standing up for those coming along, trying to lend a hand, but I'm definitely not getting any younger . . . although this advocacy work makes me *feel* younger.

"*I was so much older then / I'm younger than that now,*" sang Bob Dylan. It feels good to be passing the torch to the next generation, though I'm doing it for selfish reasons as well. The truth is that our young activists have tons of energy, and when I work alongside them, some of it rubs off. People helping people—that's the lineage I want to be a part of. So here's to Bonnie, one of our national treasures, someone whom I think about when the going gets rough.

Chapter 18

RAY / THE COUNTERSUIT

The going is about to get very rough as Ray Manzarek is called to the stand. The defendants are continuing their "case in chief," their countersuit, where they're asking for forty million dollars out of my pocket, based on my vetoing songs for commercials. In other words, I've been bad . . . not upholding my fiduciary duty as a partner to make money at any cost, and not saying yes to the bastardizing of Jim's words.

Briggs begins with the direct examination of Ray, my nemesis. Some define the word "nemesis" as "enemy," but I prefer Webster's definition: "formidable rival." The Dalai Lama says our enemies are our best teachers. Although "enemy" may be too strong of a word, without Ray, I must admit, there would be less honing of my thoughts and fewer challenges to figure out where I *really* stand. He truly has been a powerful lifelong catalyst for me, and maybe I should dedicate this book to him, since he has helped me define myself, my morals, and has forced me to draw the line in this consumer-obsessed society in which we live. Not to mention what a great, great piano player he is.

Briggs asks Ray, "Do you recall who first approached you about—"

"Cadillac." This sounds a little too rehearsed, as Ray is taking words out of his attorney's mouth.

"What was said?" asks Briggs.

Ray begins, "The storyboards were two commercials that eventually ran on TV—a very clever idea. Seems very, very good. I was very impressed. I thought it was a very clever use of The Doors's song and very clever commercials, and the one they had for the dealers and the convention had all the new cars, and they looked terrific. They were sensational all the way down from the big car, the big Escalade SUVs, down to the new little sports car that they were going to be putting out in a year, a year later."

Are we talking about the same company, Cadillac, where a senior GM executive called the Toyota hybrid, the Prius, a "PR gimmick"?

Ray continues, "We were very excited to get something on the airwaves, on television, on a mass market to say to the people of America and around the world—it was worldwide rights—'Hey, The Doors one more time, listen to The Doors, listen to the song "Break on Through to the Other Side," coupled with a great American car, the American car, the Cadillac.'"

"We" were very excited? The three of us never discussed television coverage, Robby was on the fence, and I said no. Not much excitement there.

"And you had discussions about this proposal with Mr. Krieger, right?"

"Uh-huh," says Ray.

"And you also had a discussion with Mr. Densmore?"

"Well," says Ray, "Mr. Krieger and Densmore, yes, together, at Robby's house one lovely afternoon. We were sitting outside and we talked about it. I said, 'Listen, these guys have a great presentation, a whole new line of automobiles.' They'd shown me the video and a couple of storyboards for a couple of commercials. I said, 'God, they need the work, all the work they can get, and this Cadillac is being assembled in Detroit.'"

I hate to bust Ray's bubble, but the Detroit CEOs are keeping the money. (In fact, there was so much hoarding they would eventually have to be bailed out!) It *ain't trickling down* to the workers.

Ray goes on, "The objection was raised: 'Well,' John said, 'Jim didn't want to do the Buick commercial,' and I said, 'That's Jim Morrison in 1968. Today he would have the smarts and the brains to realize that.' Jim was a very intelligent guy. He knew about marketing. He knew how to get things across to the public. Jim would say, 'Listen, let's get it on TV because TV is where it's at right now. TV is communicating to the mass market. This is the perfect opportunity,' and Densmore said, 'I don't want to do it.'"

"Did he explain why he didn't want to do it?" Briggs says.

"It was the idea that Jim wouldn't want to do the Buick commercial, ergo, that same Jim Morrison thirty years later would not want to do the Cadillac commercial, which made no sense to me because it was assuming that Jim Morrison would not be able to develop from, you know, admittedly all our antiestablishment hippie stance is what was going on in the sixties, that Jim would not see the writing on the wall."

What is that writing? Was it that peace, civil rights, women's rights, and all the rest of it are passé? As Elvis Costello wrote: *"What's so funny 'bout peace, love, and understanding?"*

Sounds more like graffiti to me. But then, Ray was always the ultimate survivalist. Family was always first with him, which is not a bad instinct, per se. But that trait makes it extremely hard to turn down $, even when you don't need it. *More, more, more.* It's challenging the genetic code, crossing very old boundaries. Kind of like eating dessert even when you're full. This impulse to stock up for the winter when you have a football field of equity that'll last all the winters of your and your kids' lifetimes, is the survival instinct working overtime.

"What did Mr. Krieger say?" asks Briggs.

"Mr. Krieger was on the fence. He hadn't made up his mind one way or the other. He was open to it, and I told them [Cadillac], because John was very concerned with an internal combustion engine, which is what we all drive . . ."

No, that isn't true. I bought the very first hybrid car (a combination of gas and electric) many years ago.

"But he [John] was very concerned about the hybrid car. I asked, 'Are you guys developing any kind of hybrid car?' They said, 'No, not at the moment, it's not part of our new line that's coming out. We're going from the Escalade all the way down to a little sports car, but the next generation is going to have an ecologically friendly hybrid car.'"

Briggs says, "Mr. Densmore testified that he wanted to be the protector of the legacy of The Doors, and by having blocked this Cadillac commercial, that somehow protected the legacy of The Doors. Do you believe that?"

"No," says Ray, "absolutely not. I think that *diminishes* the legacy of The Doors. There was another one John turned down that I thought was a large mistake. We don't sell any records in Japan. This was maybe fifteen, twenty years ago. For some reason or another, the Japanese just never got behind The Doors. I don't know why. And the Japanese love television. They're a nation of television because, after all, Sony and everything else, the Japanese control the world with television outside of whatever is south of Europe.

"So Japan calls and says, 'We want to use 'Hello, I Love You.' What could be better for Japan as a light little, happy little *'Hello, I love you, won't you tell me your name?'* Perfect for the Japanese. It had two kids skiing down the hill in Hokkaido and curving to *'Hello, I love you, won't you tell me your name?'* You get to the bottom of the hill and it's open ski, and the next shot they're sitting around the fireplace in their after-ski outfits, and they're smoking a Peace cigarette. The cigarette is called 'Peace.'"

Promoting cancer sticks for the youth? Can't imagine why I didn't agree to that.

"They're having a cocktail," Ray adds, "and smoking a cigarette. The fire is going on. I thought, *That's perfect for Japan. That's exactly what we should be doing, because we don't have any record sales.* The Japanese see something on TV, that's what they go for. And here's 'Hello, I Love You' on the TV set, and John said, 'Absolutely not. Absolutely not.' I can't but feel that John has a political agenda, and he's rejecting these things not because of their worth to the Doors catalog, but because of his own political agenda, which is his association with, you know, various groups, various anarchist groups that he knows about and supports."

I want to yell out, *Excuse me, Ray, but what the fuck are you implying? The Sierra Club, Rainforest Action Network, and Heal the Bay are anarchist groups?* How can this be the same keyboard player who was in a band where his "friend" Jim wrote,

Dead president's corpse in the driver's car
The engine runs on glue and tar
Come on along, not going very far
To the East to meet the Czar

Oh, I guess that's just more of that sixties antiestablishment hippie stuff.

"In your opinion, Mr. Manzarek," says Briggs, "would Mr. Morrison today support Mr. Densmore's view that his poetry, his music, should not be used in tasteful ad campaigns such as the Cadillac commercial?"

I don't know where he got the word "tasteful," as if he's some sort of casting director.

Ray is quick to say, "Absolutely not. Jim Morrison would be all in favor of doing it. Your television set would say to you, 'Break on Through to the Other Side.' There's some thirteen-year-old kid watching it. He doesn't know what the product is. Ninety percent of the time, I don't know what the product is when they're advertising something. That thirteen-year-old kid will hear that maybe and not even be watching and he's going to hear 'Break on Through to the Other Side.' If I'm thirteen and I hear my TV saying that to me, I'm going to go, *Wow, what's that? Who? What is that? What is the product?* The kid doesn't care what the product—he doesn't even know what the product is."

"So you decided to bring this action against Mr. Densmore?" Briggs says.

"We knew it was going to continue on, and he'd just be rejecting things out of hand all the way down the line, to do it for a political agenda to look good in front of those anarchist organizations and, you know, the various revolutionaries, I just didn't—ecological activists, you know, people who burn the Volvos or burn the SUVs up in Oregon, smash windows in Washington, in Seattle, when that was going on."

What the hell is happening here? I have always been totally against any kind of property destruction. Ray knows that. Could this really be the same man who thought up that brilliant intro to "Light My Fire"? He sounds like an FBI agent infiltrating the violent Vietnam War protests and actually instigating violence. I guess Ray's attorneys believe that when you have no case, you character-assassinate, build a conspiracy theory. Never, ever could I have imagined that Ray would turn on me and become a narrow-minded, provincial, self-serving isolationist.

"Mr. Manzarek," says Briggs, "in a DVD called *The Doors: Live at the Hollywood Bowl,* there's some commentary track on it. Your voice is heard saying, 'The Doors had veto power. The way we set up the band was we were four guys and everything was split four ways, and each person had veto power. It had to be a unanimous decision. We'd go—all four of us— "Sounds like a good idea. Let's do it." If somebody said, "No, I'm going to veto that, I don't think it's a good idea," we wouldn't do it.' Why did you state that?"

"Probably high at the time," Ray dares to say. "I, you know, having no idea I'd be appearing in a court of law, you know, it's part of The Doors's mythology. It's The Doors's mythology. You know, we—there are many instances in which people said, 'No, I'm not going to do that,' and we did it anyway. So, you know, the idea of veto power, as I said, is just a, you know, just a—it's fiction. It's a fiction."

If that isn't perjury, I don't know what is. Ray just said, in essence, that if you're loaded when you sign your name, you can get out of a contract. I'd like to refresh his memory with the deposition testimony of his new lead singer, Ian Astbury (who later quit), who had a few things to say about whether or not one has to abide by a contract if you pretend to have been too stoned to read it. It went like this:

Jerry asked Ian, "Do you believe that even though you are a rock and roll star—and you are, and a good one—if you sign a contract, you're bound by the provisions of that contract just as a person who isn't a rock and roll star, aren't you?"

"I would presume so, yes," said Ian.

"At least that's your feeling?"

"If you sign a contract with someone," said Ian, "yes."

"You don't get any special privileges because you're a rock and roll star?" Jerry said. "You don't get to say, well, I didn't mean what I signed?"

"No, you don't," said Ian. "Of course not."

Ray is now being cross-examined by Jeff Forer.

"Did Oliver Stone ban you from the set of the *Doors* movie?" he asks.

"Not to my knowledge," answers Ray.

"He didn't ban you because you kept telling him how to make the movie?"

"No. I'll answer your question, sir," says Ray.

Forer pushes his point: "In your book, no less than four different occasions, did you vilify Mr. Stone and his image of The Doors?"

"Yes, I do."

"You call him a moron?"

"Well, you know," says Ray, "a harsh word perhaps."

"You call him a Nazi?"

"Well, he definitely had what I thought were fascist tendencies."

"You called him a fascist, right?"

"Yes."

"Weren't you guys paid good money to get the *Doors* movie made?" asks Forer.

"Yes."

"Why would you trash a Hollywood director?"

"Well," says Ray, "I talked to the man."

Ray and Oliver's relationship had obviously gone downhill ever since Ray had publicly dumped on Stone's movie. It was sometime in January 2007, when Oliver asked me to join him, Val Kilmer (who played Jim), and Kyle MacLachlan of *Twin Peaks* (who played Ray) to do a Q&A after a fifteenth-anniversary screening of the *Doors* movie in Hollywood.

I had given Oliver the galleys to my first book before it was published and he cherry-picked it quite effectively for material for the film, in exchange for a big thank you in the credits at the end. It was a jolt when I heard exact sentences that I wrote coming out of actors' mouths. My book, *Riders on the Storm*, had been released several months before the movie came out, garnering very respectable reviews from the *New York Times* and *Washington Post*, among others. And then, one week after Oliver's flick hit the theaters, my book went quickly to #3 on the *New York Times* best-seller list. The power of the media (with that big thank you in the credits) was palpable. And so, I felt I should be there for the screening and the talk afterward.

I was happy to see the film once again after so many years, and I think it held up very well. I was disappointed that it wasn't more about the sixties era that we came up in, but Oliver sure got the story of the tortured artist. I was amazed at the depth of Jim's intensity that he captured.

"If you don't like my foot on your chest, don't go to my movies," Stone famously stated.

I felt that Val Kilmer should have been nominated for an Oscar for fitting into Jim's leather pants. At times, he gave me the creeps on the set, he looked and acted so much like Jim—it felt like he was back!

The only time that someone else successfully filled Jim's leathers was a glorious evening on January 12, 1993, when Eddie Vedder inducted us into the Rock & Roll Hall of Fame. The honor of having him fill Jim's shoes and his leather pants for one night, possibly the only singer alive with the talent to do so, was grand. And still, he was only a substitute for Jim.

When I think back, it was the weight of fame that crushed our lead singer. Certainly, each of us has individual genes that we bring to the table. Then there are our individual up-bringings (mobile military life, for example), but the trap of being our highly famous, handsome lead singer didn't fit well with the man in leathers. At one point, he donned railroad-engineer overalls and purposely gained weight to metaphor-ically shoulder the extra pounds on his actual shoulders. He said in interviews how foolish it was of him to pose for pho-tos. Monday-morning quarterbacking is easy, but for Jim it was already Tuesday in relation to alcohol when he looked up. And he couldn't get back.

During the Q&A following the *Doors* movie, with Oliver to my right, Val to my left, and Kyle to his left, I was asked if I felt the movie was accurate. "Well," I said, "I don't remember all those naked girls running up onstage."

Oliver raised his eyebrows.

I quickly added, "I mean, if that had happened we would have stopped playing! All this to say that Oliver has created an impressionistic painting of the times . . . and it's a beauti-ful painting."

Mr. Stone relaxed.

This idea about impressionism came from my running into a couple of actor friends, Ed Harris and Amy Madigan, at a party. It was during the time that Stone was shooting *The Doors* and Amy could tell I was on edge about how it was going to turn out.

"John," she said, "they're going to take a six-year career, squeeze it into two hours, and blow it up to the size of a two-story building. Is that going to be reality? It's going to be an impression. Just let it go." That was good advice . . . which I could partially take in.

During the Q&A, I said I wanted to play my hand drum while reading an excerpt from Jim's poem "American Prayer," which the audience and panel seemed eager to hear. There wasn't a mic stand so I asked Val to hold the mic up to my mouth as I recited. He made a great roadie, and it went so well, Oliver remarked that nothing could be said after that, and we adjourned.

Chapter 19

A CRY FOR HELP

Back in the courtroom, Forer changes his tack by asking Ray, "Jim wasn't well, was he? By 1969, you knew he wasn't well?"

"I don't know what you mean by that," Ray says.

"He didn't come to you," Forer responds, "and talk to you sometime in 1968 about wanting to quit the band?"

"Jim did say he was having a nervous breakdown," Ray concedes. I wonder why having a nervous breakdown doesn't count as not being well.

"That was the summer of '68? According to your book?"

"I, of course, knew he wasn't having a nervous breakdown. He was drinking," says Ray. "I told him, 'You drink too much.' I said to him, 'Look, tell you what, man, give it six more months. If you still feel the same way, it's over with.'"

"And six more months went by, and did he say anything to you?"

"Well, he didn't say anything. I told him, 'Six *more* months. If you still feel like you want to quit, we'll go ahead. You can quit.' But he never said he wanted to quit after that."

"Did anyone get him to a doctor?"

"For a nervous breakdown?" says Ray. "I don't think he was having a nervous breakdown. I think he was having a bad hangover."

"You're not a doctor, are you?"

"No, I'm not."

"You weren't a doctor at the time?"

"No."

"You don't know if he was having a nervous breakdown or not?" Forer says.

"No. I didn't think he was. It didn't seem like it. It was kind of a bolt out of the blue—'I think I'm having a nervous breakdown.'"

"Could have been a cry for help too, couldn't it?"

"Could have been a lot of things."

"*Could have?*"

"Could have."

I find this line of questioning disturbing—not so much what Forer is asking, though. Manzarek's responses sound like a classic case of enabling—engaging in behaviors that gloss over or allow destructive habits like drugs and alcohol abuse to continue.

"He was your brother, though?"

"Well," says Ray, "you know, we put that band together."

"Yes, you did."

"Yes, we did."

"Yes, you did. Was he taking too many pills at that time?"

"Pills were around," says Ray. "Whether he was taking too many pills . . . There were a couple of incidents. You know, one at the recording studio where he had taken too many pills. But pills were very common. Whether he was taking too many pills or not, I'm not a doctor."

"Drinking too much?"

"I think he was—I think he was starting to overindulge in alcohol, yeah."

"In your book, you say:

We have to confront him. We've got to sit him down and tell him to stop drinking. Face-to-face. John breathed a huge sigh of relief. He said, "I've been waiting for you to say this for a long time, Ray."

"Well, it's time now," I said. "I was waiting for the real Jim to come back. I thought it was all a phase he was going through."

"It's no phase, Ray. It is Jim," said John.

"John saw the problem a long time, didn't he?" says Forer. "He saw what was going on, that Jim Morrison was breaking down?"

"So he alludes," says Ray.

"So *you* allude?" corrects Forer.

"There you go," says Ray. "I mean, what John saw and what John knew and didn't know, you know, I really can't say. You know, John never offered, 'We've got to get help for this guy. We've got to get him help.' You know, John just simply said, 'I can't take this anymore. We can't keep going on the road.' So, you know, what John knew about Jim Morrison, I don't know. I can't—"

"How old was John Densmore?"

"Couple of years younger than Jim," says Ray.

"And you were the oldest? By five years?"

"Yeah."

"So John was what, twenty-two, twenty-three years old?"

"Uh-huh."

"His wisdom was to say, 'I think we better stop playing.' This was wrong?"

"Pardon me? What's the question?" says Ray.

"He didn't want to play anymore because he [Jim] was getting sick. He saw Jim self-destruct and he wanted to pull the plug, didn't he?"

"Well," says Ray, "I don't so much know that he saw Jim self-destructing as he was just concerned about the tension that would go on when we wouldn't play well and the strangeness and, you know, of course, we all wanted to play at the peak of our powers."

The fact is that my heart was breaking over Jim's alcoholism and there were no substance-abuse clinics back then. I remember that I couldn't look into Jim's eyes because my young psyche knew there was something wrong . . . something very dark . . . I had a headache and skin rashes for several years before Ray, as the elder of the band, said maybe we should stop playing live. I didn't give a shit about how much more money we could make. I was extremely concerned about our singer's soul. But I will never get a chance to say that to Ray.

"I want to take you back to 1968," Forer says, "specifically to the incident in your book where Jim comes to you and tells you he wants to quit. It says:

'Ray, I wanna quit.' I couldn't believe it. We had the No. 1 single and the No. 1 album. We were realizing our goals. And this was just the beginning. The cinema was next. And then politics. Man, we had a long way to go. And he wants to quit? My mind went blank. I couldn't even think. Could you?

'Why?' was all I could manage to say.

He paced the room. His head slouched down. He half

mumbled under his breath, 'I don't think I can take it anymore.'

'But why, Jim? What's wrong?'

His head slowly came up. Our eyes met. 'I think I'm having a nervous breakdown.'

'Oh, man, no, you're not. You're just drinking too much.'

'No, Ray, I'm telling you, I'm having a nervous breakdown. I want to quit.'

'Well, let's not break it up now. I'll tell you what. Let's give it six months.'

'Okay. Six months,' Jim said. 'But I tell you, Ray, I think I'm having a nervous breakdown.'

"The ride wasn't over yet, was it?" Forer says. "Got to keep him going?"

"Hardly," Ray blusters. "That's the whole point of this, is he was, you know, I mean, it's an odd thing to say but he had an obligation to the world. He's a poet. He's an artist. His obligation is to create these beautiful things, you know. He could put words on paper and this guy was—they were beautiful. I loved the words of Jim Morrison. And to take that away and dissipate that gift was just—I'm sorry. It wasn't something that I was going to allow to happen."

"You didn't believe he was having a nervous breakdown?"

"I didn't believe he was having a nervous breakdown. I believe he was drinking too much and needed to rest. *You're not having a nervous breakdown. You've been out carousing and drinking with—God knows what you've been up to.* So that's what I thought."

"Get that saddle back on and ride another race. Wasn't time for Jim to rest, was it?" says Forer.

I am reminded of part of a speech given by Pulitzer Prize–winning poet Galway Kinnell: "There's this theory that goes around that I've heard many times that it doesn't matter how many wrecked lives lie behind us, the important thing is to get that brilliant painting, that amazing sonata, that great poem. And all sins are forgotten. But I really don't believe this. I think, actually, on the contrary, it's the absence of the feelings for others, for one's loved ones, that damages the great work."

I believe that's true of Jim's poetry, which was truncated by a shortened life.

Ray says, "Jim was a young man. Jim was like—what was he, twenty-five years old. I'm sorry. I wasn't going to allow him to waste and dissipate his talent. I think what he was meant to do was write poetry. That's what he was meant to do. And he did a great job of that. And his poetry was Doors lyrics. You know, I wanted to go into—get us into cinema and eventually into politics. I thought by the time Jim was thirty-five, somebody in show business is going to become president of the United States, I thought. That's what I thought. And it happened."

"Fascists like Ronald Reagan, you call him in your book?"

"Do I call him a fascist?" asks Ray.

"Yeah," says the attorney.

"Ronald Reagan?"

"Yeah."

"Well," says Ray, "I'm not a fan of Mr. Reagan. He was the governor of California at the time of the hippie revolution. So he was not our favorite guy."

Now wait just a minute. Earlier in the trial, Ray said he felt that today's business decisions should not be made with a sixties hippie mentality. Now he's trying to turn the tables and make it look like he's the good, caring bandmate?

"At one point," Ray says, "it's in my book, at the Whisky a Go Go, Jim took me outside and said, 'Listen, man, we've got a problem. We've got to fire the drummer. I know he's a good drummer. I just can't stand him as a human being.' And I went, 'Oh God.'"

"That's what Jim said? Couldn't stand John as a human being? John Densmore knows about this story?"

"No, of course not. I never told him," says Ray.

That's true. I read it for the first time in his book, and frankly, it made me sob. I called Robby and he said that Ray was an asshole for putting that in, that Jim could have said that about so many people over the years.

"Did he [John] know that you said to Jim Morrison, 'Think of him as your dumb kid brother'?" asks Forer. "Do you remember saying that?"

"Well, I didn't want to say that."

I bet he didn't. At least not with me sitting here.

"But you did say that?" asks Forer.

"Okay," says Ray, "I did say that."

"It's the bitter truth?"

"I said it. *You* didn't have to say it in court," Ray counters.

"You said it?"

"All right," Ray concedes, "well, I said it."

"You said it in your book?"

"Yeah, I said it. All right."

"But Jim Morrison, for some unknown reason, made his last call to a band member. Not to you, did he? Who did he call?"

"By God, he called John Densmore."

"Why did he do that?" Forer asks.

"Well, he must have reconsidered John Densmore. And at the end there, he finally liked him. Either that or nobody else was home. We didn't have answering machines. He could have called me. I wasn't home. He could have called Robby. Robby may not have been home. He called John. John was home. Great. You know, he called somebody. The point is that he called to say, 'How is "L.A. Woman" doing?' And John said, 'It's doing great, man.' They had a great conversation. 'You have to come back. We'll go on the road,' John said."

Ray continues to rewrite history. I said the album was doing great, but I did not say, "Come back, we'll go on the road."

Ray continues, "Jim, of course, never was able to come back. John suggested to him we take out the bass player, Jerry Scheff, and maybe even the rhythm guitar player."

It's hard to keep my mouth shut as Ray keeps on perjuring himself. I never said a word about playing live. It's all Ray's fantasy. Now he adds, "And Jim said, 'That sounds great, man. When I get back, we'll take it on the road.'"

"He called John Densmore. He didn't call you. How did that make you feel?"

"It made me feel fine," Ray says quickly. "I mean, who cares who he called? We had art to make together. We had a lot of things to do together. The point is not who he called. The point is the conversation that we're going on the road and we're going to play 'L.A. Woman' with the original band that recorded it. Jim was having a good time in Paris. That was the point of the conversation. Not who called who. I don't know who called who. It didn't even occur to me that it would be taken as a slight or this would be an important thing. You know, John called Jim. Jim called John. Who cares?"

I care. It's very important who called whom, because if

I'd called Jim and he had hung up on me, as Ray falsely wrote in his book, that would imply my begging Jim to come back. That didn't happen, so Ray lied in his own book. My true account (I should know because I was there) is that he called me and he was stoned. I was trying to detect if Jim was still drinking, which I sensed by his slurred speech. I knew he was going down the darkest path available.

At this point, Mr. Forer addresses the subject of using songs for commercials, and Ray jumps at the chance to paint me red by saying, "After that article in the *Nation*, I think he [John] took great pride in saying he was the one who stopped Cadillac. That made him look real good in front of the various organizations."

"He didn't call you a moron or a Nazi, did he?" says Forer.

"No. He called me greedy."

"He didn't call you a fascist like you called Oliver Stone, did he?"

"No, he didn't call me a fascist. Not yet. Perhaps he will after this trial."

"He didn't blast the Hollywood community. He just said that you shouldn't have done the deal and you didn't do it?"

"What he did was send out to the public," says Ray, "certainly to corporations, the fact that The Doors aren't going to be doing anything. And all of that had to do, again, with John's political agenda. And the fact that he said, 'I support those people up in the state of Washington who smash windows and all of that, the anarchists, the terrorists.'"

I feel sick to my stomach as the judge intervenes to announce a lunch break. Now my old bandmate has called me a terrorist. I wander down the marble hallway, recalling a quote from a well-known world leader:

The streets of our country are in turmoil. The Universities are filled with students rebelling and rioting. Communists are seeking to destroy our country. Russia is threatening us with her might and the Republic is in danger. Yes, danger from within and from without . . . Yes, without law and order our nation cannot survive . . . we shall restore law and order.

That world leader was Adolf Hitler.

Chapter 20

T&A

I step outside the courthouse feeling punch-drunk, like a prizefighter who just went fifteen rounds. I head for my usual patch of grass behind a bush next to the courthouse wall. Maybe a little yoga will center me again. I take off the jacket of my "monkey suit" and drape it over a low branch of a bright purple jacaranda tree. Before I start the same yoga routine I've been doing for the last forty years, I scan the area for jury members. My long hair is already making me look weird enough. And now that I've been labeled a terrorist by my old bandmate, it's a good bet that seeing me posing in a half-contorted yoga posture is not going to improve a juror's opinion of me.

Shit! There's that Latino juror with the ponytail. I think he's on my side, but I can't take any chances. I wait for him to go away as I mill around in place. What if he thinks I'm back here taking a piss instead of using the facilities like everyone else? Boy, this trial has intruded on my world so much, I'm paranoid enough to have removed the child's pose from my yoga routine, where I sit on my knees and lean the upper part of my body forward, arms extended, to stretch out my back. Looks like one of those on-the-ground prayers to Allah. Wouldn't want anybody from the jury seeing that after I've just been labeled a terrorist and an anarchist. T&A. I remember when T&A referred to tits and ass, not terrorist and anarchist.

But wait, maybe I *am* a terrorist, since I made friends with an Iranian musician. I met Reza Derakshani at a conference some years ago, and he asked me to arrange his music with a Western influence. He played a couple of sixth-century Persian guitars made out of gourds and he sang in Farsi, but I immediately heard how we could blend our two cultures by creating a rock/jazz/blues orchestration under his gorgeous, ancient instruments.

Reza and I made a CD and we did some gigs on the West Coast and at the Kennedy Center in DC, where I announced to the audience, "I'm aware of the political stalemate between our two countries [the Bush administration had ordered that no US congresspeople were allowed to talk to Iranian politicians]. But as public citizens of Iran and the US, Reza and I are going to have a [musical] conversation right now!" The audience roared. I've seen it demonstrated time after time that cultures that are at odds, when exposed to each other's art, often feel a healing. They are hungry for the communication, because it produces a shared sense of humanity. My real goal was to enable Americans to see the faces and hear the sounds of the Iranian people.

To begin our performance, Reza entered from the back of the auditorium, sticking a narrow, hollow reed (the *ney*) under his lip, instantly transporting us to the desert with his flute. Already onstage, I trickled in with rhythmic percussion, calling the lonely wanderer down the middle aisle to join me.

In our musical conversation, we spoke volumes about the gap between Western and Middle Eastern cultures as we recreated our youths in our minds and sounds, with Reza climbing the hills above Tehran while I climbed the Santa Monica Mountains that cut through Los Angeles.

Reza's beautiful Farsi vocals lay down in a bed of Western grooves and the hour-long set passed in what felt like minutes. The audience couldn't help but get up at the end and dance like a group of wild dervishes. When we broke for tea, the room was filled with warmth and broad smiles. Today, Reza and I email each other about gigs, not politics, because he has gently alluded to the fact that a political conversation could make life more difficult for him over there. He and I speak of Rūmī as being one of the most popular poets in America, while the American government used to speak of the poet's homeland, Iran, as part of the "Axis of Evil." I feel like an underground ambassador, once again trying to heal cultural differences with art. Does that make me a terrorist?

The warm winds gust up suddenly, blowing my jacket to the ground. I grab it, brush off a few leaves, and, giving up on finding any centeredness, head back to the courtroom for the rest of the root canal. The usual suspects take their places and Jerry steps up to cross-examine Ray.

"I want to clear up another thing," says Jerry, "before we get into the substance of all this. Am I right that it's your contention that Mr. Densmore is an anarchist?"

"Mr. Densmore told me," says Ray, "that he had contributed to the cause of those people up in Washington State who are, you know, window-smashers and the ones who are protesting at all the world treaties."

"That's not my question. My question is, is it your belief that John Densmore is an anarchist?"

"No."

"Is it your belief that somehow John Densmore supported the events—the horrible events of September 11, 2001?"

"Well . . ." says Ray. It feels like he just bit me on the back of the neck with that pause. Next, he'll be sucking all the blood out of my body.

"I'm asking if it's your belief," repeats Jerry.

"I don't know what Mr. Densmore believes."

"But you have a belief about Mr. Densmore. Is that right?"

"Correct."

"One way or the other?" Jerry says.

"About what?" asks Ray.

"About whether he supported the events of 9/11."

"I don't know what his position is."

"But you don't think he's an anarchist?"

"I don't think John is an anarchist, no," says Ray. "I think—I do think he doesn't want the two of us to use the name The Doors."

"And you think he is incredibly arbitrary and unreasonable and has poor business judgment?"

"No."

"You sued him for that," Jerry says. "You sued him for forty million dollars because he's breached his fiduciary duty and has horrible business judgment in turning down a fifteen-million-dollar commercial."

"Well, there's that Japanese commercial that we didn't do, that . . . would have raised the value of The Doors and reintroduced The Doors into the public mind in Japan for the first time."

"So here's a guy who you don't think is an anarchist, but could be behind 9/11?"

"Excuse me, sir?" says Ray.

"Who holds a tremendous grudge against you or a chip on his shoulder? Pick one."

"I'll pick the chip on the shoulder, and I don't think he's an anarchist."

"Who has cost you forty million," says Jerry. "Who has bad business judgment. Has tinnitus in his ears. Doesn't want anybody to use the name The Doors. And you want these twelve jurors to believe you when you say, 'Oh, John, please come play with the band'?"

"Of course. My God. This is what it started off in the first place, you know."

"I wanted to be real clear that that's your position," says Jerry.

"My position is that we would be more than happy to have John play in the band. We wanted him to play in the band in the first place."

"Will you pack the stadium with police because this dangerous man would be on the stage with you?"

Briggs objects that Jerry is being argumentative. His objection is sustained.

Jerry rewords his question. "Let's be clear. You don't think that John Densmore is trying to stop you from singing Doors music, do you?"

Ray says, "I think he'd like to stop the whole damn thing if he could, yeah."

"Do you think that this lawsuit is about stopping you from singing Doors music?"

"No," says Ray. "It's about who has the rights to use the name. We could go out and sing 'Light My Fire.' I could stand out in the street and sing 'Light My Fire.'"

Finally, we get back to what Briggs said in his opening statement: "Let's not be mistaken . . . Mr. Densmore wants to attempt to stop my clients . . . from playing this music." Now Ray is saying the opposite. He is *so* busted. Maybe he and his mouthpiece should do lunch in one of their exorbitant restaurants to go over all of this. Or at least have a short conference in the hallway so they can get their stories straight. Talking out of both sides of his mouth is not unusual for Ray.

"Mr. Manzarek," says Jerry, "we've just seen a portion of your deposition from April 13, 2004 . . . The whole testimony that you gave about meeting with Mr. Fink [The Doors's first attorney], and describing what you wanted in a partnership agreement, and reviewing that agreement with Mr. Fink, is a complete fabrication, isn't it?"

"That actually never took place," admits Ray.

"So when you saw that contract as an exhibit," says Jerry, "and you testified under oath, you saw the date and you just made up the rest of the story because you thought that's what fit?"

"It all blended together. Well, I don't know that I—I guess I did make up the story. I mean, it all blended together."

"So when you saw this, you just figured, *Well, I'll put my head back to 1966, and I'm just going to create this story about a meeting with Max Fink that never took place?*"

"Well, we met with Max Fink. Obviously the part about this is, you know, it seemed to be a real story as I was reconstructing it in my mind. But obviously it's not a real story."

"We're going to take a long look at myth and reality now," Jerry says, "and see what's myth and what's reality. On page eight . . ." He is referring to the CD that Ray made in 1996, for which his friend Kirk Silsbee wrote liner notes that clearly describe The Doors's policy of individual vetoes. Jerry reads a quote from Ray in the liner notes: "'The Doors all had veto power. If one guy didn't want to do something it wasn't done, that's the way it's always worked with The Doors. It was a four-way split of all the money, total democratic with veto power.'"

"Well, that's the myth," says Ray. "The myth is that The Doors had veto power, and we've always sort of—not always, but it's been talked about. It's the idea, once again, that The Doors are of one mind and they create and they're operating out of the exact same space in their minds. You know, that's part of what has been going on. 'The Doors have veto power.' People love that. It's part of the myth. This is not the reality. This is the myth. And, you know, fine. Go ahead. Put it in there. Make it seem like The Doors are terrific. Unfortunately, we're at a crossroads now, and this is the crossroads."

"Well," says Jerry, "you've got a two-and-a-half- or three-hour CD entitled *Myth and Reality*. Didn't you think that you ought to maybe tell people which part was the myth and which part was the reality?"

"I wasn't operating in a contractual mode when I was doing this."

"Didn't make any difference to you if you perpetuated this myth?"

"Some myths are terrific, you know," says Ray. "And the myth of The Doors has some things that are perhaps exaggerations that make for a great rock and roll band and make for a great story."

"When you talked about that there were four guys and each was one quarter of the pie and without one of them you didn't have anything, it's real clear the four quarters were you, John, Robby, and Jim, right?"

"Yes. You wouldn't have those Doors records," says Ray. "That was an artistic gathering. That happens once in a lifetime. And there we were, you know, together on the beach in Venice and making records in Southern California. And the musical communication was great. The musical communication between the four of us was terrific. That is why those songs are all so good."

"Tell me, what is *The Doors Collection?*"

Ray answers, "*The Doors Collection* is a DVD that was originally put together for a LaserDisc collection. That's a DVD collection from the LaserDisc."

"And this is part of the commentary track that appears at one hour, twenty-five minutes, and twenty-eight seconds," says Jerry. He has a clip played for the jury in which Ray himself states that our band was made up of four equal parts. Then Jerry says, "When Mr. Briggs read to you those words, your flippant answer was, 'I must have been high.' Were you high?"

"I could have been," says Ray. "But the point is, that's again the perpetuation of the myth. And I wasn't about to spoil the ideas about The Doors's unity of mind and everything. And I, once again, that's why we're here in this courtroom. Because with that idea in mind, one person can shut the whole thing down. And that's wrong."

"So you perpetuated that myth," says Jerry, "in your own spoken reality, *Myth and Reality*, spoken words on a CD, and you perpetuated that myth on the commentary track of *The Doors Collection*, didn't you?"

Ray begins to hem and haw. "Well, *Myth and Reality*, I don't say that. That's not in *Myth and Reality*. But yeah, that's me talking, you know. That's me just kind of babbling on, of course, you know. Ray Manzarek has a tendency to just babble on and tell stories. So, quite frankly, sir, I'm telling a story there and perpetuating a myth, and the reality is a whole other thing."

"Would you turn, please, to Exhibit 16 in front of you? Okay. Do you remember that this is an agreement that was entered into with Mr. Greene, who was your business manager, for the purpose of empowering him to negotiate deals on behalf of Doors Music Company? Do you remember that?"

"Yes. That's what it is."

"I want to focus on paragraph two," directs Jerry, "which says:

> [Bob] Greene shall have the sole and exclusive right to administer and supervise the exploitation of the composition including, but not limited to, the right to license the printing, publishing, and use of the composition, throughout the world.
>
> Notwithstanding the foregoing, Greene shall not have the right to license or authorize the use of the composition, or any of them, in or in connection with radio or television commercials, it being understood that such license and authorization shall require the written consent and permission of all of the partners of Doors.

"Do you see that?" asks Jerry.

"Yes.

"Was this a perpetuation of the fallout from the Buick situation?"

"I can't recall this contract, quite frankly, sir," Ray says.

He just said, "Yes, that's what it is," a minute ago.

"You understood," says Jerry, "or you understand from this language, that even though Mr. Greene was empowered now to make any music license he wanted for The Doors Music Company, he couldn't do a commercial unless he got all of your written consent?"

"Well, that's what it says here."

"My question to you," says Jerry, "is, we've looked at the Doors Music Company partnership agreement that required unanimity. We've looked at the amendment in 1970 that went further and said, 'Put it in writing.' Now we've looked at the administration agreement to Mr. Greene that says, when it comes to commercials, you've got to have unanimous agreement of all the partners. Mr. Manzarek, at the time that you executed any one of these agreements, did you tell your partners that this unanimous requirement was just a myth?"

"Well, certainly not on the one after the Buick commercial. But this administration agreement, this is signed in a rash of signings right before Jim left for Europe." Isn't it obvious to Ray that Jim was hasty to get all of us to agree *not* to do ads without written consent while he was gone? But he sticks to his guns: "So what exactly this contract said, I don't think anyone was really aware of it."

I continue to be amazed at Ray's audacity in overlooking the fact that the four-way veto was Jim's specific request.

Jerry says, "You've mentioned a couple of times an offer from Apple to use a song. What was Robby Krieger's position with respect to the Apple commercial?"

"I can't recall at this particular time," says Ray, relying on his selective memory.

"You don't recall him saying he was in favor of it, do you?"

"Probably not."

"When you were talking with Apple about this Apple commercial," says Jerry, "did you tell anybody that you had independent negotiations with Apple where they would pay you personally $250,000 for a song that you might create in connection with the Cube?"

"Well, that was afterward," Ray lies.

"It was the same time, wasn't it?"

"Well, it *was* at the same time, but it was after the commercial didn't—we didn't work out."

"Did you tell your partners when you were trying to encourage people to do an Apple commercial that you had a side deal for $250,000?"

Briggs objects, trying to save his client from getting caught in yet another lie, stating, "Misstates evidence. Assumes facts not in evidence. Lacks foundation." But he is overruled by the judge.

Ray does his best to answer the question that has him cornered: "I can't remember who I talked to about that. If Mr. Densmore hadn't been so adamant in his refusal—as we've talked about, for his political views and/or, you know—Mr. Densmore is not an anarchist, but those views are anarchistic views."

So here we go again. At least I'm in good company. Thomas Jefferson was accused of being an anarchist for not trusting big government.

Ray adds, "I don't want to say 'eco-terrorist.' He's certainly not one of those. But he knows the anarchists up in Washington State."

Is he really referring to the few protesters with masks who broke windows? *Give the court some names, Ray,* I think to myself. He seems to want to smear me by connecting me with them. The truth is that I don't know any environmentalists in Washington State. I know people from the Rainforest Action Network from the Bay Area who attended the protests. But their credo is nonviolence.

The trial is winding down and we are almost ready for closing arguments when Judge Alarcon says, "Mr. Manzarek, there are a number of questions from the jurors." The judge reads, "'Do you feel that the name of the band could be restructured to satisfy John and still bring the same notoriety that the original Doors name brings?'"

Ray says, "Well, again, quite frankly, I think the band—I think we are The Doors. Robby Krieger is the writer of 'Light My Fire.' I want to play these songs with the band that we created . . . The Doors is who we are."

Ray's comment almost makes me feel sad for him. How long will it take for him to understand that "the band that we created" is gone forever?

"Your Honor," says Jerry, "with all due respect, I don't think the question has been answered."

Briggs protests, "With all due respect, I think he answered the question."

The judge restates the original question, "So is there some way that the name could be changed to satisfy Mr. Densmore and still bring the same notoriety?"

Ray answers quite simply this time, "I don't think the name should be changed."

The judge asks another juror question: "'Do you use the name and font type because you are The Doors and have the right?'"

"Yes. Exactly," says Ray. "Exactly. I mean, we have the right to use any font we want. And we choose to use that one. It's cool. And that's the one we use."

Jerry steps up to finish his cross. "I didn't hear the answer to part of this juror's question, 'If you got offered fifteen million today by Buick (not Cadillac but Buick) for 'Light My Fire,' would you do it?'"

"Well, once again," says Ray, "we'd certainly have to consider *not* doing it, given the history of The Doors."

"How would you vote?"

"Well, again, it would depend on the automobile, what the new Buick line was."

"You wouldn't reject it out of hand."

"I don't think a partnership should reject anything out of hand," says Ray.

"You think a partnership should consider the pluses and minuses?"

"I think all of these things should be judged, each according to its merit."

"How many times," says Jerry, "did you ask John Densmore to join you at the meeting with Cadillac so that he might have the benefit of seeing what you saw?"

"Well," Ray hesitates, "I assumed that was going to be the next step. I did a preliminary and the next step would have been to show it to John and Robby. There's no point in bothering everybody all the time."

"The guys flew out from Cadillac land?" asks Jerry. "You knew they were coming? They didn't just show up and knock on your door. They had an appointment to see you?"

"Yes, yes . . . Again, I didn't know about the people coming from Cadillac land. Somebody, whoever the heck it was that instituted it, got this idea going, said, 'A couple of people want to come over and show you some stuff.'"

"How many people were there from your side?" asks Jerry.

"Me."

"How many times did you try to call John Densmore and say, 'John, the Cadillac and the advertising people are coming over. Why don't you take a look? I think this could be interesting'?"

Ray seems irritated as he responds, "I had no idea if it was interesting. I was going to take a look at it and see what it's like. 'Hey, this is interesting.' Then John and Robby and I got together at Robby's house and then John shot the whole thing down."

"Is the answer 'none'?" asks Jerry.

"What's the question?"

Jerry repeats, "How many times did you call John to ask him to come over and meet with you when the Cadillac people showed up?"

"I didn't call Robby or John. I did the preliminary investigation."

We are finally near the finish line. The judge turns to Briggs and asks, "There are no further witnesses, no further exhibits?"

"No further exhibits, Your Honor."

Mr. Forer is next: "Right. Nothing additional."

Jerry tells the court that he has nothing additional either, and the judge informs the jury that *all* the testimony in this case is over. It has lasted three months and involved forty witnesses as well as hundreds of exhibits.

The next thing the jury will hear are three sets of closing arguments, from Mr. Jerry Mandel, Mr. Jeff Forer, and finally Mr. William Briggs. As I watch Ray walk back to his seat in the courtroom, I can almost see his youthful shadow moving beside him. We were of like mind once upon a time.

For a drummer, the space between one beat and the next is extremely important, since the space implies the feel of the entire composition. If you play on the front of the beat, as in military music, Irish music, polkas, etc. (the style I learned in my high school marching band), the feel is rather controlled. I used this style way back when I played at bar mitzvahs. On the other hand, if you perform with the accent on the back of the beat (if you don't hit the next beat until the last moment), the feel is very laid-back, as in the blues, R&B, ballads, etc. I certainly got this style down from performing for years in bars.

When The Doors got started, we covered the blues a lot until we had enough originals, so our foundation was first built on a laid-back feel. Then the originals, with Jim's percussive lyrics, pushed the pulse forward a little. Thank God Ray and I were in the same arena when we wrote the music to these words. Together, we chose to forego a bass guitar player after Ray found a keyboard bass, but the luxury of having two minds hold down the groove was gone since Ray was split between playing the organ with his right hand and the piano bass with his left. Traditionally, bass players and drummers are like brothers, working in the basement, cooking up the groove, so it was a challenge for me to not let the tempo speed up when Ray took a solo. He would get excited like most soloists do when the spotlight hits them, and his left hand, which was supposed to be in the "pocket" with me, sped up.

But for the most part, the two of us heard things the same, due to our mutual love of jazz. In fact, it was almost telepathic. I love dynamics, which has always made me different from other drummers. God knows, I'm not the fastest drummer, but Ray and I would cue the band in and out of dramatic volume changes, which allowed the music to breathe. For example, after Robby's solo on "When the Music's Over," Ray and I would take it down to a pianissimo (extremely quiet) bass and simple drumbeat. It was very effective after a loud guitar solo and this is what made The Doors's songs breathe so much.

Novelist, essayist, and film critic Steve Erickson dramatically captures this notion with the following words:

The absence of the bass [player] left black open swaths of silence in The Doors's music. Driving Sunset Boulevard at night, rounding the curves and cliffs of the Palisades, one could be certain that if the vehicle were to suddenly go out of control and sail off the side of the road into space, it was The Doors that would be heard on the car radio.

Ray and I musically relished those extremes, but Ray always wanted success more than any of us, at any cost, and his salesman mentality has resulted in his being sued by the drummer of his old band. He just went too far, but soon enough, the issue will be in the hands of the jury and a verdict will follow. I'll be relieved to have this in the past so I can get on with my life. But nothing will ever be the same.

Chapter 21

MYTH AND REALITY

I enter the courtroom through familiar doors and take my place in the same security line I've stood in for the last nine weeks. It feels a little bit different today, however, as I'm filled with disbelief. I can't believe this morning will be the last time I'll have to jerk myself awake at dawn. Musicians are night people. I can't believe that years of preparation and the loss of my entire summer are finally coming to a close. Most amazing of all, I can't believe that I actually care about Jerry Mandel, a litigator!

Jerry has become a dear friend . . . even if he is a lawyer. We have connected in a deep way, shouldering each other's personal trials outside the courthouse. He has educated me in a world about which I knew nothing a short time prior, a world I'm eager to leave. But because of him, I'll be leaving with respect for the few judges and lawyers who try to do their best in a sometimes hopelessly gridlocked system.

Jerry told me this is the second-longest trial of his entire thirty-year career and, as tough it's been, I'm kind of excited to hear his closing argument, the culmination of a ton of work and research. It's a little bit like seeing live theater, only the subject is much too close to home for me to relax and enjoy it.

The order of the closing arguments is preset: Jerry will go first, followed by Jeff Forer for the estate, and then we'll hear from William Briggs. I cringe just thinking about the diatribe Briggs will unleash, but at least I won't be on the witness stand, in his line of fire. This time, he'll be directing his energy toward the jury.

The jury. I said a silent prayer as I got dressed this morning. Will they get my position now that they've had an inside peek at the supposedly glamorous life of "rock stars"?

After I'm cleared through security, I take the elevator to the fourth floor, and for the last time, I walk down the cold marble hallway. I smile at a memory of a couple of jury members I saw last week who were pitching pennies against the wall to kill time. We were on a break and I wished I could join in. They saw me give them a one-second smile in reaction to their game, and they smiled back. I quickly looked away since "no contact" is the rule. Now the ball is in their court.

We take our seats in the usual places. Jerry looks at me, smiles, and rises. Hope he slept well last night and feels alert and ready, because This Is It!! Jerry begins to speak in a steady, self-assured voice that lulls me into listening to him. Here are some meaningful excerpts from his closing arguments:

"We've been here for about nine weeks. There have been by my count thirty witnesses in this trial. There have been hundreds and hundreds of exhibits that you have seen and that you have heard. It has been, in the way of trials, a pretty comprehensive trial. And I'll tell you this, if John Densmore has to make new friends like Ray Manzarek said, let me tell you something, I want to be the first guy in line to be his friend."

In previous testimony, I stated that a number of friends had called me thinking I was part of the Doors of the 21st Century tour. Ray's comment was that I should get new friends.

"He's the kind of guy you want as your friend," Jerry continues. I start to get a little misty around the eyes. "He's the kind of guy who has principles and integrity and could have shined all of this on and taken the money and run, but he stood up and he is standing up for what he believes is right. And if his worst crime in the world is that he's a tree hugger, I want to hug him too. Because that's the kind of person he is.

"And the Coursons, sure, they could have stayed away. They could have grabbed the money. They could have done whatever they've been doing and just let Ray and Robby run the show. They didn't want to do that. It wasn't right to them. It wasn't right to get railroaded. It wasn't right to watch John get sued. I'm proud to represent them. I'm proud to have spent my summer here defending their honor and representing their honor. It's not just about the dollars. It's not just about the money. God knows you've heard about the money and you'll hear more about the money. It's about principles. It's about promises. It's about integrity. That's what this case is about.

"There's been a lot of trash talk in this case. There's been a lot of character assassination in this case. I don't know why. Frankly, I find it offensive. I don't know why we get to a place where each witness has to be trashed. Each one has to be challenged. Where the character has to be challenged because that's the way you're going to win. I don't think so.

"'No, there are no partnerships,' they say. But you've seen the written documents. You've heard the people talk. They've said paper is unimportant. 'We don't care what's on paper. It's just paper. We live a real truth.' They laugh off the things that hurt them. 'Oh,' Robby says, 'I guess I just forgot to fix that thing I told them I'd fix.'

"Or how about this one: 'Don't believe what I say. I was high at the time.'

"They got a little misdirection for everything that doesn't work for them. We have a morality and ethics in our society that give us an expectation of how we should deal with other people, how those people should deal with us. It's not a bad thing. It's a good thing. But then you get this weird element that has come into this trial. This 'I'm a rock star' theory. We have rules. We have morals. We have ethics.

"And you know what, ladies and gentlemen? They apply to you. They apply to me. They apply to John. And they apply to Mr. Manzarek and Mr. Krieger. And I don't care if they're rock stars or not and you shouldn't either. They don't have special rules because they are good musicians. Maybe they should be held to a higher standard. Maybe because they are rock stars and they're icons and they're idolized, they should be held to a higher standard.

"We talked about identity theft in the opening statement and we still talk about it today. The name 'The Doors' is property in these United States. And as you now can see, it's very, very, very valuable property. And rock stars are no less obligated to respect that property than you and I are obligated to respect the property of anybody else or any other business or any other partnership.

"The absolute cornerstone of this business, The Doors, is, 'All for one, one for all, and if anybody has a veto, we won't do it. We will respect and honor that veto.' It's the foundation of what started in 1965. It's been hugely successful to date. But they want to make the rules different today than they've been for thirty years and there is only one reason they want to do it. That is because the green bags have been waved in front of their eyes and, as Jim Morrison said in 1969, 'Ray, it's just about the money for you, isn't it? It's just too much, isn't it, Ray?' When he, as Ray said, thrust that dagger into their hearts and said, 'I don't trust you anymore.'

"That's the reason to change the rules that have worked so successfully for thirty years?"

Jerry faces the jury directly here, making eye contact with each of them. "And you remember when you were being interviewed to be a juror in this case, Mr. Briggs told you that his clients had to work to put food on the table and would you excuse them for not being here? Food on the table? At $150,000 a night, they're putting on quite a spread.

"But the rightful owner of the benefit of that logo, the benefit of that name, is a partnership, ladies and gentlemen. And if Jon Pareles of the *New York Times* is right and what this band is, is 'a passable tribute band with a valuable trademark,' that valuable trademark is owned by a partnership and we need you to tell us who that partnership is. We need you to tell us who has the rights, who has the right to vote.

"Well, it's worked pretty good for thirty years, wouldn't you say? Wouldn't any one of you like to have been a partner of The Doors? I would. I can't sing, but I'll tell you what, I love that money.

"They just want to ride into town on their high horses and tell everybody else how to run the business because it's the Ray and Robby Show. When Jim came to him and said, 'I'm having a nervous breakdown,' Ray said, 'Oh, let's keep playing. Let's keep playing. We owe it to society. We owe it to America. We owe it to people who read your poetry.'

"It wasn't until years later that he finally had to admit, 'I was wrong. The guy was really having a breakdown.'

"[These guys] just come into town and say, 'We change the rules, and if you dare stand up and question why . . . It must be a grudge match. You must be an anarchist. You must be a communist. How dare you stand up and say we can't change the rules?'

"It's not going to fly in this courtroom, ladies and gentlemen. I don't think you're going to let it fly. It doesn't make sense. He doesn't have that power. And rather than follow the rules that have worked for thirty years, these guys come in and say, 'We're going to change the rule based on four really great arguments:

"'One: I'm a rock star and agreements don't apply to me. That is their big argument.

"'Two: We're just dumb kids. We were really stupid when we signed these papers. What did we know?' Let's see, Robby Krieger went to college. Ray Manzarek has a bachelor's degree in economics and a master's degree and was thirty-one years old when he signed a 1971 partnership agreement, and he wants you to believe he was just a dumb little stoner boy.

"Their third argument: 'It's just paper.' So if times are tough, ladies and gentlemen, and you can't make the mortgage payment on your house and the bank comes, you just tell them that they can't take your house because it's just paper that you signed. And I'm sure they'll be receptive to your argument, don't you think? Hasn't worked for me.

"And then the fourth argument they have, my personal favorite: 'I was high. If I said something that hurts my case, I was high. That's it. I could have been high two weeks ago. I could have been high two years ago. Could have been high thirty-two years ago. But I was high.'

"So that's it. There's their four big arguments.

"I want to talk about Ray Manzarek. He was the last wit-ness. There are three Rays that testified here. There's the Ray Manzarek that testified in his deposition that you watched [on tape]. There's the Ray Manzarek that testified when Mr. Briggs asked him questions. And there's the Ray Manzarek that testified when I asked him questions and Mr. Forer asked him questions. And they weren't all the same Ray Manzarek.

"I think Ray Manzarek is totally, completely, absolutely, unequivocally unbelievable and a liar. I don't know how I can be any more clear. And I mean it. He lied about the una-nimity requirement, saying it's a myth that there's this veto that other people have perpetuated. In his own spoken word CD, *Myth and Reality*—what an amazing title, *Myth and Re-ality*—he says, he's quoted in his own liner notes: 'The Doors all had veto power. If one guy didn't want to do something it wasn't done, that's the way it's always worked with The Doors. It was a four-way split of all the money, totally demo-cratic with veto power.'

"Ladies and gentlemen, I don't know how it could be more clear. And his excuse is, 'Oh, gosh, that is just a liner note. I didn't write it.' And, 'Gee, I must have been high at the time.' Come on.

"Todd Gray walked in here, who is The Doors's webmas-ter, and said, 'I introduced him [Ray] to Tommy Gear to do the graphics. I didn't have time. I introduced him to Tommy Gear.'

"Tommy Gear walks in and says, 'Oh, yeah, I met Ray twice in his home in Beverly Hills. We went over the draft of logos and the little insignias.'

"But in his deposition testimony, sworn testimony, he [Ray] says, 'Nope, never met him.'

"He thinks that Jim, who he knew so, so well, would do the Cadillac commercial. Gee, that's odd. He thought he'd do the Buick commercial too. I think it sort of backfired on him. Don't you think? When your partner [Jim] says he wants a referral to five lawyers so he can sue his partners, I think he didn't know his partner very well.

"He [Ray] said he knew his friend Jim best. Yeah, he knew him best. Except when he came to him and said, 'I'm having a nervous breakdown, I want to quit.' But in his own book he says, 'Now I know.' If he knew him so well in 1969, how come he didn't realize it then?

"He acknowledged in his testimony—here's a quote I had read to him and he acknowledged it:

It was a four-man band. Everyone was important. You know, each one was a cardinal point of the compass. North, South, East, West. Each one was a facet of the diamond. And without any one of The Doors, The Doors wouldn't be The Doors.

"Well, I guess he's changed his mind. On his *Myth and Reality* clip, *Myth and Reality* CD, he makes the following statement: 'You remove any one of those quarters and you don't have anything.'

"Maybe he should have said, 'If you remove any one of those quarters, you don't have anything unless they start dangling $250,000 a night in front of you and you can go hire a singer and come and join and tell John Densmore to shove it.'

"The greed gene. You don't have anything. Unless the money gets too good. It's just too good, isn't it, Ray? The money's just too much, Ray. It seduces you. It seduces you to change your story. Oh, what a tangled web we weave.

"My personal favorite exhibit in this entire cased is Exhibit 85. The exhibit everyone dared to deny because they never ever thought that Stewart Copeland was going to walk into this courtroom and testify, and he did. Exhibit 85: Stewart Copeland's memo to Ray, Robby, Ian, and Tom. Every single person to whom this memo is addressed denies ever seeing it, denies ever talking about it, denies ever discussing it, because they never thought Stewart would come here.

"He was going to be a Door. He was raising all these questions. And every single one of these people denies getting it. And Tom Vitorino [the manager of Ray and Robby's group] actually had to say under oath, 'Oh, gosh, I don't know if that's me. Am I *that* Tom? Oh, gosh, I don't know.'

"This is a huge memo. Huge because it shows that this was on their minds. It shows that they made a conscious decision after the issues were raised. It shows that what they engaged in was willful, conscious, and deliberate. They made the decision. The issue was raised. They chose the decision. And, ladies and gentlemen, they've got to live with it.

"Ian Astbury, he appeared by deposition. And actually, he also appeared live, as you know. He did get a percentage of the profits. He has his own corporation that contracted in Europe. I thought one of the most interesting things about Mr. Astbury was his relationship with his partner Mr. Duffy in the band called the Cult. Remember his testimony? He'd been on hiatus for ten years.

"'Mr. Astbury, do you think Mr. Duffy could go out and call himself the Cult of the 21st Century?'

"What was his answer? 'That would be ludicrous. It would be absurd.'

"Next, Abe Somer. You'll remember that Mr. Somer was The Doors's attorney from 1967 or so until 1982, 1984. He has no ax to grind here. He represented everybody. He has no reason to take one side over the other. But he was very, very honest in saying there was always unanimity. Anybody had a veto. He was there at the time of Buick. Abe Somer terminated the new Elektra contract between Elektra and Robby and Ray and John and left a whopping $750,000 on the table—that's like eight million in today's money. Because they didn't think they were good enough without Jim to keep calling themselves The Doors.

"Robby Krieger. He was sure honest about commercials. Of course he was opposed to Cadillac. He was opposed to Apple. And he was at least honest enough to walk in and say, 'Yeah, I've got twenty-twenty hindsight.' That's Robby Krieger. He's honest enough to say that.

"Unfortunately, he's not honest enough to avoid suing a partner when he knows that he doesn't even have the votes. Doesn't even have them to give up. Robby Krieger, who didn't even vote for Cadillac, who didn't even vote for Apple, has the audacity to sue John Densmore for not voting for it. What is wrong with this picture here?

"Maybe Ray and Robby thought they'd just come to town, steamroll everybody. Hell, it's just a bunch of old people who were the parents of Jim and Pam. 'They're not going to care.' They're eighty, eighty-five. One of them is ill.

"But you know what? Somebody does care. John cares. And the Coursons cared. And the Morrisons cared. And they're standing up in front of that steamroller and they're saying, 'You know what? There's rules to play by here, folks. There's promises that were made. And we're going to enforce those.'

"I say, thank God for John Densmore and thank God for the Morrisons and the Coursons, who have the integrity and the principles to stand up when it would be so easy to look the other way.

"I'm proud to be part of them. I'm proud that they're our clients. I'm proud that it's not always about money. I'm proud that there are people like that in our society, who do things for principles and promises and integrity.

"Thank you, Your Honor."

Now it's Jeff Forer's turn to present his closing arguments for the estate. He begins, "Remember that John Densmore testified that he was hurting because Jim was an alcoholic that needed help? Do you remember that? It was early in the case. He knew they had to stop performing so that Jim could get better. Do you remember that? John was really heartfelt about that. He was ridiculed for stopping playing, for not playing in the Seattle concert because he was sick to his stomach.

"But he actually cared. He actually cared about something more than just the performing and the money. And you know what? At the age of twenty-two or however old he was, maybe he couldn't formulate it. Maybe he couldn't address it. Maybe he couldn't deal with it. But he knew it was wrong. And he tried to stop it.

"But Ray didn't stop it. Ray knew differently. Ray knew that there were things to do.

"We heard testimony from Lou Reisman [the Morrisons' other attorney] that he asked Ray Manzarek if he would please take down the picture of Jim Morrison that they were using at the beginning of their concerts . . . This was before the estates filed their lawsuit. Mr. Manzarek was at Mr. Reisman's office and Lou asked him to do just that, and Ray refused.

"Mr. Reisman told Ray Manzarek that left him no choice but to proceed and file a lawsuit. Ray Manzarek didn't care then and he doesn't care now. He was finally able to control Jim Morrison, probably for the first time in his life, and he liked it. He wanted to use the picture, and by God he would. He'd refer to Jim as endorsing the concert. 'Jim would love it.'

"The Doors are synonymous with Jim Morrison, everybody knows that. You say the word—the term 'The Doors'—and people don't think of Ray Manzarek. They don't think of Robby Krieger and they don't think of John Densmore, and they are wonderful musicians. Maybe they should think about them, but they don't. They think of Jim Morrison.

"And if the advertisers use Jim Morrison's picture to sell tickets or they use Jim Morrison's voice on promos or the image of the lizard to sell the T-shirts, that would be okay. Hell, if it can sell tickets. If it sells merchandise. Because according to Ray Manzarek, Jim Morrison would love it. Ray knows. Ray knows.

"Robby Krieger watched it all go by and does nothing. Remember: to *not* decide is to decide. And Robby Krieger is as culpable as Ray Manzarek for *not* deciding. It's time to get off the fence. Robby Krieger, Ray Manzarek, and Ian Astbury, the three of them, added instant legitimacy to the band by using the late and great Jim Morrison as a prop. That is offensive.

"I want to tell you that during that thirty-year period of time, the Morrisons have not filed a lawsuit against anybody. They don't do that. They're not like that. But they're principled people. He was the youngest admiral in the navy. You heard his war record. You heard his service record. This is not a guy that trifled. He's a man of principle.

"So finally—and I think this is a fundamental difference and it happened in depositions. It happened in trial. The defendants would always ask somebody, 'Did you expect Jim Morrison to be there?' Everybody said, 'Ha ha ha, he's dead.'

"How about John? 'No one cares about the drummer,' Bill Kirby [The Doors of the 21st Century's promoter] said on the witness stand. Well, that's not the problem. The problem was that it was The Doors that were playing. And Densmore wasn't there. Morrison wasn't there. Manzarek would say, 'If we're not The Doors, who is?' And that showed the world that The Doors endorsed this group. And nothing is further from the truth.

"So the reputation of The Doors is what they stole. That's what was the misappropriation. That's what was the misrepresentation. That's what they held themselves out as. 'Hey, if we're not The Doors, who is?' Well, they're not The Doors. It's Ray Manzarek and Robby Krieger and Ian Astbury.

"That's it, Your Honor."

Chapter 22

STRANGE DAYS

It's time for high drama as Briggs takes a long swig on his Red Bull. He rises, buttons his ultra-expensive suit jacket, and begins to pace around the room. I have to hand it to him, he's got attitude. The trial is ending and Briggs is up. He looks at the jury members with a sad kind of smile, clearly manufactured to create a particular mood in the room. Here are some of his closing arguments, with comments from Yours Truly sprinkled in . . . the comments I was not allowed to make while this man was lying to the jury with such self-righteousness and arrogance.

"Ladies and gentlemen," he begins, "I come to you today with a saddened heart. And the reason for that is, I've spent fifteen years in this profession. One of the things that I was taught in school, one of the things I learned while practicing in this profession, is that our system of justice is supposed to be about equity.

"Our system of justice is supposed to be about fair play.

"When I left last Friday, my head was hanging down. I was somewhat depressed. Those notions that I held dear, those notions that I was taught, had been shattered. Mr. Densmore's counsel comes into this courtroom and he says to you, 'My client Mr. Densmore believes in the truth.' Well, if that were true, ladies and gentlemen, he would not have fought so hard to prevent you from learning it.

"Now, ladies and gentlemen, I was so despondent when I got home that evening. And as I was putting my daughter to bed, she said to me, 'Daddy, what is court?' She's four years old. She wanted to know why I missed an entire summer with her. She knew that I went to court every day. But she didn't know what it was . . . Those of you who have children know that they're naturally curious. And she said, 'Daddy, what is court?'"

It's hard to take Briggs seriously with a chorus of violins playing in the background. I imagine him billing Ray and Robby four hundred bucks an hour for "the entire summer." That's one more reason for me to win—so I don't have to cover the other side's court costs. Mine are exorbitant, so theirs must be off the map at this point.

Briggs continues, "So I said, 'Bella'—her name is Isabella, so I called her Bella—I said, 'Bella, a court is a place where people go to have their disputes decided in a fair fashion.' But I started to quietly shake my head. I did not want to disillusion her.

"Then she said to me, 'Daddy, what is a jury?'

"And that simple question, that one question, brought it all back to me. Because you see, ladies and gentlemen, that one question helped reinvigorate my faith in this system. Because you, every single one of you sitting in this box, are the judges of this case.

"There's been a lot of testimony. But the fact is that veto power doesn't matter. That's right. This veto power, if such a thing existed, if such a thing was even practiced—we'll get to that in a moment—it doesn't matter."

Let's get to it right now, I think to myself. Briggs wasn't in the garage in Venice with us. I was. It *did* exist. It was practiced and each of us had equal VETO POWER.

"Unanimity here doesn't matter," Briggs says. "None of those features matter. And the reason is simple. Because you have to ask yourself, ladies and gentlemen, what was the reason John Densmore said no to these opportunities? That's what our lawsuit is about.

"It's not that there was some so-called veto power. It's not that there was this unanimity requirement. That's irrelevant. What is relevant is that Mr. Densmore jointly owned an asset with someone else. And when you jointly own something with someone else, the law says you have duties. The law says one of your duties is that of loyalty. The law says one of those duties is not to put your own interests above that of someone who you jointly own the property with.

"Here Mr. Densmore put his own interests above that of my clients. Here Mr. Densmore put his own interest above that of Robby Krieger, Ray Manzarek, and even the estates. It doesn't matter that the estates decided not to sue Mr. Densmore. The fact of the matter is, Mr. Densmore put his own political and social beliefs above that of my client."

It is so frustrating to hear him ranting endlessly about putting my interests first, since this entire lawsuit is about upholding *Jim's* interests and putting *them* first. I guess it's considered un-American *not* to be greedy. Maybe that is really what this lawsuit is about.

"But this is one of the things they didn't tell you. Every time my client gets up onstage and performs, every time Robby Krieger gets out there and performs for someone, the estates and John Densmore are paid. They were paid a per-formance royalty. So they got paid for these performances."

That would be real nice, I think to myself, *but there was never such a thing as a performance royalty.* If there was, I have to ask, when, what, and where is the money? I never got a nickel. Can lawyers be sued for not telling the truth in a court of law? Where does perjury begin and end? Does it only apply to the client? It appears that way.

"I told you," Briggs says, "that what we are seeking from Mr. Densmore is an amount that each of you feel appropriate. And here's the reason why: Back in 1965, two guys got to-gether on a beach in Venice. And you've heard my client tell the story. And he certainly tells it a lot better than me. They got together. They eventually hooked up with Robby Krieger and John Densmore.

"Remember, they all created it together. Remember that agreement made back in the garage. If there's anything that we can agree on in this trial, it is that, yes, Jim Morrison said, 'Twenty-five, twenty-five, twenty-five, twenty-five. That's what we're going to do. We're not going to get into these disputes about who wrote what. We're just going to divide it equally.' That was the basic agreement.

"And you heard the judge's instruction. A partnership is for profit. That's the purpose of it. You don't go into a partnership to lose money. You don't go into business with someone to lose money. I mean, would any of you do that? 'Oh, I'm going into business with somebody and my pur-pose or my intent is going to be to lose money.' That is not done."

That wasn't the purpose of The Doors's partnership ei-ther. Just the opposite happened . . . we made tons of money from the business we created together, because it was our intent to make money. And judging from ongoing royalties and commissions, we are still doing it.

"Keep this in mind," says Briggs, "we as attorneys are a careful breed. We prepare documents for our clients."

I nearly choke when I hear this. His own client, Ray, said it was "just paper" when he was on the witness stand a day or so ago, in an attempt to belittle the importance of contracts. I guess Briggs and Ray never took that lunch to get their stories straight. Well, as hard as it is to hear these lies and discrepancies, I have to remind myself that in this case, they all work in my favor. If they are such blaring lies to my ears, they must sound the same to the jury.

Briggs carries on as if he hasn't just contradicted his own client. "We want to give them all kinds of options. And in giving a client an option, we think of various scenarios that may come into play. We give them options.

"Now, they've come into court. They've tried to show you a bunch of documents. 'We're a partnership here, we're a partnership there.'

"We understand that for the most part The Doors did not license their music for commercials. Okay. If that's what they do, then this is what happened with Cadillac and Apple. We all understand because it was taught at an early age there are certain wants and lifetime opportunities that come around. It's like hitting the lotto. These happen only once. Some call it grabbing the brass ring. Some of a different generation call it the golden ticket. Whatever it is, it happens once in a lifetime. And when it comes around, you grab it and you don't let go.

"When Cadillac came around with its offer for fifteen million dollars, ladies and gentlemen, that was one such opportunity."

I thought that the extraordinary success of "Light My Fire" was just such an opportunity. What about "Hello, I Love You"? That was #1. So was "Touch Me." And what about "Riders on the Storm"? The truth is that The Doors have had a number of "once-in-a-lifetime" opportunities. And, in fact, the several we've gotten, we've grabbed, and I for one will not let go. I refuse to sell off one of our babies for a larger plastic ring.

But Briggs sees it differently. "When Mr. Densmore made his decision to say no [to Cadillac], ladies and gentlemen, he did not consider the interest of either Mr. Manzarek or Mr. Krieger, which the law says he is required to do."

Of course, he is leaving out the part where Robby and I offered Ray a million-dollar loan. If that's not considering his best interests, I don't know what is, but I guess this lawyer and I have different opinions on the topic.

"He [John] did not consider the interest of the catalog, which the law says he is required to do."

Robby and I agreed that in the long run, our decision to *not* sell out for commercialism would cause the value of our songs to go up.

"The law says that if you have this property together, if you have this joint asset together, you can't engage in something that is whimsical or capricious, such as this."

On this point, Briggs and I agree in a convoluted sort of way. Doing commercials seems quite whimsical and capricious to me.

Briggs continues, "Mr. Mandel gets up yesterday and what does he say? That he's proud to represent John Densmore. 'John Densmore is a man of principles and integrity.' Tell me, ladies and gentlemen, what kind of man of principles and integrity would say one of the country's largest and most innovative companies ever should be compared to the KGB, an agency of the Soviet Union, a failed government that went out and assassinated people?"

Briggs has his people wrong. I didn't say that. That quote is attributed to the president of Czechoslovakia, who used it as an analogy to make the point that his country should slowly move into democracy. We should be able to relate. After all, we tried to bomb Iraq into democracy and it didn't work out all that well. But I have to keep my mouth shut and just listen.

"What kind of man of principle and integrity," Briggs says, "would say that banks are the center of worship of our towns? Excuse me, but I pray in a church. And I think most people do. I don't think that they worship at the altar of some bank as John Densmore stated in his article in the *Nation*."

I know what he is referring to, but once again, he is misinterpreting me. My criticism was that, in many cases, money has become more important than God, and I don't consider that a good thing.

"As for his claim that he wants to maintain the integrity of the music, well, that is a lofty goal, but ladies and gentlemen, you've heard him tell you, 'Hey, I recorded the music so people would buy it and I can't control who buys it.'

"Let's talk about the Beatles. One of the contemporaries of The Doors. Their music was used in a commercial."

The point was already made that the Beatles didn't own some of their own songs, but why bring up the truth at a time like this?

"Bob Seeger sold, what was it, 'Like a Rock.' I made a comment about it during the course of the trial. But did that hurt the integrity of his music? His catalog went through the roof."

Which makes me wonder if that's why our new box set is climbing the charts these days and Seeger's is not.

"Mr. Densmore wanted to make sure that none of those assets would ever be used. So he drove a stake in them. He drove a stake through corporate America's heart, saying. 'You will never get one of these Doors assets.'"

Now I'm not only a terrorist and an anarchist, I'm also a vampire slayer.

"What do my clients seek?" Briggs asks the jury. "We're going to rely on your judgment. And the reason we're going to do that, ladies and gentlemen, is this: We're not trying to hurt John Densmore. We're not trying to terrorize his family."

He can say what he likes now, but he was absolutely trying to make me look like a terrorist when he asked me rather casually during this trial if I had funded Al Qaeda. What a preposterous tactic, one I will never forget, and I can hardly believe my musical brothers would stoop so low. And then there is the forty million that his clients are trying to get from my pocket. Sounds like terrorizing to me.

"What we want, ladies and gentlemen," Briggs says, "and we're going to leave it in your hands, your collective hands, is a simple statement from you, as my client said on the stand: 'Tell John Densmore one man can't stop this. Tell John Densmore one man cannot elevate his own principles, his own social agenda, hidden or not, above the interest of someone else that co-owns this property with him.' You can't do that, ladies and gentlemen. You have a duty of loyalty. And when you violate that, you've got to send a signal."

This was exactly the reason Jim created four-way veto power—in his own words, "in case things got weird." Things were getting weird and that was his signal.

"We're asking you send that signal to Mr. Densmore.

We're leaving that in your hands. My clients are not here to hurt or financially ruin anyone. But we do want that signal sent."

Jim's lyric, *Strange days have found us,* is wafting through my head as Briggs ends his closing arguments.

"And again," he says, "this has got nothing to do with veto. This has got nothing to do with unanimity. It's the reason he said no. That's all our claim has to do with, ladies and gentlemen."

If that were true, then I win. The reason I said no is because of Jim's own concept, which he called "one for all, all for one." And he hated selling out.

Jim famously wrote:

I love the friends I have gathered together on this thin raft [our band]
We have constructed pyramids [great songs]
in honor of our escaping [a career in music, something we loved]

PART THREE

WAITING IS
THE HARDEST PART

Chapter 23

SCENES FROM A HALLWAY

I

Well, here I am, sitting on the cold marble bench outside the courtroom of District Division #36 on the fourth floor. I thought the trial was over yesterday when the jury went into deliberations. It wasn't. I just found out from my attorney (who apparently never takes a day off) that he and I will be sitting right here every day, possibly for several more weeks, as long as jury deliberations last. So much for no longer having to jerk myself awake at dawn or no longer having to drive in bumper-to-bumper traffic in the early morning. I still have to do both of these things because, although the testimony is over, I'm not through. Jerry feels that since the jury is working hard each day behind closed doors to come to a verdict, we need to make them know that we appreciate what they are doing.

I appreciate them so much that I wonder if maybe I should just accept my fate and enroll in law school. This trial has consumed my life for years now, and I have to admit that, these days, I've cultivated a newfound appreciation for words. As a musician, I was lost in the nonlinear world of sound, but now, language has become much more fascinating and compelling to me. I think I love words now, something that took me by surprise when my *Nation* article got worldwide attention.

Sitting alone in my writing room, I realize that I have the ability to conjure up and write down ideas that get people thinking. I really do enjoy chewing on thoughts. I guess I'm a "word man" now. Years ago, Jim wrote: *I'll always be a word man, better than a bird man.*

I keenly felt our differences back then. The three musical birds supporting the word man's words was a magical combination. Jim's words were just so strong, he needed three birds to express them. Now, however, I consider the rest of the poem,

Words dissemble
Words be quick
Words resemble walking sticks
Plant them, they will grow
Watch them waver so

My *Nation* piece wavered across the globe.

So, Jerry and I are here along with the jury, keeping a daytime vigil in the hallway. There are no lit candles except inside our chests, and there is nobody else around. Certainly not the opposing litigators. They probably have bigger fish to fry, or bigger and richer celebrities to hook. This hallway is so deserted, it feels like we're sitting on a long, empty lane of a bowling alley, waiting for . . . will it be days? Weeks? Until the jury comes out and hopefully bowls a strike in our favor . . . or . . . or . . . Will I end up having to take out a loan to buy groceries? Will I get to continue my "shameless" tithing to charities and causes I believe in?

The jury members see Jerry and me each time they take a break or go to lunch. But just for a few minutes. We sit here all day to make an impact for a few minutes, and then we leave and go home, just like the jury does.

II

Guess what? It's been almost two weeks and I'm still sitting on this marble bench. Only it's slightly warmer because I've been here for so long. Maybe I should put out a little tin cup for donations because some of the people who work here smile and stare at me each time they walk by. I've become a permanent fixture in this hallway. The guy in the snack shop knows me, the security guards know me, and Jerry has even introduced me to a few judges.

I take a break and hurry to the men's room because nature is calling. But it's almost noon and I don't want to miss seeing the jury (or rather, having the jury see me) when they leave the courtroom. I'm standing at the urinal wondering how much more of this I can take, when Jerry rushes in and says, "They're out!"

Oh shit, they broke a little early today. They missed seeing me sitting on my bench, which is strategically positioned so they have to pass by me. Was I here all morning for nothing? I skip washing my hands and run out of the men's room, breaking into a fast walk. I don't want it to be so obvious that I'm trying to get in front of the folks exiting the jury room. Oh well, win some, lose some. Jerry has a slightly disappointed look on his face. At least they saw him sitting on the bench. I think I'll go back into the men's room and wash my hands.

III

It's been three and a half weeks and I'm still sitting on my "spot." I discovered that the horrible, bright neon lighting that runs down the entire hallway is really good for one thing: clipping my nails. I clip away and reflect on my life, as I have a strong feeling that something important is imminent, as in THE VERDICT. Release. Only now Jerry tells me that this case has been so complicated, the jury verdict is less relevant than the eventual "judge's statement of decision." Whatever the hell that is. So it isn't the end, after all.

As I look shocked, Jerry goes on to explain that after the verdict is read, the honorable Judge Alarcon has to decide which issues are "equitable," meaning which issues are about money. Then he will write a statement that could take months to fashion. When Jerry finishes walking me through this, I am so fed up, I stand up and announce, "I'm going home." This was supposed to be the climax of the ordeal, but that's still far away and I feel like I've already reached my limit.

I start to say goodbye to Jerry when Mr. Forer stops me in my tracks. He rushes toward us with great anticipation and says he just heard that there will be a verdict in a couple of hours. Holy shit! The culmination of years of preparation and work. But then, maybe it won't be the culmination at all, since Jerry has pointed out that how the judge rules in his future written statement is most important.

Forer's announcement proves to be more than a rumor. During the next hour and a half, the deserted bowling alley transforms from a morgue into a bustling train depot. The opposition shows up without their clients . . . no surprise. The hallway is packed by the time we all enter the courtroom to hear the climax, or rather, NOT the climax.

Once we are all in our seats and the judge enters the room, he turns to the jury foreman. "Have you reached a verdict?" he asks.

"We have, Your Honor."

What happens next is more confusing and frustrating to me than any one day of the trial. And more surprising, since there are several issues at hand here. The jury is on the fence, some for, some against. But no monetary awards have been decided upon, due to the fact that because there were so many issues on which to vote, the jury got confused by the complexities.

Apparently, though, they are finished and it is in the judge's hands to figure out the real verdict and the monetary awards and penalties. But who won and who lost? There's no telling how long it will take for the judge to make his final decision, and I get to sit here in limbo. For two weeks? Three months? Six months? A year?

As I head back home after the anticlimax of hearing the jury foreman state their nonverdict, I think about Ray and Robby. They weren't sitting on the bench with me during the last several weeks. They were probably out playing music illegally somewhere, as if the trial had never happened. For them, it was a two-day affair, not an entire summer of agony like it was for me. I finally pull into my driveway and wonder how I'm going to explain to my wife and friends that, although the jury has reached a verdict, nothing has been decided. I realize that Ray and Robby were right not to show up today. The final climax, yet to come, is as elusive as ever.

Chapter 24

A REALLY BIG STEP

I sit in my home office, my desk piled high with "before," "during," and "after" paperwork from the trial. There are literally mounds of legal documents for me to review and loads of new bills to pay. How ironic that I went to jail to save trees, and here I am, staring at the demise of an entire forest that my actions have generated. Thank God for recycling.

It's been six months since the "nonverdict" was read, and my attorney and I are waiting to hear the judge's written decision. There will be no formal gathering for this final ruling on my case. And there is no set date when it will occur. Anything goes, and Jerry checks the court website every few days to see if Judge Alarcon has posted his decision. When he does, Jerry and I will meet on our own to commiserate or celebrate, whatever the case may be.

Talk about delayed gratification! I can't help but manufacture reasons why this is taking so long. Some of them are negative, as I imagine the judge carefully crafting a biting document that will break me financially and emotionally. On the other hand, maybe (hopefully) Alarcon is taking his time because he wants his "statement of decision" to be ironclad and to sway in my favor. Either way, we are expecting about a fifty-page document, which will act as a template for any future appeals.

I've been going about my personal business, reviewing my finances, trying not to face the possibility that I may have to seriously downsize my lifestyle . . . as in having to sell everything to make ends meet. I have no idea if my financial outlook is about to change for the better or the worse, so how can I make any plans or decisions about the future? I only know I've grown attached to my house, my family loves it too, and I hope I don't have to put it on the market.

When the phone rings, I pick it up. It's Jerry, and he says he has some good news. He insists I hightail it to his office, and without another word, I jump into my car. Oh my God. I try to drive the speed limit, but now, after six long months, I can hardly tolerate the fifteen minutes it takes to get to Jerry's building.

When I walk into his office, my attorney is smiling like a Cheshire cat. As soon as I see his face, I pull out my hanky and start dabbing at my eyes.

"It's a slam dunk, John," Jerry says, waving a document at me. "The Honorable Gregory Alarcon has written a ruling in your favor that is impenetrable. It is so thorough and knowledgeable, he should write the liner notes on your next box set!"

There are some smaller decisions about minor issues that have gone to the other side, but in the scheme of things, they don't matter. What does matter is that the larger and more relevant issues have been decided in my favor, the issues that prompted me to file this lawsuit in the first place. Jerry reads me the highlights of the decision that has marked today as one of the best days of my life. All decorum leaves me as I blubber into my handkerchief. Here come da judge!

> *For the reasons set forth in this court's Statement of Decision dated July 21, 2005, the court issues the following order.*
>
> *The court finds that use of the name* The Doors *by defendants is a violation of B&P Section 17500. The court finds Manzarek and Krieger libel for false advertising.*
>
> *Effective immediately, Defendants Ray Manzarek, Robert Krieger, and those acting in concert with them . . . are hereby permanently enjoined from performing, touring, promoting their band as* The Doors, The Doors of the 21st Century, *or using any other name that includes the words* The Doors, *without the written consent of all the partners of the old Doors partnership . . .*
>
> *Effective immediately, defendants Ray Manzarek and Robert Krieger are hereby personally enjoined from using the name, likeness, voice, or image of Jim Morrison to promote their band or their concerts.*
>
> *IT IS SO ORDERED.*

And finally:

> *With respect to the Cross-Complaint of Manzarek and Krieger, the court orders that said Cross-Complainants take* nothing *as result of their claims.*

Jerry puts down the paperwork and smiles broadly at me. That pretty well sums it up. I do not have to beg, borrow, or steal forty million dollars to give to my former bandmates. In fact, I am required to give them "nothing" in the decision of the judge.

And they have to pay my court costs. That sounds really good to me. So good, I feel like I just drank a bottle of really fine champagne. I let out a long sigh that has been waiting for years to be released. I feel free from all of this, from fear and abuse and being called names. Can this really be the end?

Apparently not, as Jerry says three words that stop my heart for a moment: "They will appeal."

"Really?"

"Probably. Do you think their attorneys will take this lying down?"

"No," I say, still smiling. "I was really looking forward to recycling all the legal crap I have lying around."

"Not yet, John. Not yet. But today was a big step. A really big step. Congrats."

We give each other a giant hug and I'm out the door. I have some celebrating to do and I have to return to my everyday life, even though once again, this is not the end. Maybe there is never a real end to anything. There are just pauses to catch our breath, lick our wounds, and celebrate our victories.

Chapter 25

INTERLUDE

I value writing as a new creative outlet, but at the same time, I miss my old one. In my opinion, the linear legal system needs more flow . . . like music. I've spent almost a year twiddling my thumbs, waiting for some movement toward the appellate court decision. The appeal. This court is on a level above Judge Alarcon and has tons of cases to review. Jerry made sure I knew this would take time, but sometimes in my darkest hours, I think this cloud cover will never lift. And then, if the appellate judges flip the decision, the clouds hovering over my head will turn into thunderheads.

I'm sure Ray and Robby's legal beavers have been furiously writing up a storm about how Judge Alarcon messed up in his decision. The way I see it, however, he wrote about as clear a ruling as can be; but the other side figures, *Let's spend another year or two on this and possibly several hundred thousand dollars in the process.*

My lawyer told me that sometimes an attorney will tell their clients when it's a lost cause and they shouldn't appeal. I wish the esteemed barristers from Century City would tell it like it is for once and say, "It's over." But for them it isn't, since I'm sure they're filling their clients' ears with ideas like "reversal and revenge." And they're still filling their pockets too. Where are the elders in the legal profession? Are there any?

There are certainly elders in music, which reminds me of the time Robby and I met Ravi Shankar when we studied at his Kinnara School of Music in between Doors tours. Robby took sitar, and I, of course, was fascinated with those extremely difficult little Indian drums: the tablas.

Many years later, in 1995, there was a seventy-fifth-birthday celebration for Ravi Shankar in Los Angeles. An event that was scheduled to begin in the afternoon and go into the evening, all of India's greatest musicians and singers gathering in one place to play for the "master." Mr. Shankar himself wasn't performing. It was a tribute to, as the late, transcendental George Harrison put it, "the godfather of world music." I got a pair of tickets from Alan Kozlowski, who had produced several of Ravi's CDs, so I figured the seats were going to be good. But I didn't know how good . . .

My friend Andy Krikun, who had studied Hindu music, walked beside me as we ducked out of the hot San Gabriel Valley sun and into the cool confines of an old performance space in Pasadena. Indians were swarming around the foyer and you could feel the anticipation in the air.

Descending the aisles, we looked for row B . . . Could that really mean the second row? As we made our way toward the front of the auditorium, Andy and I noticed Mr. Shankar sitting in the first row, being greeted by all the illustrious musicians in attendance. We checked our ticket stubs, and sure enough, our seats were located *directly* behind the master, in the second row! We felt like two teenagers who had front-row seats at a Lakers game as we gawked at our heroes. But this time they weren't sporting tennis shoes. In fact, all the performers were barefoot in their gorgeous saris and Nehru jackets. I looked over at Andy and we simultaneously broke out into wide smiles, as if we'd just landed in Mumbai.

The concert offered stellar performances from all of the greats, but a gesture from each of the participants toward their musical guru shocked me. After every musician finished a set, they walked down the stairs from the stage, approached Ravi, got down on their knees, and then prostrated themselves in front of the master. He was very appreciative and tried to stop them, but he knew this was something they insisted on doing. He also knew he was expected to receive it with grace, and so he did. After a few performances, the gratitude became palpable as the musicians kept calling the master "Raviji," a Hindu sign of respect.

These gestures were mind-blowing to witness from the POV of a sixties radical (me), particularly when The Doors had invoked the lyric, "'Father?' 'Yes, son.' 'I want to kill you!'" Jim's Oedipal Greek metaphor told us to cut the umbilical cord once and for all, because the politicians and army generals were false kings who lied to us.

As I recall this story, it's not like I want my kids to prostrate in front of me to show some respect. I'm just trying to figure out how to lead the youth on an honest path, having been wounded in my own youth by deceitful superiors. To witness real mentorship, such as Ravi Shankar's relationship with his disciples, touched me deeply, and I know why. It's the Indian musical tradition of surrendering to a living guru who guides the student with discipline . . . but never abuse. And then it's the maturing of the relationship, where the student rises and surpasses the master, who looks on with pride.

My mentor, Elvin Jones, my main man, the polyrhythmic "jazz machine" behind John Coltrane, broke on through to the other side on May 18, 2004. The motor behind Trane laid it down on drums so heavy, so strong, that his pulse will be felt for centuries. I feel so blessed to have had my path cross Elvin's several times in my life. Originally my teenage idol, he became a friend and the most emulated musical thread I've got going.

It was 1963 when I nervously showed my fake ID from Tijuana to the doorman at Shelly's Manne-Hole in Hollywood. The jazz club bouncer looked at it, gave me one last glance that said it was fake, and let me in to see my hero. At sixteen, I had already pored over all of Coltrane's Impulse! LPs, while my ears were being fed candy. Now I was going to see The Man. He sat behind one of the greatest jazz quartets in the history of the art form, and he did it with a huge grin. The Beatles hadn't hit yet, and Elvin was my muse.

Elvin Jones blazed a new path for all the rest of us timekeepers. He was the first to free up the job of clockwork, improvising continually but never sacrificing a strong sense of pulse. His constant "conversation" with Coltrane later inspired me to try to have a musical dialogue with Jim Morrison. Not a word was spoken, but so much was said. Elvin played so loose, it gave me the courage to literally stop the steady rhythm on "When the Music's Over," during Jim Morrison's rap about the earth, and just jab at my kit in quick expressive grunts. Elvin churned rhythms like an eggbeater, and served up multi-meals within every four bars. With his beats perpetually on the edge, he sounded like he was going to fall into his drum set, but he never did.

Between sets at the famous Manne-Hole jazz club, I went back to the bathroom, not because I had to relieve myself, but to get close to the dressing room. I heard voices and laughter from behind the wall—my heroes. I opened the dark redwood door to the head and occupied myself washing my hands until I heard the same voices coming out of the opposite room.

Not wasting time, I spun around and grabbed the knob, wet hands and all. I could hear the musicians passing by on their way to the stage, but I couldn't get the door open! Wiping my hands on my pants, I used both to turn the knob. When the door opened, Coltrane was standing right in front of me, looking at who was coming out of the bathroom. My reverence told me to chill, and I quickly shunned eye contact. I motioned that the bathroom was free, but Trane walked by, heading for the stage. I noticed that everyone sort of quieted down when he passed. I looked at Elvin's face, and he smiled at me!

My book *Riders on the Storm* captures my obsession:

> *Anytime I would drop the needle on [a Coltrane record], the bellowing, driving energy would make me imagine I was actually inside drummer Elvin Jones's body. The tempo pulsed in my veins . . .*

Other than dissecting every nuance of his style on records (down to his moaning between quarter notes), this was the first flesh-and-blood contact, the first of several to come. When the last set was over, I lingered in the back, hearing Elvin say to Trane, "Hotel, hotel." I repeated the phrase over and over to my friends the next few days. They thought I was nuts.

My next "live" contact with the most seminal jazz quartet in history was a year later at UCLA's Royce Hall. They burned such a hole in the place that half the audience was gone before they finished. Some fans just didn't understand. If Coltrane hadn't helped define bebop and "cool" jazz with Miles Davis, he wouldn't have had permission to go "outside." Knowing his history, I ate up all of Coltrane's experimental excursions into space. It was actually "inner" space, as exemplified in one of his then-recent titles, "Chasin' the Trane."

At Royce Hall, they played that one for about forty-five minutes. In the middle of the tune, pianist McCoy Tyner laid out, leaving the rhythm section, bassist Jimmy Garrison and Elvin, to face off with the leader. Coltrane turned around and, with his back to us, entered a duel with my percussion master. It was twenty minutes of the most primitive, emotional catharsis I've ever heard coming out of any musicians. Elvin's stamina was a perfect match for the tenor player.

After the concert, people were allowed to wander up onstage, so Yours Truly sheepishly played the role of groupie. This wasn't a rock show, so crossing the line between artist and fan didn't involve climbing the Berlin Wall. I still lacked the nerve to actually *say* anything to my teacher, so I just watched as Elvin used a hammer to remove the nails he'd pounded into the floor to keep his bass drum from sliding. The man played hard!

The next physical contact was many years later. Coltrane had died, and in the eighties, Elvin's Jazz Machine was initiating lots of new young players. I was in New York and ventured down to the jazz club Slugs on the Lower East Side. With a redbrick wall as the stage backdrop, Elvin's sound was projected louder than ever. I could tell it was a little too much for some of the patrons, but my craving for his rhythms was satiated . . . for a while. I thought back to early Doors rehearsals, where we fashioned the solos in "Light My Fire" after some of the chord changes in "My Favorite Things, Pt. 1."

Coltrane had taken a corny Broadway tune from *The Sound of Music* and made it his own.

In 1995, I caught Elvin at the Vine Street Bar & Grill, a jazz club just a couple blocks from the old Manne-Hole. I was especially nervous this time. Toting my autobiography under my arm, I headed backstage to actually *talk* to Elvin, after witnessing a performance that had as much power on drums as I'd seen thirty years earlier down the street. By this time I'd received many accolades about *my* drumming, but this was jazz. This wasn't rock and roll. This was the root of all my learning about the craft of drumming.

With trepidation, I introduced myself, which didn't ring any bells for Elvin, so I quickly held up *Riders on the Storm* and said, "This is for you . . . it's my autobiography about playing in a rock band . . . In here I wrote that you gave me my hands." I was prepared for condescension, jazz being the higher art, but that wasn't a quality in Mr. Jones's repertoire. He was so incredibly kind and gracious, I was once again humbled to be in his presence. He spoke in a quiet way, thanking me for comin' down. I felt complete. I had honored the man who had taught me so much.

Several years later, the Machine was playing the Jazz Bakery in Culver City, and I felt another pilgrimage to Mecca was due. Elvin's playing hadn't deteriorated in the least, and after the last set, I went backstage for an autograph. His eyes lit up when I asked who some of his mentors were.

"Sid Catlett, yeah, Big Sid Catlett, among many others."

Ignoring the concern about looking like a fifty-year-old groupie, I asked for autographs on my old Coltrane LPs that I had brought with me.

"Don't be embarrassed by that," Elvin beamed as he John Hancock'd my collector's items.

His wife tried to move the party along and get the living legend home . . . There would be no late-night meals with the godfather of the skins tonight. As we walked toward their wheels, my guru let me take the cymbal bag from under his arm and carry it the rest of the way. It was only a few yards to the car, but I'd waited thirty-five years to have the honor.

I don't know if any young litigators look up to their superiors with that kind of respect these days. All things do come to an end, however, even when we think they never will. Approximately five years after the first day of the trial, on May 29, 2008, with all principals present, in a two-to-one decision, the California Court of Appeals upheld the decision of Judge Alarcon.

Now, it's over, really over.

This is the end.

Chapter 26

THE GREED GENE

'd like to try to explain to Ray and Robby why I felt forced to take a stand against them and what they were doing, but our relationship has been rather strained due to this litigation. Maybe the best way to accomplish this is to revisit the technique I used in *Riders on the Storm*, in which I wrote a series of letters to Jim Morrison. In Jim's case, the letters were written to a dead friend. In this case, I'm writing to two lost brothers and to the memory of our lost relationships.

Dear Ray and Robby,

I'm hoping that this letter might help you understand me. You obviously don't, because after I won the appeal, you two booked another tour USING THE NAME AGAIN. The judicial system calls that "contempt" of a California State injunction forbidding you from using the name The Doors ever again. The only remedy would be a $1,000 fine or jail! You obviously were banking on the idea that the PR would be so terrible for me and for our legacy if I ever took you to task that I'd never enforce the penalty, which was true.

Then, my trusted barrister told me that you would probably take your appeal all the way to the Supreme Court! The absurdity seemed comical, but he was right. It was another half a year until the Supreme Court of California denied hearing the case. It was over . . . it was finally, really all over.

So let's go back in time for a minute, to reflect on where we started. Have either of you forgotten that rock and roll began in a garage as a rebellion against the stiff, consumer-oriented fifties? When rock started out, its rebellion was bouncing off the status quo. I remember in the 1953 film *The Wild One*, Marlon Brando was famously asked by men in suits, "What are you rebelling against?"

Decked out in his black leathers (an outfit Morrison copped), sitting on a large Harley-Davidson, he retorted, "Whatya got?"

Eventually, the youthful rebellion of the sixties actually won—we stopped the Vietnam War—until the black magicians of Madison Avenue realized the enormous amount of money that could be made off the counterculture, as they attached a virus to our message of "love." But Jim, of course, was the underbelly of the Flower Power movement.

Do you remember, Robby, after Jim came to one of Guru Maharishi's lectures, he said he didn't want to learn to meditate? He just wanted to look into the teacher's eyes and see what was there. He said that the little man from India had "something." Whatever that something was, the guru was the catalyst for bringing the four Doors into their first rehearsals together. After all, that's where I met Ray . . . in a meditation class with Maharishi.

I guess it was the darker side of that "something" that I saw in Jim's eyes when his pupils were pinned wide open from a large dose of LSD. I once joked to him that they might get stuck, and Jim wasn't amused. Expecting a belly laugh from my comment and getting a blank stare, I quickly looked away from our front man. I was the only one in the band who directly confronted Jim on his path of Dionysian dismemberment. I *saw* his fate of living a short life, inflaming his iconic destiny, but there was nothing I could do about it.

Everyone tries to alter the negative paths of their close relations, so as to bring them in line with one's own vision, but it seems that try as we might, fate exists solely between the individual and the divine. When I confronted the "Greek god," there was some backlash. Later, when Jim complained to Ray about me, I was very hurt. It took all this time for me to understand that I was *supposed* to hold up a mirror for Jim while I supported his lyrics with my rhythms.

In hindsight, it seems that at various times in our career, we were all scared of Jim . . . scared of his self-destruction, scared of his tearing down everything that we'd built, scared of his power. But his destiny was to blaze a trail of excess, scorching and burning his way to an early demise. And that made him even more famous. Or rather infamous—famous for the wrong reasons.

When I think back to 1968, I recall that the band had just become big enough in Europe to garner a tour. But while performing in Germany, we encountered a very quiet audience, which was unusual for us. I was thinking that maybe Jim's wardrobe (his requisite black leather pants and boots) dredged up old Nazi vibes from deep in the crowd's psyche. Whatever the reason, Jim got so frustrated that he unscrewed the mic stand from its base, walked to the back of the stage, and stood in front of my drums. Then, wielding the mic stand in his hand, he suddenly ran toward the audience as if he were going to impale some of them on his "javelin." It freaked me out.

Remember, I was just a flower child from the West Coast and somehow I wound up in a band that sometimes elicited violent overtones, although the Germans took it like they knew the territory. We were getting very popular and I was seeing firsthand how the masses like to build celebrities way up and then shove them all the way back down. On top of that, Jim liked riling people into a frenzy, so maybe some NRA dude in the audience would try to take Jim out. Or maybe Jim would take somebody out. That had been my mother's fear about her son, my brother. After he committed suicide, we spread salve on our wounded psyches by imagining that he was finally at peace and the possibility of his hurting others was gone. Sometimes darkness gets so close, it's almost visible and downright palpable.

Michael Ventura, novelist, essayist, and film critic, who wrote a piece for our box set, beautifully set the stage:

> Early on, before their first recording session, John Densmore had this realization: "I'm in a band with a psychotic. I'M IN A BAND WITH A PSYCHOTIC. I'm in a room with a psychotic." Densmore, Robby Krieger, and Ray Manzarek deeply loved Jim, but Riders on the Storm makes it clear that they were also afraid of him. Unlike in The Doors [Oliver Stone's movie], John never did acid with Jim because he didn't trust him. Listen to Densmore talking in his memoir about the recording session that produced "The End."
>
> Densmore writes: "We walked out into the blinding light of the neon lobby and bought some junk food . . . Jim began chanting 'FUCK the mother, KILL the fa-

ther. FUCK *the mother, KILL the father.' He looked deranged. He caught me staring at him, catching his eyes for a split-second glance, and he responded, 'It's my mantra, man. Fuck the mother, kill the father.' Although I knew Jim had taken acid, at that moment I thought that anything was possible with this man. He could murder somebody."*

And they weren't even famous yet.

Jim's genius, for some reason, came in the Dionysian package of man's benefactor and man's destroyer. Yes, it's true, Ray . . . something in my young psyche knew what was coming. I'm very sensitive to people on the edge. I recognize them quickly, and my first impulse is to try to help. If they're going down too fast, my second impulse is to get away because the peripheral intensity can pull others down with them. When I told Keith Richards about Jim's spaced-out, drug-induced performance at the Hollywood Bowl, he said, "Jim's dead, we're not!" I'm sixty-seven years old now; I like being an example of the longer road, and I can listen to Jim's words and say, "That's the real gold. It will make you shine."

When I think back, Robby, Jim wasn't the only one who had some self-destructive tendencies. I've always been aware of your distant personality, not really here but swimming in the world of sound: a true musician. Others have judged you as being on drugs, but I knew better . . . until fairly recently. Remember in the nineties when I orchestrated an intervention with your family and friends, because of your excessive drug use? You seemed pretty close to the edge. I don't know if that came from a hole in your psyche or from a spoiled rich kid's upbringing, but some say that the intervention possibly saved your life. Your dad told me I was the definition of a true friend. I had hoped later for a thank you from you, which never did arrive, but upon reflection, I realize that I was naïve to expect it. I had simply done what I could, and the truth is, it was kinda for me as much as you . . . protection against guilt if I lost you.

Later, I was worried again when you began nodding off during our mediation conference, a tendency that continued during the settlement conference as well. Instead of a "thank you," The Doors of the 21st Century's recent tour was a spit in the face, but I received it stoically, like a member of the punk group Fear, who encouraged such behavior from its seething mosh-pit fans.

When I really think about it, I don't believe I could handle losing you, Robby. I mean, we really were kindred spirits, holding each other's hands through Jim's craziness and Ray's arrogance. Okay, it's hard to admit but I probably wouldn't be able to handle losing you either, Ray . . . assuming, of course, that everyone is going to cross over *before* Yours Truly. The truth is that, way deep down, I have a reservoir of cherished memories of our early days together: rapping with you, Ray, excitedly over our favorite jazz musicians; sitting on Venice Beach, watching the planes take off from the south at LAX and hoping that someday we'd be on one of them; dreaming of the future, hoping this little dream of ours would actually come to fruition. It did. We had our glory days.

Remember when Bruce Springsteen approached us at our induction into the Rock & Roll Hall of Fame and said he wanted to pay his respects and that I was a very unique drummer? Sounds like I'm bragging, huh? I guess I'm still hurt that you and Robby thought you could replace me. But then there's the ridiculous idea that you guys thought you could replace Jim!

Up until Jim's estate and I sued you, you two tried to re-live the past. I really do wish you all the best as the Manzarek & Krieger Band (founding members of The Doors), but now, with our age and success, we should be examples of how to lead.

Remember Jim's lyric:

Dead cats, dead rats . . .
Sucking on the soldier's brain . . .
Fat cat in a top hat
Thinks he's an aristocrat
Crap, that's crap!

Well . . . we're "fat cats" now. I know we sixties survivors didn't have real mentors around us. *Don't follow leaders, watch the parking meters*, as Bob Dylan said. But we did it without a roadman, which, as you know, is another word for a guide in Native American Church ceremonies. It was metaphoric for the times, but actually, these days hip-hop artist Jay-Z is talking about the same thing:

So it's best for those to not overdose on being famous
Most kings get driven so insane
That they try to hit the same vein that Kurt Cobain did
So dangerous, so no strangers
Invited to the inner sanctum of your chambers

Hip-hop has parented a lot of young people.

Michael Meade said, "Elders are people that have ex-tracted some wisdom from the damage of their own lives, and have begun to imagine what will be going on after they're gone." So we need to think about giving back.

Try donating 10, 15, 20 percent when you're in the highest tax category . . . or any category. I don't care if the tithe is for charity or to salve the conscience of someone in their twilight years. Turn that battle between your primal instincts (which have already won over and over) and your better selves into a waltz! It doesn't have any effect on your (or my) life, except a nice deduction from your taxes. Think like the Mormons do! They tell their parishioners to give 10 percent to the Church of Latter-Day Saints. I'd suggest you try to find something *not* connected with organized religion, though some churches do very good things. It's just that the trap of "*Our* God is better than *theirs*" is extremely dangerous.

I know, Robby, it sounds like I've got my hand in your pocket. Or I want to put the government's hand in your pocket. I certainly can't, and shouldn't, tell you what to do with your dough, but think of it this way: Money is like fertilizer. If hoarded, it stinks . . . but if it gets spread around like compost, new ideas are jump-started. People don't want a handout; they want a hand up. We will probably always live in a hierarchical world (survival of the fittest), but if we treat each other with respect for the diversity of talents in the human race, people might smile more. After all, we share the same biology. Therefore, basically we're all on the same road. One might be on a freeway while another is on a dirt road, but we are all walking essentially the same path from cradle to grave.

This rap, by the way, is metaphoric for our country too. Michael Meade tells us that currency comes from the word "current," and it's supposed to flow like a river. If that's true, then we need a laxative for our "credit freeze," busting the rocks and boulders that corporate beavers have used to dam things up. I hope rock and roll is smarter than just turning its heroes into rich people.

As I sit here writing these words, a movement is forming on the streets all over the US, from Boston, Massachusetts, to Kona, Hawaii. It's even gone global. Inspiration from the social media–driven revolts in the Middle East is fueling the anti-greed protests that began on Wall Street. It started out as a cross section of youthful liberals, elderly folks, and even some Tea Party members, angry at the disparity between classes. The mantra for these Americans from all walks of life is that the richest 1 percent own and control the other 99 percent. Are you guys aware of this?

When I was a kid, I was part of the 99 percent. The freeway rammed through our lower-middle-class house, and we had to move. Since my twenties, due to the success of our band, I've been part of the 1 percent. Well, not really the 1 percent. I'm not a billionaire or a corporation, but my pockets are pretty deep. Even with that kind of insulation, I've never forgotten where I came from and I've been fighting for the 99 percent ever since I became wealthy. It's scary to admit that I'm an "M" (the M-word, as in millionaire), but people with dough must come out of the closet and stand next to the working class if we're going to bring back the middle class. This would help our kids as well. Besides inheriting our dough, they will inherit a lopsided world if we don't try and make it more equitable.

In our era (the sixties), two radical Catholic priests, Daniel and Philip Berrigan, poured homemade napalm on draft files as a protest against the Vietnam War. Today, the LA branch of the recently disgruntled public have plans to take trash from the southern part of the city, which is blighted by foreclosures, and dump it in front of a bank. This is because the protesters blame banks for causing urban decay.

People also have grouped outside the mansion homes of

several CEOs of banks, demanding they fix the economic meltdown, which they caused and then accepted bailouts with no damage control. The ratio of payment of CEOs vs. workers in Japan is the lowest in the world: 11:1. European countries are around 20 or 30:1. The United States gets the award for having the most disparity of any country on the globe: 475:1. Your kids and mine are going to need extra locks and bolts on their doors if we keep going the way we are.

Van Jones, Obama's "green czar" who got dumped due to conservative commentator Glenn Beck's red-baiting, predicted this uprising on Tavis Smiley's PBS show months before it happened. I know that I've been writing about this monetary gap between classes for years. Jones said that the "banksters" should be on the streets with the homeless based on their performance, but we bailed them out. Even Federal Reserve chairman Ben Bernanke said of the protesters, "They blame, with some justification, the problems in the financial sector for getting us into this mess . . . And at some level, I can't blame them."

As I wrote years ago:

Capitalism is getting so top-heavy, our economy will be getting a continual backache from all the silicone. With double-digit deficits up top, it's soon going to be a bust! We're the wealthiest nation in the history of mankind. It's a huge banquet, milk and honey are flowing, but many are not allowed at the table. It is not a Beggar's Banquet, one of my favorite early Stones albums. Twenty percent of US children live in poverty. They are going hungry. The upside-down pyramid isn't going to hold.

Back to Wall Street . . . or just outside Wall Street. The

citizens' list of grievances include: racism, President Obama, Republicans, Democrats, hunger, the wars in Iraq and Afghanistan, workers' lack of rights, the prison industrial complex, low taxes for millionaires, and the country's financial system. I went down to Occupy LA, and one veteran held up a sign that read: *4,477 = 99%* . . . referring to the number of soldiers killed in Iraq and the 99 percent who have to scramble for 1 percent of the pie. He said, "I'm here because I did two tours in Iraq and I saw a lot of people die. Why? Why did they die? The answer is that they died for corporate America, so it's time to bring a change."

Even if this movement falls apart, they've already made their point. It's on the tip of the world's tongue. Another woman exercising her right to democratic action said, "There are so many issues at stake, but it all comes down to money."

When I look back at the purpose of this book, I wrote it for two reasons: First, to clear my name and set the record straight about what happened between us. Second, we have to start talking about this greed thing . . . otherwise my children and everybody else's are going to be living in a world far worse than the one we are living in today.

Yes, yes, true giving is anonymous and I don't like red-carpet philanthropy any more than anyone else. Even if critics label this entire book with that moniker, the real reason I'm mouthing off here is to try to set an example, get a dialogue going. Believe me, I don't like revealing that I've got some bucks. But writing this book, putting Yours Truly up to the scrutinizing eye of the public, is one way to keep myself in check, because this money addiction is as strong as heroin, and you have to live more than one donation at a time. The altruistic feeling doesn't last long and greed waits behind your shoulder, looking for an opening. Did you ever consider that having piles of loot at the conclusion of your journey can be toxic to crossing over? Spanish poet Antonio Machado puts it beautifully in his poem "Portrait":

> . . . *my youth twenty years on the earth of Castile;*
> *what I lived a few things you'll forgive me for omitting . . .*

> *In the end, I owe you nothing; you owe me what I've*
> *written.*
> *I turn to my work; with what I've earned I pay*
> *for my clothes and hat, the house in which I live,*
> *the food that feeds my body, the bed on which I sleep.*

> *And when the day arrives for the last leaving of all,*
> *and the ship that never returns to port is ready to go,*
> *you'll find me on board, light, with few belongings,*
> *almost naked like the children of the sea.*
> (Translation by Robert Bly)

The whole point of this diatribe is to get rid of some luggage, physically and mentally. Ray, maybe you were right when you criticized me for being married several times. God knows, I tried to honor the institution, but due to the stress of five years of litigation, my third marriage crumbled. My road just didn't turn out like my parents' road, which lasted for forty years of marriage.

By the way, just a couple of nights ago, guys, Jim came through to me in a dream! We were recording and his performance wasn't up to par. He wasn't drunk, though. He was peaceful and calm; he just couldn't focus. And he was apologetic about it . . . he was sorry. I'm sorry too.

Sorry it was so hard for us to support his vision.

Sorry that our road has become one of separation from the brothers and bandmates I grew up with.

Sorry was the feeling I got from Jim's dream, but he had no regrets. Sorry, but not sorry. The truth is that we took the road that was laid out for us, we're still on it, and who knows where it will turn. Like the words that Jim wrote, I, too, love the friends Jim gathered on the thin raft. We floated down the Ganges, the holy river of life. Our raft was seaworthy only for a short crossing, though, due to the captain's directions, and the weather was bad. Quickly, everyone went overboard, and to the surprise of some, the captain couldn't swim.

> Come on baby, gonna take a little ride
> Down, down by the ocean side
> Gonna get real close
> Get real tight
> Baby gonna drown tonight
> Goin' down, down, down

When I confronted Jim about his drug and alcohol use, it was my effort to throw him a life vest, but he wasn't interested. His fate had been written and he followed it to his destiny. The destiny of we three remaining sailors isn't finished. Fate is still pushing us around and hopefully forgiveness is in the wings. I just needed to have available (for those who are interested) my story of what I went through. And here it is.

Now, I'm going to tell you what I love about you both.

Ray, I felt *totally* in sync with you musically. It was like we were of one mind, holding down the pocket for Robby and Jim to float on top of.

Robby, my meditation brother, your solos soared like

Coltrane. Your intuitive songwriting ability was beyond comparison.

Ray, thank you for introducing me to Jim. I was so pleased when you and Jim saw what I saw in Robby.

Robby, I cherish the years we were best friends. I always felt you were the brother I lost, and I was the one you lost.

I now know that our songs are going to be around after we've exited this global stage, and I am, as I know you are, extremely proud of our accomplishments. We can be remembered as even more "special" if we don't pollute our gold, and if we remember to be generous with the fruits.

Sincerely, and with deep respect for your artistry,
John

Afterword

News flash: Robby Krieger and the estate of Ray Manzarek have each sold their respective ownership of The Doors's catalog! Wow—I'm now in bed with the buyer, a corporation. But I still have veto power to stop "anything getting weird," to quote Jim's rap about why our band should manage ourselves.

I asked Robby again, what did he need to buy with all of that money? This time, he said he was going to give a lot to charity.

Good! He's taking my idea of many months ago when I'd proposed, "Let's show these rockers how to do it, if they're going to 'sell out.' Sell 100 percent with restrictions, and give half to charity." Robby seemed to like the idea, but he didn't say anything about it for months, and then all of a sudden, I heard he's sold his quarter with no restrictions.

I email Robby right away:

So you sold your one-fourth with no restrictions? Not even "Light My Fire"? The song that Jim got so upset over being considered for a Buick car commercial? A song which he didn't write [Robby primarily penned that one]?

Maybe you're relying on me to protect that song . . . so you can get the max $$.

His email back:

So yes I'm selling along w Dorothy [Ray's wife]. Lucky we have you and Anne [Jim's sister] to hold the line. I'm sure that if you guys sell, it will be with restrictions, so we'll still be covered! You still have veto power, and the buyer understands that.

Wow, again. Is this a comedy skit from *Key & Peele*, where the miscommunication is hysterical? I'm thinking, *What about Jim's wishes? He's our ancestor!* And Robby may be thinking, *I'm feeling pretty good, 'cause I just made my pockets even deeper!* The "Jay-Z Syndrome." As Ray would probably say, *It's better to have deep pockets than not, John!* True, of course, but I'm kinda with Yvon Chouinard on this one. He's the CEO of Patagonia, who at eighty-three just gave his entire company to charity. He said he hopes that gesture will help make a future world where the balance of just a few very rich people and a lot of poor people evens out a little.

Then, just as I'm feeling like that last "Door" open, John Fogerty of Creedence Clearwater Revival has bought *back* his songs from his record company! After a thirty-year struggle, he succeeded in doing the opposite of all his peers, who are selling their songs to hit pay dirt. His quote sums it all up for me: "I'm the dad [of these songs]. I created them . . . They never should have been taken away in the first place. And that hijacking left such a massive hole in me."

My warning is this: if a songwriter feels any remorse over letting the ownership of his or her songs go, he/she can fill that hole with money, but I think there will still be a void. At my age, humor is becoming more and more important, therefore I appreciated *Rolling Stone*'s headline in the article about the sale that Robby and Ray's estate just completed—"Break on Through (to the $$)." I think Jim was more accurately writing about breaking through to a newer, hopefully higher, state of consciousness: *"Gate is straight, deep and wide / Break on through to the other side."*

Acknowledgments

First and foremost, I want to thank Andrea Cagan for all the meticulous editing, encouragement, guidance, and humor!

Second, there would be no book without Jerry Mandel, my trusted barrister who stood by my side for years and has become a great friend. He's still there.

So is my soul mate, Ildiko von Somogyi.

I'd also like to thank the following people:

Jeff Forer, who represented the Jim Morrison estate.

Steve and Clara Morrison, who have now been united with their son Jim.

Penny Courson, whose daughter Pam has also been united with Jim.

Anne and Andy.

Emily and James.

Paul Fedorko, for representing me in the past.

Jennifer Gates, for representing me in the present—she gets my prose.

Kenny Nemes, Jeff Jampol, and Max Michaels, for their eye over the entire book project.

Friends and fellow writers Sam Joseph and Bernie Schwartz, for editing.

Stewart Copeland, Anthony DeCurtis, and Nigel Williamson, for their testimony.

Luka D., for staying on my case.

Leslie Neale, Brad Schreiber, Jim Southwick, Andrea Grefe, Jerry Swartz, Randall Wixen, Marilyn Jordan, Kelly, Rio, and Samara.

Don Sloggy and the Lost Dogs.

I would like to thank Akashic Books for TOTALLY getting what I'm up to here!

I want my readers to note that the testimony covered in this book is just a small portion of the weightiness of the entire trial.

I would like to thank Shepard Fairey for his unique eye that so masterfully shaped the cover of this book. He got inside The Doors.

And finally, all the fans who stayed with me through thick and thin. And also, beneath the intensity of this project, all those who I have carelessly omitted.

Permissions